POCKET PILGRIM

A wobbly journey along the
Camino de Santiago

G.F. Murphy

Kindle Direct Publishing

For Pauline - Always

CONTENTS

PROLOGUE

Writing a book as a first time author was, for me at least, a very testing experience, and at no time during the exercise did I feel I had passed the exam. My apologies then, for any slaughtered syntax or grammatical gaffes. I hope my little story manages to emerge through the debris.

The front cover shows a spray of paint to illustrate the books title; this can also be taken as a metaphor for its contents. I never felt during my writing, that I had given full weight to the uniqueness and splendour of the Camino de Santiago. My words, I often felt, were little more than a mess of graffiti, when compared to those needed to describe the true glories I discovered along the way of this incredible journey.

I dont think I was a very good pilgrim either! OK, I completed the expedition and fully absorbed the experience. However, when measured alongside my fellow 'peregrinos', I felt a bit of a fraud. I saw such dedication, commitment and passion in others; far beyond anything I brought to the journey, thats for sure.

I never thought of myself as being a proper pilgrim; I believed I lacked the genuineness or substance to be the real deal, as it were. A bit like a pocket pen knife or a pocket dictionary; functional yes, but not quite as good as the real thing. Yeah that's it........ I was just a pocket pilgrim really.

The front cover photograph features the monument at the end of the Camino in Muxia, towering over the North Atlantic coast. Muxia was the final town on my long Camino journey.

This striking sculpture, 'A Ferida' (The wound), by Spanish Artist Alberto Banuenos, is a wonderful piece, and I beg Alberto's forbearance in my my untidy appropriation of his work in the design of the books cover.

FOREWORD

S t Augustine, the great philosopher and theologian proclaimed in one of his many famous observations: 'The world is a book, and those who do not travel read only a page'. Well, I couldn't agree more! I have been lucky enough to have travelled extensively throughout my adult life, and this journeying has rewarded me with some of my most memorable and life enriching experiences. It was about time I thought, to add another page to the book of my own travelling life.

It was mid-summer, and following a maelstrom of last minute planning, I stood on the verge of a long dreamt of and very special journey. For the next month or so I would be walking the Camino de Santiago; the ancient pilgrimage road to the city of Santiago de Compostela, located in the north western Spanish province of Galicia.

There are many different 'Camino' routes and many starting points in Spain and elsewhere in Europe. The Camino Portugués, Camino Norté, Camino Primitivo, to name but a few. All sharing the same destination and purpose, and all eventually coming together in the great cathedral city of St. James the Apostle. My chosen road is the 'Camino Francés' or 'French Way'. This is the oldest and most popular of all the routes; travelled these days by thousands of people each year and down the centuries, by millions.

I would begin my walk in Pamplona, the great Basque city lying under the shadow of the Pyrenees in eastern Spain. Ending, hopefully, in Santiago de Compostela in about 30 days and around 800 Kilometres of dedicated hiking.

The French Way traverses east to west through four very different provinces: The craggy mountains of Navarre; the sumptuous, wine rich hills of La Rioja; the hot, flat cereal plains of Castilla Y León; and finally, the hilly farmland and cattle country of Galicia.

These regions boast widely differing geography, distinctive personalities and cultures, and indeed, languages. Each reflecting the wonderful diversity found on the Camino, and which I was so looking forward to experiencing and enjoying on this long journey across northern Spain.

From reading the experiences of others, it was clear that those who undertake what is a pretty tough and demanding journey, do so for a variety of reasons. For many it's simply the challenge, for others it's a great adventure, some see it as just a walking holiday, and plenty more observe its original purpose as a religious or spiritual pilgrimage.

As for myself? This was a journey I had been desperate to undertake for many years, and with a fusion of motives for doing so. It would be fair to say though, that whilst very keen to experience more adventure and challenge, I was more motivated by the opportunity this journey offered to take some time-out from the demands of my world, to evaluate and reflect on the course of my life, and hopefully, have the opportunity to think carefully about the way I wanted to shape the years ahead.

According to accounts I have read, many make the point that the mindset they brought to the beginning of the journey and the motivation for undertaking it, was very different to how they felt at its end. I think anyone who contemplates a long and challenging expedition such as this, must be looking for some kind of outcome, or a pay off if you like, that will give real meaning and context to their experience.

I too was hoping for such an outcome. I hoped that throughout this journey and at its end, I could discover something about myself. Something that would act as an inspiration and catalyst for change at this significant point in my life. At some point during this expedition, I would turn 60 years of age.

I also expected to have a bloody good time too, and a lot of laughs and a glass or two along the way. I can quote Augustine, but a Saint I certainly aint!

I had arrived at this point with several conflicting ideas about what, exactly, was going to unfold. I had read a lot about the Camino and had a very good idea as to what it entailed, but I was still left with many questions. Did I have it in me to make it all the way across Spain to Santiago? Unlikely I thought at first, it seemed such a huge distance. How far did I think I would get? Should I set a target of miles or think in terms of landmarks? I suppose I should have had all this worked out beforehand, but because in the end I had thrown this trip together so quickly, I was winging much of it and I would be literally learning as I went along. Well, as they say, good luck with that.

Everything I have written here is taken from my contemporaneous journal of my expedition, and into which I diligently entered the details of each day's travel, observations and experiences. I also managed somehow, to decipher the dozens of notes, jottings and scribbles I made along the way, just as little moments or events took my eye or amused really. I have also relied heavily, on the memories evoked by the many photographs I had taken during this wonderful journey.

In addition, if you will allow, I have been bold enough to embellish some of my stories and experiences with a few witticisms and a bit of humour here and there to lighten the load and the road, as it were. Anybody who knows me would expect nothing less, and I hope it's a better read for it.

Where I thought timely or appropriate, I have also introduced some personal observations on important historical topics or contemporary issues I encountered on this fascinating journey. I hope that these little flourishes too, help add substance and interest to my storytelling.

If you have started to read this jumble of words, I do hope you can bear with it to the end. I would very much like for you to share my journey, the many adventures I had along the way and my eccentric musings set alongside them. Who knows, you yourself might be inspired to get your boots on, pack a bag and set off on your own Camino adventure. I really hope so, I think I can recommend it!

ONE

San Sebastian

and

Pamplona

My journey begins in San Sebastián. This a beautiful Spanish seaside resort situated on the Bay of Biscay and about 20 kilometres from the French border. San Sebastián (Donostia to the locals) is one of the most famous and popular tourist destinations in Spain, and the crowds I encountered during my short visit left me in no doubt of that.

In the middle of the holiday season it was, unsurprisingly, heaving with tourists. The beaches were as busy as any I've seen on the more familiar 'Costas' to the south, and the streets of this atmospheric little city were thronged with tourists and locals, many sampling the famous and seemingly countless 'Pintxo' bars of the old town. *Pintxo* (pronounced, 'pincho') are basically bite sized snacks, served mostly but not always on little sticks, and made up from a bewildering selection of local foods and garnishes, each as mouthwateringly delicious as the next. If you find yourself in the Basque country, don't make the mistake of ordering *'tapas'* as you might in Benidorm. If you do, you will stay hungry!

I had wanted to journey to San Sebastián for some time, and it was a happy coincidence that gave me the chance to make this visit, and also use it as the jumping off point for my pending expedition. I spent a day and a night in this fabulous little resort and enjoyed every moment. It is a destination I can recommend without any hesitation . It was getting late in the afternoon on that first day, and I was keen to sample some pintxos and a few glasses of wine myself. At length, I found a nice little bar tucked away in a corner of the old town, luckily managing to snag a table shaded from the fierce heat of the blazing sun.

Sat close by at the next table was a handsome young couple. The lovely lass must have eyed the book I was reading, politely asking if I was from England. I agreed that I was, and we were soon happily chatting away.

It was immediately evident that the young lad had a very bad stutter, causing me to take a few sizeable and nerve-settling gulps of wine. For as usually happens when I get involved in conversations with people who stutter and stammer, my own tongue and teeth become twisted as I try to adjust and accommodate.

I don't know why, but it happens to me every time and I am always angry with myself, particularly as I ordinarily think of myself as a good communicator under most circumstances. As you will have noticed of course!

My problem is, I am never sure of the correct way to properly engage with people who are so unfortunate to have this difficulty. Is it the right thing, for example, to just ignore it and press on regardless? Or does one make adjustments and pause helpfully at the appropriate moments? I always think the former as being extremely rude and the latter as unforgivably patronising, which is why I am, shamefacedly, always thrown when speaking withpeople who stutter and stammer. Why this should be the case I have no Idea, but there it is.

I have always felt that people who have even more serious and obvious afflictions are best placed to deal with this situation. For example: if your ears are missing or your face is otherwise horribly disfigured, or if you have just a couple of stumps for arms, you can sort of take the 'afflicted folks high ground' as it were. You could rightly say: "Think yourself lucky mate; it might take you three quarters of an hour to say: 'Meet me Monday morning at Tottenham Tastee Treats and we'll have a hot hamburger with haloumi', but at least you can tie your own shoe laces". That sort of thing.

This also got me thinking about the words chosen to describe what must be such a frustrating condition. What lexicographic loonie decided to pick the names 'Stutter' and 'Stammer' as descriptors? Both replete with letters that give sufferers the most difficulty! And yet it is no different in other languages. The Spanish for stutter is 'Tartamudear', stammer is 'Balbucear'. In German, they are 'Stottern' and 'Stamme' respectively. What were these people thinking of?

There are plenty more examples: 'Dysarthria' is a condition in which the sufferers have problems in expressing certain words. What, like Dysarthria you mean? Here's my favourite, and this is true I promise. 'Pneumonoultramicroscopicsilicovolcaniosis', is a severe illness caused by the inhalation of minute dust particles, and causes extreme shortage of breath. If you had this disease you would never be able to say so. Both of your lungs would surely collapse in a heap of powdery dust and die in the attempt. Unbelievable!

You will get used to these little diversions from the subject and into my peculiar world view. I can't help it you see. Once my mind flutters off into these flights of fancy, I just have to wait until it returns to its roost in its own good time. Once I've ran out of steam, I usually settle down again and return to the story.

After a pleasant couple of hours nibbling on *pintxos* and sipping red wine, I ambled well sated and burping through the packed narrow *calles* to the little hostel I had checked into earlier. The 'Hostel Balea', was just a short walk along the river bank from the old town. It was very pleasant and good value at just 25 euros, and would do me nicely for my one night in the city. Following a refreshing little nap, I took a leisurely stroll back to the bay area to sample whatever night life was on offer.

San Sebastian must be where every Spaniard under 25 congregates for the summer! Wherever I turned I was faced with lively crowds of ridiculously good looking young folk, all determined it seemed, on getting pissed and mental as quickly as possible.

I felt incredibly ancient amongst all this vitality, but absorbed myself into their scene with as much brio as I could muster. I realised it had been quite some time since I was last out boogying, but I was still surprised that I appeared to be the only person attired in platform soled shoes, flared jeans and penny-round collar shirt. It was too hot for a tank-top.

It really was a very warm night; pleasantly tempered though by a gentle, salty breeze wafting in off the Atlantic, and I very much enjoyed perambulating along the promenades and curves of this very fetching bay.

It was very, very busy too. Every bar and patio was packed, and it took me ages to find a place in which I could both comfortably sit *and* recognise the music. After a few glasses of rough but interesting wine, I decided on one last spin along the river promenade before calling it a night. As if on cue, the sky erupted with a spectacular firework display and everyone around me began to applaud. Well really, this *was* a surprise! How splendid it was for my short visit to be recognised in such grand style, a couple of free drinks would have served just as well.

Acknowledging the acclaim and pointing appreciatively to the pyrotechnics, I humbly bowed my way back towards the hotel. What kind and thoughtful people are *Los Donostiarras*. I must remember to write a letter of appreciation to the Mayor.

The following morning burned bright with both sunlight and anticipation, and I passed a pleasant couple of hours pootling about the hot streets, eating up a bit of time and some more delicious *pintxos* before it was time to leave. I returned briefly to the Hostel to pick up my back pack, trudging heavily back into the centre and the cool shade of the underground bus station.

My original plan following my brief spell of R&R in San Sebastian, was to travel onwards by bus to Saint-Jean-Pied-de-

Port on the French side of the Pyrenees. Saint- Jean is the official starting point of the Camino Francés, my chosen route for the pilgrimage to Santiago de Compostela. As is often my way though, on the short and picturesque journey from San Sebastián to Pamplona where I planned to swap buses, I had a change of mind.

Looking at my maps, I could see that from Pamplona the bus would embark on a short but dizzying journey across the Pyrenees to Saint-Jean, where as I have stated I planned to begin my journey. It occurred to me then though, that this seemed a pointless trip to undertake. Upon my arrival in Saint-Jean, I would do nothing more than turn around and walk straight back over the mountains to Pamplona. Madness surely?

So, what to do? I knew that Saint-Jean was the 'official' start to the route and I should probably continue on to there. On the other hand, I was shortly to arrive in Pamplona, less than 60 kilometers into the Camino Francés. Was it such a big deal? At that point, I was far from convinced I would be able to complete the long journey across Spain to Santiago anyway, and I'm afraid to admit I easily talked myself into the Pamplona option, not really feeling it would make much difference in the long run.

Having made my decision I soon thereafter arrived in Pamplona, and following a long walk from the bus station to the city centre (why couldn't they put the bus station *in* the city centre?) I booked myself into a small and inexpensive hotel, and for what I thought might be my last night of real comfort for quite a while. I spent the late afternoon and early evening dodging rain showers, as I attempted to explore as much of Pamplona as I could in the few short hours available to me, and before I was to begin my journey.

Spending most of my time in the old city amongst the delightful narrow streets and busy plazas clustered around its centre, it took mere moments for me to take a shine to this lovely city. The main square in this part of Pamplona is the Plaza del Castillo; wide and spacious, and decorated with a plethora of bars and restaurants around its perimeter. Sitting just off the plaza, the standout buildings were the Gothic cathedral, which regrettably I didn't make time to visit, and the intricately designed Baroque influenced Town Hall; colourfully bedecked with large flags representing city, province and of course *Euskal Herria*, or Basque Country to you and me.

Pamplona, capital of the Navarre province is an ancient city and can trace its origins back to the Roman era. Down the centuries, it has been conquered and ruled by many different occupiers, the richness of its long and diverse history evident everywhere. Splendid buildings, with distinctive and varied architecture adorned every street and square. Balconied apartments above the shops and cafes gave the city a genuinely 'lived in' feel. Pamplona had a nice, easy going atmosphere, and I very much enjoyed my aimless wanderings through its streets, stopping occasionally here and there at a nice little bar for a beer or glass of wine.

Pamplona is of course, famous for its 'Bull Run' in July each year. The *encierro* is held during the festival of San Fermín and has long since become an international tourist event, attracting tens of thousands to the city annually. There have been many injuries and sadly deaths down the years, as the young men of the city rise to the centuries old challenge of 'running with the bulls'. It was difficult though on this particular day, to imagine such carnage and frenzy amongst the quiet and stately streets I happily explored.

That got me thinking. Nothing profitable usually comes from that activity, but anyway.

Having been raised on a strict diet of Dinnefords Gripe Water, porridge oats, Bill & Ben The Flower Pot Men (what *did* 'flobalob' mean?) and Dandy and Beano comics; excitement was brought into my life as a young boy via TV episodes of Thunderbirds, Batman and The Man from U.N.C.L.E. As I got older and a little more adventurous, 26-a-side football matches in the street, or clay-bunging fights in the fields at the back of our houses, raised the excitement stakes considerably.

Incidentally, clay-bunging for the uninitiated, is an Olympic standard sport where the assailant, sorry I mean competitor of course, selects a long, thin pared-down willow branch and tops it with a blob of softened clay. The objective then, is to whip-flick your weapon and direct your clay 'bullet' at high speed towards your selected target. A direct hit on exposed flesh would sting like hell, and leave a mark that would still be visible five days later. Many a sobbing, wounded child was sent off crying to his mum as a result of a direct hit. It was brilliant!

My teenage years presented two major challenges: Finagling my way into pubs for under-age drinking sessions with my mates, and insinuating my fingers and other desperate appendages into the soft fabric of girls underwear and associated parts. A session of the former often preceding, indeed necessitating, any attempt at the latter. Both of these were high risk and high adrenaline encounters, and probably represent the zenith of ambition and achievement of my adolescent years. Listen, it was the 1970s, what can I say?

Yet all these dangerous activities seem small beer indeed, when compared to the growing-up-dreams and death defying deeds of those brave young Spanish lads, intent on pitting their wits and foot speed against those massive, sharp-horned beasts.

History tells us, that this all started during the time when bulls were brought back in from the fields for mating, and the young men of the town would show off their bravado by running in front of them. Over time this developed a competitive edge, evolving into the tradition and spectacle we are familiar with today.

Nowadays, the participants must be over 18 (ladies too, oh yes) and not under the influence of alcohol. For my own part, a vast intake of strong drink would be *essential* to get me to run in front of a highly sexed, rampaging ton of beef, whose sole intention was to separate me from my large intestines. All very macho and exciting I'm sure, but I bet none of those Pamplona boys have ever had a serious go at clay-bunging. Now that could really take your eye out.

To its citizens, Pamplona is known as *Irũna*. This is a passionately Basque domain, and its distinctive language and culture is inseparable from the city and region. Basque ideology and its nationalist politics are complex, and its cause is deeply ingrained within its people.

The Basques argue that they are an ethnic-indigenous people, historically deserving of separate recognition as an independent nation. The Basque influence is spread over seven different regions; four in Spain and three in France, all hugging the Pyrenees which is at their identifying, geographical centre.

The background and history is, as I have said, complex to say the least, and has been molded and shaped by successive national governments and their policies towards the region. The modern 'campaign', as it were, can be traced back to the middle and late years of the 19th century, where changes in laws and relationships between the Basque provinces and the Spanish crown, dramatically changed the political landscape between both parties, effectively beginning the struggle which continues to this day.

The early 1960s saw the establishment of ETA; a para-military organisation aimed at achieving Basque autonomy. Towards the end of that decade, violence had become an important weapon in ETAs continuing struggle, leaving its deadly mark throughout the region and elsewhere in Spain over the following years. This continued until the longed for cessation of hostilities in 2011.

Following the death of Franco and Spain's return to democracy, the Spanish Basques at least, achieved a remarkable degree of independence and self-government which continues to this day. This sense of nationalism and ethnicity is visible throughout the region, and particular in its major populations such as Bilbao, San Sebastián and of course, here in Pamplona or more correctly, Irũna.

I really would have liked to have seen more of this very likeable city, but not wishing to be out too late, I made my reluctant way back to the hotel and an early night. Sleep didn't come easily though, my mind was a whirl of conflict as I grappled with the hesitation and indecision that was forming a hard knot in my stomach. Eventually though I drifted off, but only to a series of strange dreams and fearful apparitions dancing across my half-conscious mind. Bathed in sweat, I awoke at first light feeling not at all rested, and with the slow realisation that a great and compelling test was about to begin.

So, what brought me here and why? If you hang on a minute, I'll tell you.

In Around 1140 AD, an illuminated manuscript was produced called 'The Codex Calixtinus'. It was originally attributed as being the work of Pope Calixtus II, but is now generally recognised as being an anthology of individual works, brought together in this one book by Aymeric Picaud; a French scholar of that period.

The purpose of the book, was to give spiritual and practical advice to medieval pilgrims embarking on the Way of Saint James to Santiago de Compostela, and is often referred to as the 'Liber Sancti Jacobi', or the Book of Saint James. A very early edition of this book from around 1150 AD, is held in the archives of the cathedral at Santiago.

The book consists of five volumes: Book of the Liturgies; Book of the Miracles; Transfer of the body (of St James) to Santiago; The History of Charlemagne and Roland; and finally, A Guide for the Traveler. This last book does exactly what it says on the tin, and gave an abundance of practical advice to the medieval pilgrim intent on the journey to Santiago. Where to stay and get food, which shrines to visit on route, the nearest Tesco, the location of mobile phone charging points and cash machines etc. This last part of the volume, centuries past and to this day, achieved great fame. It is often held to be the world's first tourist guide book, and is rightly considered as a great historical work of learning, magnificence and beauty.

My own little story has no pretensions of achieving such reverence and recognition (give it time though) but it pretty much follows the same route along the Camino Francés as described in the Codex Calixtinus. A large number of the towns and cities described in the Codex appear in my own narrative. Many of the ancient churches and other wonderful buildings I visited along *The Way*, feature in that venerable tome too.

So, with old Aymeric dead these many centuries past, I decided it was time that the Camino had a new hero and travel guide. With all due modesty, I could think of no one better than my good self to give the job to. This then, is my visitation and re-experiencing of a near 900 year old story, the parenthesis of which are formed by: Aymeric Picaud, the great medieval monk-scholar and pilgrim, and me; a manic, wandering, garrulous fool, giving forth on this and that as the mood takes him.

Now then! If you are thinking of abandoning my little tale in favour of the Codex, I should point out a couple of important differences before you make your final choice.

Firstly: Aymeric's publication is written entirely in Latin. A dead language understood only by the Pope, a sprinkling of bearded academics and of course, Stephen Fry. My offering, however, is written in a *kind* of English that even a six-year-old can understand. Mainly of course, because it appears to have been written by one.

Secondly: the oldest copies of the Codex are locked away in cathedrals, abbeys and dusty libraries etc. and can only be accessed by esteemed scholars and very nosy people with lots of money. My story, however, is instantly accessible on-line, and after I've signed a lucrative publishing deal, will be available in all good bookshops and attractively priced.

Still with me? Grand, let's get cracking then. It might be better if you made some sandwiches and a pot of tea before you settle down. There are hundreds of kilometres to walk and many stories to share along the way, you'll be glad of a butty and a brew.

Oh, and you might want to keep a bottle of something stronger to hand to sustain you through some of the more, er, challenging passages........ Better make that two bottles.

TWO

Pamplona

to

Urtega

A melancholy mood hung over me like a shroud this morning, uncertainty and doubt, creeping in like an unwelcome guest. Not the best frame of mind with which to begin the day, nor indeed, the journey I was about to undertake. Feeling robbed of sleep and leg weary even before I'd set foot on the trail, I looked through the window of my small room onto a morning of leaden, rain threatening skies. I really could have done with some sunshine to brighten the day, and my humour.

Giving myself a shake and a good talking to, I pulled myself together and concentrated on the tasks I needed to complete before setting off. I lingered luxuriously over my usual early morning bathroom theatrics, thinking that from now on I would probably be digging holes in the ground for latrines whilst fighting off wolves, bathing in ice cold streams, and attacking my beard with blunt scissors and a butter knife. Feeling that a good breakfast might put me straight, I sought out a nearby café and shoveled down some bacon, toast and coffee. Better, much better.

I returned a little lighter in spirit to the hotel and following several aborted attempts at packing my rucksack, I had finally satisfied myself with what I felt I would both need *and* be able to carry, it was a fine balance. Having no other choice but to dump the few items of clothing I couldn't take, I bagged them and dropped them in a dumpster on my way out. Nothing to shed a tear about, the total value of my discarded stuff probably about three quid. What am I saying? The stuff I had retained wasn't worth much more, apart from my boots of course. Beyond value!

Whilst in San Sebastián the previous day, I had spotted several walkers who were clearly travelling the Camino Norté; the coastal and northern pilgrimage route to Santiago. Each of them I observed, had a large scallop shell tied to their packs, and I recognised this as being the famous symbol of St James and of the Camino. Passing a souvenir shop on my errands this morning, I saw a selection of those same shells and I bought one to tie to my own pack.

What a difference this single, simple act made to my mood. Now equipped with a badge that proclaimed my membership, as it were, I somehow felt that I now properly belonged on the Camino and that I was part of something important. It was a similar feeling as to when I first received my 'Sooty and Sweep Club' badge, in about 1962. Very emotional.

On leaving the hotel, I stopped for a while in a small park close by to make some final adjustments to my kit and to focus my thoughts. 'OK, let's do this', I cajoled myself, but without too much conviction I have to say. I made a last check of my map, dragged a worryingly heavy pack onto my shoulders and took the very first of the million or so steps that lay ahead of me on this journey. Like it or not, I was on my way.

I cast my mind back to a January day nearly thirty years ago. I was sat on a jumbo jet at Heathrow airport, awaiting take off on a flight bound for Australia. At that point I wasn't sure for how long I would be going, it may have been for good, and my mind was in a torment.

In the moments before push-back, I was overwhelmed by what I can only describe as a panic attack. I was shaking from head to foot, sweat poured from me, I was literally fighting with myself to stay in my seat. Every fiber of my being just wanted to get off that plane, to call the whole thing off, to just go home. I remember a young Irish couple sat next to me and in the process of emigrating, bawling their heads off. Not helpful, not helpful at all. Once the aircraft began to move however, the panic quickly subsided and I was just fine after that. What *was* all that about? It was however, a moment indelibly printed on my memory.

At the advent of this journey I wasn't having any panic attacks, I wasn't struck with any morbid fear, but I was consumed by doubt. I had a few moments where I thought: 'I don't have to do this, I might not be up to it, I could call it off, I could just go home'. But, like that moment at Heathrow all those years ago, once I got going I felt fine, confident enough to at least give it a go. No turning back now lad, it's time for take-off.

I discovered a little surprisingly, that I would be joining the Camino right at the end of the street where I had stayed the previous night. This first section of the footpath, would form part of the main artery through the city from east to west.

I had envisaged that the trail would somehow end at the edges of the towns and cities *en route,* and be picked up again at the outskirts upon leaving. That wasn't the case here or on any other part of the Camino, the path was continuous and unbroken over its entire length. The Way of St James had been part of the landscape for centuries, long before a good number of the towns and cities it carried were plonked upon it. Indeed, many of these places owed their very existence and prosperity, solely to the commerce the Camino and its pilgrims blessed them with.

Despite having good maps, I was conscious that the route could become complicated and difficult to follow, especially in negotiating a way through large towns and cities such as Pamplona. This would certainly be the case, if it wasn't for the presence of the simple but iconic trail markers synonymous with the Camino. All pilgrims soon become familiar with and are very thankful for, the way signs of the yellow arrow or the shell, guiding them through the busiest cities, the remotest hamlets and most isolated stretches on the trail.

The hero in this particular history of the Camino is one Don Elias Valina Sampedro, a parish priest in the Galician village of O Cebreiro (which will be heard of again later) and who was a great student of the Way of St James. Don Elias as a devotee of the trail, was convinced that the Camino needed reviving, and in 1984 he set about his mission to clean up and restore the signage on the French Way.

His most significant task, was to paint the bright yellow arrows that indicate the correct route to take at tricky spots along *The Way*. Don Elias, brushed his way along the extensive route in his little Citroen motor car, daubing scrounged paint on roads, trees and buildings and anything else he felt useful to his purpose. He was also instrumental in setting up little groups of supporters who would maintain and add to these markers over time, to the extent that these days they are an integral and much-loved feature for every pilgrim on the Camino.

All Camino travelers should give their thanks to him, I certainly did and many times too over the course of my journey. Don Elias died in 1989, without really seeing the full impact of his work and his legacy. It can truly be said however, that he left his mark on life in more ways than one!

The day's first task of course, was to find my way out of the city. Thankfully, the pavements were dotted at regular intervals with brass inlays of the shell emblem, and I found it was easy enough to negotiate my way through the streets and towards the outlying countryside.

Approaching the edge of the city, the route took me through a large, social housing development and for quite a distance too. The brass inlays of the city centre pavements had, for some unknown reason, been replaced by painted footprints and arrows. They worked just as well though, and I was soon passing through the modern looking towns of Cizur Menor and Cizur Major.

These estates were busy with new constructions and roads and were so anonymous, that neither really warrant any further comment here.

Not yet used to keeping my eyes open for the arrows I lost the trail for a while, but realising my mistake quickly enough, I recovered my ground and was soon back on track. So far, the Camino had been pretty uninspiring during its long trek through the suburbs, when suddenly! I reached the edge of a housing development, passed through a gap between two gable ends and onto a dirt track set down on a broad plain. I did a quick double-take. A huge, ugly council estate behind me and in front, a vista of meadows and mountains. Fantastic.

A blue sign atop a wooden marker pole pointed the way to the first destinations on my itinerary today, comforting proof that I was now well and truly on my way. Having left the confines of the city behind, I felt I was now on the true Camino of the wilderness, the Camino of centuries and pilgrims past. It was a nice, memorable moment to mark this early stage of my journey.

Although it had been a relatively short walk out of Pamplona I was already in need of a rest, as much to get the pack off my back for a while as anything else. I realised in the initial stages at least that this would be an issue, as I got used to the combination of carrying the weight of my pack over long distances *and* in the heat. It would get easier of that I was certain, but right then? It was hurting.

A nice and steady walk along a gently rising, well-trodden path, was my introduction to the many harder kilometres I felt certain lay ahead. Seeing my *first* fellow pilgrims on the trail was an encouraging moment too, *alth*ough they were mainly cyclists at this point. Each of them ch*eerily* offered the traditional greeting of 'Bon Camino' as they pas*sed by*; a wish for a good and safe journey invariably exchanged betw*een* travelers everywhere along *The Way*.

I was beginning to feel much more positive now, certain that I was doing the right thing and that I was where I wanted to be. Slowly but surely as I grew into the rhythm of the walk, the clouds of doubt from earlier were being dispelled, as indeed were the real ones above me. It was turning into a very hot and sunny day.

I was heading for what I had originally chosen to be my rest stop for the night, the small, isolated village of Zariquiegui, sitting peacefully just over half-way up the mountain. As a Camino novice, I had no real idea where or when would be a good time to call an end to my first day. My map showed Puenta la Reina as the suggested end to this section of the trail, but at 24k from Pamplona seemed a big ask at that time. I was quickly to learn that the section guides in my map book were exactly that; a guide or indication as to what would be considered a good days walk, depending on terrain etc.

From the second day on, I would mostly stay within the general frame work of the daily guides, but happily, they allowed for a lot of flexibility. At that point then and to as yet my untrained eye, Zariquiegui just looked and felt like an appropriate place to stop.

The trail was now growing steeper with every step, but the burden was thankfully eased by the fantastic views opening up around me as I climbed ever higher. Pausing briefly to look back down the trail, Pamplona was already 10 kilometres behind me and quickly receding into the distance.

Feeling pretty tired by now but quietly determined, I decided upon reaching Zariquiegui that I still had enough gas in the tank to press ahead and take on the first big climb of the journey. Apart from anything else, I had only walked 11 Kilometres so far, nowhere near enough for a day on the Camino. Having had a relatively late start, I decided I would push on into the evening, confident enough that there was still plenty of daylight to work with before I would have to call an end to my first walking day.

Following a rest and a bite to eat, I began the very steep ascent along the rough track to the top of Alto del Perdón. The uneven trail was surrounded by thorny bushes and scattered rocks as I followed its course up the mountain side, but the backdrop was now beginning to blur. I could feel my field of vision gradually narrowing to the path beneath my feet, my eyes fixed solely on the sloping trail as my energy drained away. It really was a very stiff pull up to the top and my pack felt like a ton weight, with the straps biting painfully into my shoulders. For the first time but certainly not the last, I found myself having to dig deep for the reserves of energy and determination that I needed to drive me on.

Drawing then, on the experiences gathered over many years and thousands of miles on my walks back home, I straightened up and pressed on. I clambered and tottered unsteadily up the final metres, cheeks blowing with relief as I finally crested the peak. Once I had got my breath back, I allowed myself a small fist pumping celebration. The first of the countless mountains and hills I would encounter over the coming weeks, had been conquered!

The heights of Alto del Perdón (Mount of Forgiveness) provided my first taste of the knockout scenery I had hoped for, and it took a while to take it all in. The vast basin in which Pamplona sat stretched for miles beneath me, and out towards the brooding massif of the Pyrenees to the east.

On the other side of the mountain lay the dale of Valdizarbe; long and wide and fading into the distant haze. It really was quite stunning. On the peak itself, thrumming with the sound of the many nearby giant wind turbines, was set a little shrine, a covered lectern describing the peak and its history, and two or three monuments.

The most interesting and impressive of these, was an enormous artwork strung across the peaks edge on the Pamplona side. It was a series of sculpted metal figures in silhouette, depicting a caravan of pilgrims and pack animals cast just as they would have been on pilgrimages spanning the ages. The entire piece was simply but beautifully characterised, graphically encapsulating both the long history of the Camino and its relevance for modern day travelers.

This artwork, created by Vincent Galbete, has been part of the Alto del Perdón landscape since 1996 and bears the inscription: (translated from Spanish) 'Where the path of the wind crosses that of the stars'. Unadorned words, but very effective and really quite poignant. A reminder if one was needed, that I was embarking on a journey first travelled many centuries ago, and by countless thousands since.

My mind drifted briefly, as I tried to conjure those sculptured shapes into real life. What must it have felt like to be stood on this exact spot eight or nine hundred years ago? What thoughts must have occupied those modest and unworldly pilgrims, as they pondered the unknown and possibly dangerous journey ahead? Were they frightened or excited? Was their faith enough to sustain them through the hardships and sacrifices they would have to endure?

With all the modern aids and relative certitude of safety and security attached to my own journey, I still felt exposed and a little tentative as I stood and pondered over the kilometres ahead, and back through those ages past. I truly hoped I would have the self-belief, strength and determination, to be a worthy follower in the ancient and humble footsteps of those long ago pilgrims.

I crossed over the mountain top road (access for the wind turbines) and peered out over the western side of the peak, taking a much closer look at the valley unfolding below. I paid particular attention to the path I would shortly be taking on, tumbling down the mountainside and across the distant plain. It was an awesome sight and I was irresistibly drawn towards it, itching now to be on my way again. And so, with enough naval gazing for one day, I dragged my 'ton weight' pack onto protesting shoulders, and set off on the last leg of today's journey.

The climb I had recently completed was to be matched by an equally steep and long descent, this would carry me most of the way to my revised overnight destination of Uterga. Hefty sections of the long climb down were over rough stones and rutted dirt track, and it was pretty tough going, any slip could end in injury. I was also by now, really feeling the effects of the long climb up, the strain on my knees and thighs particularly telling.

Despite the difficulty and having to concentrate on virtually every step, it was fabulous to see the broad, fertile valley below drawing ever nearer and gradually clearer. Unknown hills were emerging and sharpening in the distance too, as the sun slowly lowered, painting a moody and forbidding backdrop. This was how I imagined the Camino would be, and even though I was but halfway through the first day, I was already completely hooked.

Eventually the steep decline eased, evening out onto a short, straight and dusty track. It was then just a couple more kilometres, before another gentle climb led me up a rise to the little *pueblo* playing host to my first night on the Camino.

I entered the small village of Uterga feeling very tired, carrying stiff legs and with an aching back, but nonetheless, really chuffed with myself and my efforts on this first day. A quick scout around revealed the village to be little more than a small, unpresuming affair, thankfully removing the need for any post-hike sight-seeing.

Feeling incredibly knackered and very thirsty, I soon found a table outside a modern looking bar/restaurant and launched myself into several well-earned, life restoring cold beers. Once rested and revived, I walked the short distance across the street to check into my first Camino albergue, my first *cara-vanserai* as a pilgrim. I have to say, I was just a little apprehensive of what I might find.

The albergue 'Casa Baztan', a large, three-storied structure was surprisingly quiet I thought, with only half a dozen occupants in a place I guessed, for 50 or more. This was my first stay in one of these places, and I was very pleasantly surprised and impressed with its layout, cleanliness and great facilities. I really hoped this augured well for the rest of the trip.

The young *Hospitalier* in charge of the albergue greeted me very warmly as I entered through the doors, beckoning me towards the front desk to check me in. "Hablas Español?" He asked, rightly sensing my mastery of his native tongue. "Sí, pero por supuesto!" I was confidently able to confirm, continuing in my best Spanish to explain my day's journey and how I had arrived at his impressive dwelling and what pray, were my instructions? With a furrowed brow, he exclaimed that I should wait a moment and disappeared into a back room.

A couple of minutes later, he emerged holding a map, two eggs, a ball of string and a bicycle pump. Laying these items on the desk he said: " Eet is difficult, but I think thees what you ask for, but I am sorry, I no 'ave any burnt lemons. I think I call my sister, she speak Norwegian". How extraordinary! Perhaps it was my accent?

After the formality of noting my UK passport details, the freshly summoned sister then added the first stamp to my *Credencia*, my 'Camino Passport'. A single impression on a field of empty and pristine pages, that hopefully by journeys end, would be full of the unique seals I would collect from every city, town and village I would visit on the long road to Santiago.

Apologising for her brothers laughable inability to decipher my Spanish, she asked me to repeat what I had said earlier. "Ahh, no problem, I understand" she exclaimed confidently.

Excusing herself, she returned moments later with a photograph of the King of Spain, a chess set, a violin and a toasted cheese sandwich. What on earth is *wrong* with these people?

The near empty ground floor dormitory where I was to sleep was lined with neat rows of double bunks, with blocks of spacious lockers placed around to hold packs and valuables under lock and key. In Britain of course, none of these would have worked, with locks busted and keys missing. Here, every locker was in good order and clean too. The shower rooms and toilets were just behind the main bunk room, and were absolutely spotless.

I was very pleased to have found such a nice place on my first night, it really was most reassuring.

From the outset this morning, it had been a fast-changing day of appreciating and adapting to the demands of the trail, added to by a growing realisation that I would need to up my game considerably in the days ahead. I also felt that too much of the day had passed me by, and I hadn't been taking in enough of the scenery or atmosphere of my surroundings. I needed to relax a little, let the hiking come naturally and appreciate the environment more. All part of the learning curve I knew, and something to put into practice in the coming days.

Feeling exhausted and footsore after a long hard day, I stowed my gear, had a quick shower and was soon settled in my comfy bunk bed.

In the moments before sleep closed in, I thought back to how I had felt that morning, uncertain and cautious to say the least. Just a single day on the trail however, had transformed my outlook.

I knew that there would be many more difficulties and challenges ahead, but I now felt much more confident that with sufficient determination, dedication and spirit, I was capable of achieving real success on this journey.

The measure of that success would of course be determined in the weeks ahead, but I was definitely prepared now to give it my best shot.

Distance walked today – 22 Kilometres. (22)

THREE

Urtega

to

Lorca

Fearing that through downright tiredness I would over-sleep I had set my alarm, but I was awake well before it's jarring tones could disturb the quietness of the early morning. The first hint of daylight was just beginning to show through the dormitory windows, as I dragged my stiff and aching limbs from my bunk. After a wash and brush-up I packed my gear and was ready to go, but first I thought, a quick brew and some breakfast. I hadn't eaten much at all the previous day.

In the quiet and otherwise empty dining room I met a young Austrian girl, Anna. She was just 19, and like me had walked from Pamplona the previous day. She was a lovely lass, and I would see her often throughout the course of the journey. I was a little surprised to hear her say she was travelling alone, but over the next few days I discovered that this would not be at all unusual. I had the pleasure of coming across many young girls travelling solo on this journey.

Should I rephrase that last sentence?

Anna explained to me with great amusement, that her mother was going crazy with worry about the terrible things that might happen to her, vulnerable and alone in the Spanish wilderness. She had soberly reminded her mum that she lived in Vienna; and could be raped, robbed, stabbed and murdered, or indeed all of these terrible things on the way home from the bus stop where she lived. None of which however, were likely to happen up here on the Camino. All true I'm sure, but my image of the city of Hapsburgian palaces, wedding cake buildings, waltzes and romantic strolls along the Danube, was shattered forever.

We chatted for a while over coffee and toast, her English was excellent, and she told me how she had just left high school and was off to University in September. I questioned her as to how she had come to be spending a chunk of her holiday alone on the Camino? I assumed that teenaged girls recently released from the shackles of school, would be indulging in the flesh pots of Ibiza or the like. She replied with a non-committal shrug, so I left it at that.

I had the feeling there was a bit more to Anna's story than met the eye, but that was none of my business. On the Camino your private world was sacrosanct, and quite right too.

As she questioned my own plans, I was unsure of whether Anna was fishing for some company on today's walk, we were certainly travelling the same route. Perhaps a little guardedly or even selfishly I decided not to pursue this line, as in these early days at least, I really wanted to walk on my own. Feeling a little guilty I guess but nevertheless, as soon as Anna left the dining room to get her gear together, I quickly slipped away to set about my second day on the trail.

I did think it would be typical of my bloody bad luck, that later on some thoughtful soul would pull me to one side and say: "Do you remember that girl you were talking to at breakfast this morning? Well, she has been found stabbed, raped, robbed and murdered; alone and friendless in the wilderness just like her Mother said would happen. Maybe you should have walked with her?" Thankfully, I had a lucky escape; no such bulletin arrived and I could breathe easy.

Today's first goal would be the small town of Puente la Reina. My map indicated that this section of today's walk should at least be gentle enough walking, which, I can assure you suited me just fine. I was very much hoping for an easier day after the stresses and strains of the previous one. I was to discover in the days and weeks ahead however, and not missing the irony one bit, that yesterday's little saunter was to be amongst the easier ones I would undertake.

From Uterga then, it was a nice enough walk through the meadows with which to begin the day. Passing firstly through Muruzábal and skirting an impressive looking winery set just off the trail, it was then onto Óbanos, which, my guide book proclaimed importantly, forms the junction of the Camino from Somport and Roncesvalles and the 'Camino Arigones'.

Whilst I wasn't expecting to encounter a great, thronging crossroads such as once might be found at ancient Kashgar on the Silk Road from China, I did think that this confluence might cough up a few extra hikers onto the trail, which to this point at least, had been much quieter than I expected. However, quiet it was to remain. Neither pilgrims nor spice laden camels come to that, were to join my caravan of one as I journeyed on.

I stopped for a little rest at the outskirts of the village, keen to unload my pack for a while and massage my tender shoulders. After the early sun it had become quite cloudy but remained very warm, and my shirt was darkened with sweat. I hung it on a bush for a while to dry out, whilst I set about beating the stiffness from my throbbing neck.

I was surprised at how quickly I had begun to feel the demands of the hiking this morning, and this was fairly easy going stuff right now. I was only five or six kilometres into my days walk and I knew I would need to concentrate my effort, not allowing my focus to be distracted by a bit of tiredness or a few aches and pains. Come on lad, buck up!

Moving on after my short break and self-bollocking, I steadily worked my way down the lush greenness of the gradually shelving slopes of the Baranco de la Tejeria, the air fresh and pure, with a quiet peacefulness reigning. It really was very pleasant walking, just what I needed to get myself settled and find a good rhythm. A few minutes later down the gentle incline, and I was entering through the historic portals of Puente la Reina.

This was a beautiful medieval town. The main street was long and dark and flanked by ancient and attractive stone buildings, many sporting ornate balconies overlooking the cobbles. As I ambled down the street, I could not but admire the cleverness of the locals, in the way that they had incorporated modern businesses into old and original structures, *and* without any of the senseless despoliation of acres of glass frontages that you see almost everywhere. Alas, I couldn't linger too long as I needed to push on, but I took my time wandering down this lovely thoroughfare, with its lively and varied architecture and atmospheric feel. It was absolutely splendid.

At the edge of the town, and having just crossed its magnificant 11th century Romanesque bridge, I was approached by a scruffy looking man, somewhere in his late forties I would guess. He was clearly equipped for walking but all his gear was random and tatty, sitting awkwardly on his skinny, bedraggled frame. Without any pre-amble, he probed at me via grunts and gestures for money and/or food, making it clear he possessed neither. Taken aback somewhat at encountering this type of behaviour on the Camino, I quickly gave him some change and with his mission completed, he bowed his thanks and off he went.

I was to encounter this fellow (he was French, I discovered later) throughout the entire journey and he was always scrounging, although very cleverly. Approaching pilgrims outside bars or albergues, he would theatrically and with much pathos, demonstrate the reason for his plight and need for money. He was clearly a con artist. He would frequently produce a tattered piece of paper purporting promises of money being payed into his bank account the following day, and could he "borrow" some money in the meantime. Get real!

He was often and surprisingly so in my view, successful in his pleadings, although I think most people just wanted rid of him. He tried it with me a couple of times along the way (I don't think he was too hot on remembering faces) but I was not so easily taken in. Here he was on my second day out, and I was to see him for the last time in Fisterra on the Atlantic coast over a month later, still at it.

Having said all that, I did make a point of studying his technique very closely, in case I might need to indulge in a bit of judicious begging myself later in the journey!

Resuming the Camino, I followed the course of the Río Arga which briefly led the way out of town. Onwards then, through the village of Mañeru and up through the taxingly steep streets of Cirauqui; a nice *pueblo* boasting a well-preserved selection of Roman roads and bridges. This was an intriguing looking village featuring an impressive Gothic church at its summit and which I would have loved to have explored. I longed to linger, but there was to be no time for sight seeing today, I really had to press on.

There were several climbs on this section; some short, some long and all tough going, and across a terrain that lurched along like a stretched out roller coaster. I plodded on regardless, but not without a bit of discomfort accompanying my efforts, I have to say. I was really feeling the bight of the backpack on my shoulders even though it was still early in the day, and my neck was aching terribly. Far from perfect, but I just had to ignore these little irritants and push on.

The weather in the first part of the day had been ideal for walking; overcast and not too hot. Gradually though the clouds began to recede, and around 1.30pm cleared to blue skies and hot sunshine.

By now, my shirt was once more completely drenched in sweat, so I stopped to change. I applied sun cream and lip protection, put on my cap to shield from the sun and set off again. Immediately on completing all this palaver, the sun retreated behind the gathering cloud that had sneaked up in the meantime, and wouldn't be seen again until early evening. Why did I bother? Unbelievable! I had a feeling that this was going be a long day.

The lengthy and strenuous climb up to Lorca did for me. I had intended to press on to Estella, only another eight or nine kilometres further along the trail, but by 3.30pm I was completely buggered. After only the briefest of deliberations, I decided that Lorca would need to be my stopover for the evening. I wasn't discouraged by any means. I knew I would get better at this, fitter and more able to complete the distances required each day. Bloody soon though, I sincerely hoped.

I immediately found a very nice albergue on the edge of the village, and imaginatively named, 'Albergue de Lorca'. It was owned and operated by a very nice Oriental lady and nominally at least, her Spanish husband. His role it seemed to me, was to sit at the bar whilst his wife did about fifteen different jobs!

She didn't seem remotely put out and besides, she was soon joined by a local chap who took over the bar and front of house bit, whilst she retired into the kitchen to take charge of the cooking bit. The husband meanwhile had lit a cigarette ('No Smoking' law selectively applied here, apparently), poured himself a beer and sat back on his stool, exhausted it appeared, by watching the efforts of his wife and staff. Nice work if you can get it.

This hostel was a small and narrow building, opening up towards the rear to accommodate dining tables and chairs. It was clean, comfortable and most hospitable. The small dormitory and bathrooms were to be found up a single flight of stairs, and set directly above the bar-cum-restaurant below. It really was a very nice and cozy little place in which to rest up.

My new Chinese friend offered to show me around the facilities and to where I would be bunking that night. She also showed me the cubby hole by the doorway where I was to leave my footwear. There, placed neatly side by side were a dozen or so pairs of boots. Why couldn't I take my cherished footwear upstairs to the bunk room? The obvious was soon explained.

From long experience, it was recognised that the addition of several pairs of stinking boots to the already, shall we say, challenging air of dormitories in albergues along the Camino was to be avoided at all costs. Sure enough, at every albergue I stayed in thereafter there was an area, often outside, where walkers were to leave their malodorous boots. No exceptions! I gave my own boots a good sniff, just to check their whiff factor, as it were. I got a generous blast of 'Eau de blue cheese and pickled onions'. What's so wrong with that?

Cleaned up and refreshed by a couple of cold beers, I set out for a brief but unrewarding look at what little there was to see in this tiny *pueblo*. A short walk along the street revealed just one other albergue and bar, and this directly opposite my own hostel.

Finding nothing else of interest and with a strong, cool breeze building, I returned to the albergue for the *'menú del día'* dinner I had reserved and paid for earlier. I was very hungry, and sat down to a wholesome three courses with plenty of wine to help it along, all efficiently served by our happy, smiling hostess and her friendly assistant. It was most enjoyable, and I left three clean plates as evidence.

I shared a table and enjoyed a lively chat with three young Italians, one guy and two girls. Lucky lad. They were all in their early thirties, professionals and with great futures by the sound of it. They were lovely people, full of spirit and joy, how I envied their enthusiasm for the life ahead. Just wait until they have been bitten on the arse a few times by life's blood sucking midges, I thought, that'll soon wipe the smiles off their faces. What a cynical old git I am!

A strange interlude. This was the same day as the tragic road bridge collapse in Genoa, I had seen the horrific scenes earlier on my phone whilst checking the news. I mentioned this warily to my Italian friends, in case they didn't know. "Ah yes, we heard" replied one of the girls, nodding sympathetically "A very sad day, but you know in Italy, these things happen from time to time" With that, she carried on talking about the extortionate price of lip stick in Milan or some such. A subject clearly more interesting to her pals too, than tragedy, death and injury to their compatriots. Extraordinary.

happily wined and dined, my lovely dinner companions bade me goodnight and retired to their bunks. I lingered for a while longer, finishing off the last of the excellent Rioja our hosts had provided, also thoughtfully helping to see off the remnants of the wine left on the adjacent tables. Better washing over my tonsils I thought, than gurgling down an unappreciative plug hole!

It had been a tiring but very enjoyable day, and I was feeling much more comfortable with my situation now. To re-enforce my thoughts from the previous night; I felt at this point I had a better understanding of what to expect, and I think the shock, if you like, of the first couple of days had now evaporated somewhat. I was very much more certain now, that everything would work out just fine.

Enjoying a last chat with the Italians, I decided in an act of terrible revenge for them being intelligent and beautiful, full of vitality and more importantly young, to recount that I had also seen on the news, that the price of pasta and tomatoes in Italy had trebled during the day and unfortunately, further large increases were expected. I clambered up to my bunk to the sounds of much weeping, wailing and beating of Italian chests. The worst kind of news travels fastest and cuts deepest, it would seem.

With these last mischievous thoughts bouncing around my weary brain, I realised my day was done. It was still daylight, but as would become the pattern over the coming weeks I was fast running out of steam. It was only around 9.00pm, but man, was I ready to sleep!

Distance walked today – 22 Kilometres (44)

FOUR

Lorca

to

Los Arcos

Although I was up ready and good to go at first light, my young Italian friends had already left. I wouldn't see them again on this trip, which was a shame. I liked them a lot and they laughed at all my jokes. Clearly, highly intelligent and sophisticated people of taste and refinement. No really.

As I gathered my gear together in the early morning bustle of the dormitory, yawning 'bon dia's' were whispered between the reluctant and shuffling early risers. Not wishing to hang around, I shrugged on my pack and quietly made my way out of the albergue into the early morning chill. The nascent morning sky was barely lit by a sun yet to break over the hills behind me, as I headed out towards Estella. This would be my first port of call on the Camino today.

The previous three days had been predominantly overcast; not too hot and usually accompanied by a nice fresh breeze, but not today. As the morning progressed, the sun gradually eased over the shadowy hills, imprinting itself onto a vast and cloudless blue sky. The heat was building steadily too with the passing of each kilometre, ominously so in these early morning hours. By midday, it would be almost 30oC.

The road out from Lorca was steep and immediately challenging, and I was soon perspiring with the effort. Although a hard climb up it was thankfully short, and I was soon on a long, easy descent running closely alongside the N-111A.

About 6k out from Lorca, I encountered the village of Villatuerta and paused briefly here to admire the striking architecture of its Gothic church, sadly closed at this time.

I'll mention straight away that I am a devotee of Spanish architecture; be it Moorish, medieval gothic, post renaissance or modern. The Camino in this respect is a huge treasure trove. From the simplest of ancient village streets to the mightiest cathedrals, there was usually something to admire, enjoy and remember in most places along the route.

Principally due to the history of the French Way, but also in respect of Spain's Catholic traditions; ancient churches, cathedrals, monasteries and convents etc. are all prominent along the Camino. During the course of my journey, and as you will see, I spent as much time as I could admiring the many architectural delights I discovered along the way. A lot of these visits would be to these various religious houses. Not in preference to or ignoring any other structures, but because in many of the places I passed through or visited, it's local church or monastery was often the *only* building of any architectural merit or interest!

From Lorca then, I swept quickly past the Ermita de San Miguel (without pausing to admire anything, thus contradicting myself immediately) marching stoutly on for another hour or so along an undulating yet undemanding trail, before arriving at Estella just before 10.30am.

This is a really pleasant, medium sized town, which over the centuries had gradually expanded around its medieval centre. Estella boasts a regal history, having once been the ancient seat of the Kings of Navarra. The narrow Río Ega rippled slowly through the centre of the town, with a large 12th century castle providing an impressive back drop. It really was quite delightful, and an excellent spot for a break.

From the get-go this morning, I had been experiencing problems with my backpack. It just wasn't sitting comfortably at all, and I took the opportunity of this short rest to have a look and sort it out. I discovered that the straps were out of sync, one being an inch or so longer than the other and felt certain that this was the cause of the discomfort to my neck and shoulders. That needed sorting.

I felt an instant improvement after that little adjustment, my pack felt better balanced and closer fitting and this cheered me up no end! I hoped that would help with my aches and pains, and from that point on I checked the alignment of my pack regularly. A salutary example of the old adage of having to learn your lessons the hard way.

Rested, revived and comfortable at last, I pursued the short climb out of Estella, quietly easing through an eye-catching stretch of trail that wandered peacefully amidst leafy, wooded glades. Simply beautiful.

Through the gaps between the spreading and densely leafed trees alongside the trail, I snatched occasional yet incredible views of the Sierra de Andia mountain range rising away to the north. A formidable and rocky barrier to the Atlantic Ocean beyond. Pushing steadfastly on up the slope, I was soon into Ayegui. Here, the town marker proudly announced that this was kilometre 100 on the Camino Francés. Great, I thought, only about another 680 to go!

Just beyond the outskirts of Ayegui I came across a signpost and turnoff to the Monastery at Irache, and which had been a subject of eager discussion back at the albergue in Lorca. Apart from its many historical and architectural delights, the monastery also housed capacious wine cellars and a bodega, from which Camino pilgrims were offered free wine! My feet twitched and turned instinctively, like a diviners wand towards water and this fine institution. Disappointingly, the miserable, sensible person in charge of my thinking today, strongly advised against such a foolhardy deviation from the trail. He was right of course (smart arse) once in amongst the cool caverns of the bodega and supping on free wine, my walking day would be over before it had properly begun.

By the time I got to Los Arcos and as you will see, I bitterly regretted not taking advantage of the free refreshment on offer.

Yet another long and testing climb led up to the village of Azqueta, settled tantalisingly part way up the mountain. I found some welcome shade by the side of a church and sat on the grass for a while, admiring what was clearly a fine-looking little *pueblo*.

From inside the chapel I could hear the service celebrating the feast of the assumption, an important religious holiday and fiesta in Spain. Lulled by the drone of the congregation and the stifling heat, I almost nodded off! My tranquil was shattered however, by the shouts and screams of children rushing noisily from the church and charging about in the little square. No doubt excited by the promise of treats to be had and games to be played at the fiesta to follow. It was a wonderful scene and brilliant to watch.

Enlivened a little by my short break, I moved on. A short sharp descent pointed the way down the valley from Azqueta, followed immediately by a long and fairly steep climb to the crest of the peak, where awaited the *aldea* of Villamayor de Monjardín.

The views from here were simply breathtaking. The ruins of a large castle sat on top of a nearby hill, etched like a child's drawing onto the skyline and dominating the surrounding area. The lush green valleys, grape laden vineyards and deeply forested hills sweeping up from them, appeared boundless. From this high point, I could make out the roofs and church spires of distant hillside villages poking through the trees. Occasional glints of sun reflecting from speeding cars, picked out the numerous roads that snaked their way through this hilly terrain. It was completely mesmerizing, and I was reluctant to drag myself away from these stunning views, but I just had to press on.

I was panting and sweating a waterfall, hands on hips as I wobbled into the village. With the heat rising unremittingly I talked myself into another break, ducking into the dark shadows alongside this villages impressive church. Sitting gratefully under a large parasol outside a nearby shop and listening to the gentle strains of the feast day service from within, I wondered if the priest from Azqueta had driven at top speed to say mass here? Surely these days, these little mountain villages must have to share a regional priest, as it were? If this was the case, it must be a tough gig to take on in the snowy wastes of winter.

It was only 1.30pm, yet I was already feeling the combined effects of the climbing and the heat, and was sorely tempted to call it a day. More so, as there was an albergue just opening its doors invitingly across the plaza. But this just would not do!! I *knew* that I would have to get used to putting in the kilometres and not submit so readily to tiredness. Buck up lad! With that self-administered reprimand, I pulled myself up onto weary legs, my pack onto stiff shoulders and with a wistful glance back at the albergue, trudged gamely on.

At this early stage of the journey the main battle was with my mind, and I must train myself to ignore and not be held back by my physical struggles. 'Overcome, adapt and keep going', would be my mantra from hereon.

My previous mantra being a less inspiring 'Fuck me I'm tired, shall I pack it in?'. I like a good mantra.

A close study of my maps, revealed the next accessible town on the Camino to be 14 kilometres distant at Los Arcos. It appeared from the cross section that after a sharp descent, the trail then rolled out over a wide, gently descending plain, before dropping sharply for the last few kilometres into the town. I was very certain, that I could knock off this distance easily enough over the course of the afternoon. I was soon to be disabused of that notion. It was amongst the most grueling and punishing short walks I've ever undertaken.

Following the descent from Villamayor, the Camino roamed its way through open farmland. This was mainly of recently harvested corn fields and occasional vineyards, with fields of sundry crops scattered either side of the trail. There was absolutely no shade at all, natural or otherwise; just an endless white strip of winding track, disappearing into the distant heat-haze.

I was walking almost directly into the sun by now, with the temperature at least 30oC. It quickly became apparent, that the afternoons walk wasn't going to be anything like as easy as I thought. It took me five hours of arduous and energy sapping hiking, to cover a distance I would normally do in little more than three.

At some point on this grueling slog, a pick-up truck towing a caravan of sorts swept past me, heading back down the road towards Villamayor. A little further on, I spotted where it had come from. Just off the trail was a shelter for a pop-up bar, the pop-up bar that had just driven past me! I had just by minutes, missed the chance of cold drinks and food, and who knows, maybe a spot of light cabaret? All that remained was an empty, open sided cabin in which I gratefully took shelter from the sun.

The place was deserted and I completely stripped off, both to cool down and to hang my sweat sodden and dripping clothes on the nearby fence to dry out. It wasn't a pretty site. Even with my clothes off, I still looked as if I needed ironing.

I was hoping my naked cavorting would be spotted and re-ported to the police. At the very least I would get a lift into town and maybe a cool, dark cell all to myself. Captive bliss.

In the absence of sirens, flashing lights and a comfortably handcuffed drive, there was no choice but to push on, and so I did; but with an aching, creaking slowness. By the time I stumbled into Los Arcos, my finger nails were growing faster than I was walking, and I crawled into the town a sun-shriveled, gibbering wreck.

The first building I saw, shimmering mirage like on the very outskirts of the town, was a refuge provided by the 'Friends of the Camino'. I have never been so pleased to see a converted garage.

Staggering the last few metres on legs barely able to function, I fell inside the shelter seeking out the darkest corner. I stripped off my shirt and sat unmoving for what seemed like an age, guzzling bottle after bottle of water from the drinks machine, desperately trying to cool off and re-hydrate. Occasionally, the *Hospitalier* on duty in the refuge came by, switching his broom over the spotlessly clean floor whilst eyeing me suspiciously. I think he was just checking to see if I was still alive!

This really had been an early examination of my endurance, mental and physical and I hoped I had passed, because I was certain, very certain by this time, that there would be a lot more days like this ahead. Well, I thought cheerlessly, that's something to look forward to isn't it?

Hobbling into the town centre on shattered legs and sore feet, shoulders throbbing under my rucksack, my spirits were soon lifted as I approached the main street. The town was decked out in all its finery, flags and bunting hanging from every building, and I was met full on by a seriously up and running fiesta in honour of the holy day. It was rocking! The towns folk were dressed in white from head to foot, garishly trimmed with red neck bandanas and sashes. The kids were tearing around buzzing with excitement, laughing and shouting, cheeks bulging with sweets and pastries. It was a glorious riot of colour and noise.

Numerous food stalls and a bewildering variety of others were closely packed around the central square where the evenings entertainments were unfolding, crowds of eager customers surrounding each one. The plaza had been turned into a mini arena, its small wooden stands packed with those lucky enough to get in. The main event would be the running of the bulls through the streets later in the evening. Similar to the more famous version in Pamplona, but on a much smaller scale. Sadly, I wouldn't get to see this spectacle, it would all happen long after I lay unconscious on my bed.

Luckily, I had managed to snag one of the last couple of bunks at the albergue operated by 'Los Amigos de Camino'. This was a lay brotherhood of volunteers, much respected for the work they do in their society hostels and on the Camino itself.

The 'Albergue de Peregrinos Isaac Santiago' was large, modern, very well appointed and operating under very strict rules and regulations; the list of which was sternly read out to me before I was allowed over the threshold. A little extreme, I thought, even for the exacting requirements of a pilgrim hostel.

Whilst chatting briefly to the *Hospitalier* in charge of check-in, he enquired as to which part of England I hailed from? On hearing I was from Derbyshire, he was beyond excited to tell that me he and his wife would be walking in the Peak District the following summer. I told him they were more than welcome to come and stay with me as long as they were in bed by 10 pm, no smoking, no drinking or talking, and definitely no shagging after lights out.

Feeling much livelier after a shower, I quickly returned to the town centre to sample, if only briefly, the wonderful atmosphere of the fiesta. It was fabulous; a real family, civic and religious occasion, all brought together on this most beautifully warm and scented Spanish night. Quite simply, fantastic.

I was really growing into the spirit of this pilgrimage now, I would be very happy to do the hard miles in return for evenings and events such as this. I didn't, of course, expect to be greeted by a fiesta every night, but I certainly intended to enjoy this one. At least for as long as I could remain upright!

It was difficult to decide where to go, entertainment and attractions were all around. A band playing here, or a conjuring show over there? Art and craft stalls to browse amongst, or maybe the flamenco dancers? It was excellent, and it wouldn't be the only time on this trip, that I would be seduced by the wonderful warmth and community spirit of small town Spanish life. I could live in this lovely little place, I thought. I could fold myself easily into the fabric of this way of life, and not look back at all. Dreams, dreams.........

I have been a regular visitor to Spain over the last fifteen years or so, sometimes staying for months at a time. I speak a little of the language, and I can identify so easily and readily with the people and their culture. Spain is such a vibrant country, rich in its regional diversity and geographical make up.

Up here in the northern mountains is as different to the Spanish 'Costas' as could possibly be, yet wherever I go in this lovely country I find the people warm, generous and unfailingly welcoming. Without any doubt, it is clear the Spanish take great pride in their families and their communities, embracing and celebrating their vitality and importance. This was all encapsulated beautifully here in Los Arcos, in this festival of faith, people and place. Just brilliant.

Mingling amongst the crowds for a while and enjoying a delicious, Spanish style hot dog (with fiery salsa, not watery ketchup) I soon began to wilt. I sat for a while outside a busy little bar on the plaza, and it took only a couple of gigantic glasses of excellent Rioja before I could feel my body crying out, no, *pleading* for rest.

Half-heartedly then, for it was a fabulous evening with much more to see I knew, I dragged myself wearily back to the albergue. After first drugging the guard dogs and cutting my way through the razor-wire fence, I shot out the searchlights in the watchtower and crept unchallenged back into the prison hut. Steve McQueen was still up, bouncing his baseball against the hut walls and catching it expertly in his mitt.

Distance walked today – 31 Kilometres (75)

FIVE

Los Arcos

to

Viana

To my great surprise I was wide awake at 6.30am and actually felt ok, Miracle! I expected to be crippled with stiffness and beset by little agonies after yesterday's trials. But following a thorough inspection and feel of all the vital parts, I passed myself as fit and well. I think my body was slowly getting broken in and tempered by the rigors of the trail. I felt in good shape and all set for another day.

The morning had broken overcast and cool and threatened rain. Before rejoining the Camino, I decided to spend an hour in the town to re-charge my phone (I had forgotten to do it overnight) have a brew and a snack, and watch the weather for a while before moving on. I had my waterproofs so it wasn't really a problem, I think I was just delaying the moment in which I needed to get my legs pumping again. I needn't have worried about the rain though; by the time I set off the skies were beginning to clear, promising another hot and sunny day.

My target today was Logroño and about 28 kilometres of steady hiking. My map indicated there were a couple of big climbs to negotiate during the first half of the day, par for the course I realised by now. I didn't want to shatter myself as I had the previous day, so I had identified a couple of bail out points along the way should I decide I needed to stop earlier. I would see how I went along. I was very much aware at this stage, that I was still in the process of testing and stretching my capabilities on the trail, mindful of the need to make sound judgements along the way. There was still such a loooong way to go!

Today at some point on the Camino, should all go to plan, I would leave Navarre and pass into the province of La Rioja, land of its eponymous and famous wine. Rioja wine, with its many layers and styles had long been a favorite of mine, and I was looking forward to sampling a few delicious 'copas' amongst its famous vineyards and estates. Bring it on.

It was a gentle enough start with which to begin the day along a fairly even and easy-going section of the trail. After two or three kilometres the terrain began to steepen, and I embarked on a long, steady climb from Desvio por Senda up to Sansol. There was little to detain or distract me here so I pushed on, descending quite sharply to the valley floor below and across the bridge straddling the Río Linares. Another sharp climb out of a kilometre or so, brought me to the small and somnolent village of Torres del Río, nestling quietly part way up the steep mountain side.

I stopped here for a brief rest, taking the opportunity to admire the splendid views of the soft hills stretching around the compass, vine rich and verdant. I spotted the tower of what appeared on closer inspection to be an architectural little gem of a church, and I thought I would risk a moment or two having a look round. On approaching however, I discovered that there was perhaps a service or official gathering of some sort in progress. Looking at the assembled cars It may have been a funeral, and I didn't think it appropriate to intrude just to have a gawp round. What a thoughtful chap I am!

I also took the opportunity to check my feet, which had been worryingly buzzing and burning all morning. To my dismay, I found a huge blister on my left big toe, bearing the size and appearance of a plump gooseberry. Luckily, it wasn't too sore yet, but I would need to treat it and cover it up properly later. Excluding beer and wine, obviously, the health of my feet was a top priority on this journey.

A short distance out from Torres del Río and set in and around a tight loop in the path, I came across the most extraordinary collection of small stone towers and cairns. These were obviously built by passing pilgrims over time, and repaired and maintained similarly I thought.

There were dozens of stacks and little mounds of carefully picked stones, piled into what at first view appeared as caricature pagodas. It was all very quirky and absolutely superb. Before moving on, I carefully and artistically added my own little creation to augment, and if I may say, improve the display. Walking away and dusting down my hands with the satisfaction of a job well done, I looked back just in time to see my sculpture totter for a moment in the gentle breeze, then collapse. Art for art's sake? No.

From that point on, there was a *lot* of climbing. Firstly, a sharp ascent to Ermita de la Virgen, with its ancient but now abandoned convent, and from there, a roller coaster descent and solid climb up to the peak adjacent to the carretera de Bargota, intersecting here with the high point of the NA-1110 main road.

It was becoming seriously hot now; fired by a burning sun emerging cautiously from a previously overcast sky, greedily sapping strength from already tired limbs. The heat was manageable, *just*, relief provided by the constantly present and cooling breeze. This really did make a difference and was very, very welcome.

I was currently and always would be on the Camino Francés, travelling predominantly due west. At day-break the sun would rise behind me, traverse around my left shoulder throughout the morning until around one o'clock, whence it would then start to beat squarely on my left side. From that point, the fireball growing in strength by the minute continued on its arc, and if I was still walking by mid-afternoon, it would be beaming full on my face. That's when things really did start to heat up and get uncomfortable. But hey, this is Spain in mid-summer. You know you have to expect it, and you have to deal with it as part of the challenge otherwise my friend, you would make no progress at all. Well, at least that's what I was trying to tell myself.

◆ ◆ ◆

From the peak of the road, it was a nice and steady descent down the long and rugged path that snaked through the Cornava Ravine. On the way down, I passed through a mixture of heavily scented pine forests, fruit orchards and vineyards, varying the scenery nicely. The trail was bursting and brilliant with a rich variety of plants, shrubs and flowers, each flaunting its own distinctive appeal and aroma. It was all quiet dazzling.

Despite my earlier intention of reaching Logroño today, time and tiredness had conspired against me, and I decided on the road leading to Viana that I would have to rest up there for the night. I wasn't too disheartened, I had put in an honest day's walking, and I could easily make up the distance to Logroño the following day.

A fair bit more climbing followed, tediously crossing and re-crossing the road, following its course down the hill on the long and uneventful approach to Viana. A couple of kilometres on and I could see the town emerging on the plain in front of me, and very pleased I was to see it too. It had been another long, hot day on the Camino, but I was still striding out smartly as I entered the town at 17.17 pm precisely.

Viana is yet another beautiful little medieval town set amidst a cluster of hills and numerous vineyards, but it is surrounded by an unforgivable ugliness of modern constructions. Buildings seemingly thrown up at random with little if any thought, and with as many different styles of concrete prefabs, industrial units and unappealing apartment blocks you would wish to see in one place. Unless of course, you were driving a demolition truck. None of these buildings were either remotely sympathetic to the town's ancient architectural origins, or even to each other for that matter. To me, it gave the whole town a harsh and unsightly edge.

Once through this misery however, Viana revealed the medieval splendour of its old town, neatly contained within the formidable walls that had witnessed many battles down the centuries. Viana's location made it a prized asset, and it had been fought over many times by a succession of monarchs, generals, re-enforced concrete oligarchs and blind town planners.

Before setting out to find my albergue for the evening, I had brief look around the central plaza which was very fine, dominated by the church of Santa María and the town hall (as you will come to see, every single church and cathedral in Spain is named for Santa Maria. Except of course, the ones that are named after somebody else. Clear?) The church was very impressive, and housed a very famous long term guest.

Interred in the grounds was the Machiavellian character of Cesaré Borgia, who was killed in battle close to here in 1507. What, with all that shagging and pillaging, murder, corruption and general naughtiness, he must have taken his eye off the ball at a crucial moment. His badly wounded body we are told, (and this is true) was stripped by his attackers and left naked other than for a red tile covering his genitals. I couldn't find any reference as to the reason behind this peculiar act. Maybe this is where the term 'A tile on the knights' originated?

As an example of the enduring vengeance of the rich and powerful, it transpires that at the whim of whoever was in charge at the time, Borgia's remains were dug up several times down the centuries. His corpse would then re-interred either in places of opprobrium or veneration, dependent on whether the powers that be approved or disapproved of the syphilitic old sods life. They were still debating another airing for Cesaré's bones as late as the 1980s!

Viana had many fine examples of Gothic palaces, churches and buildings, and it would have been nice to explore them further. By now however, I was really beginning to tire, so I set off to find a place to rest my own weary bones for the night. I sincerely hoped that the local mayor wouldn't find fault with my own innocently aching tibias and fibulas, and order them to be dug out of my bed in the middle of the night and placed on the refuse tip or some-such place. Such are the risks of fame and notoriety in Viana it would seem.

The 'Albergue Izar' appeared as just a doorway in a terrace, and initially I had actually walked past it, so easy was it to miss. Inside however, it was great. The hostel was roomy yet cozy, and once more spotlessly clean and well equipped, as I am now rightly coming to expect of these fine places.

It was clearly an albergue popular with cyclists too. Upon my arrival, there must have been a dozen or so bikes in the racks, with another six or eight more appearing later. All these bikes clogged up the little central courtyard a bit to be honest, but I suppose they had to be somewhere safe. Some of these machines looked as if they cost thousands of pounds.

I discovered as my journey progressed, that there appeared to be some animosity directed towards the cyclists on the Camino. I noticed a few slogans and odd bits of graffiti along the way expressing this discontent. Indeed, I personally witnessed a few critical remarks from fellow pilgrims too.

The issue seemed principally to be about authenticity. Historically, the essence of any pilgrimage was to walk: to spend a period outside of your own natural environment whilst immersing oneself in the process of reflection and contemplation, slowly and over time. The inference being, that to zoom along on a bicycle gobbling up the kilometres, removes much of the background and time frame necessary for the true elements of a pilgrimage to come together and coalesce.

Cyclists of course, have a very different view. It is their contention that any form of pilgrimage is a very personal experience. Whilst many would concede perhaps, that walking the Camino carries the weight in terms of history and convention, cycling is simply a nuance of this and merely brings a different experience and level of intensity to the journey. It is, they would argue, perfectly possible to feel as much a part of the Camino and its purpose in cycling it, as it would to a walker.

They would also add, (as would I) that surely the point is about personal motivation, dedication and emotional commitment, rather than the method employed to deliver their purpose.

Cycling is not an easy option either, although it is certainly much quicker. I'm told that many cycling stages on the Camino Francés are as difficult as those experienced on the Grand Tours, indeed, some sections over the years have featured in the *Vuelta a España* in reality. Definitely not for the faint hearted, I was seriously assured.

Towards the end of my own pilgrimage, I met a guy who was tackling the final 100 kilometres from Sarria to Santiago, by being pushed in his wheelchair by his wife and young daughter. No doubt the Camino 'purists' would frown on that too.

I guess it's all down to opinions. Mine, for what it's worth, is that it should be left entirely up to the individual, and we should all respect each other's choices as being part of the whole and not separate from or outside of the 'true' Camino experience. There is enough friction and petty minded prejudice to be found in life as it is, without seeking to introduce it into the beauty and simplicity of the Camino, especially just to score cheap, pretentious points. I think I've finished now.

On a more basic level though and on balance, I think I would rather have sore feet than a sore arse any day. If for no other reason; massaging your feet in the dormitory at the end of a long and trying day is a lot more acceptable than...... well, I think you get the picture!

Dismounting from the cycling issue and from my own high horse, I shall now return you to my exciting evening in Viana.

After showering and changing, I whiled away an hour or so sipping on a beer or two in the little quadrangle, writing up my notes whilst lazily watching people coming and going. I wasn't motivated to launch myself into another tour of the old town, lovely though it was. Instead I found a nice little bar close by and relaxed for a while with a couple of glasses of wine, browsing through a few brochures I had picked up from the albergue.

Whilst there, although not feeling particularly hungry I thought I should eat something, and in doing so, breaking a strict rule of mine: if not hungry, don't eat. I grazed without enthusiasm on a cheap plate of food, the details of which I was forgetting as I ate. I would have been better to wait and have something in the morning, at least I would have been ready for it and enjoyed it.

I was pretty tired by this time, but feeling very good about how things had gone so far, and despite a few aches and pains, I thought I was adjusting to the demands of the Camino nicely. Neither wanting nor needing anything else, I called it a night and retired to my bunk for a good, well-earned rest.

I can't leave the restless bones of Cesaré Borgia though, without this little observation.

Cesaré was the illegitimate son of a pope, not so unusual during those times it would appear. His high and corrupt connections led him to being trained by the church, and he was ordained a cardinal whilst still in his teens. A life of piety had no appeal for this young man however, and he set off on a military career where he would become adept at all the dark arts of ruthless power grabbing, murder, bribery and corruption. It was even thought he had an incestuous relationship with his sister Lucrezia, and he was syphilis ridden from his early twenties.

With all this in mind, I was delighted to observe that in one of the histories of Cesaré Borgia, it describes his career as 'Politician'. Sounds about right don't you think?

The next day, I would first make the short hike to Logroño and then maybe consider having a day off, mainly to give some respite to my growing collection of blisters. At that moment they weren't too painful, but I didn't want them getting any worse. I would see how I felt in the morning.

Blisters, for most hikers on the Camino are to some extent an inevitability, given the punishing daily demands on ones feet. I was lucky in that after decades of dedicated walking, the soles of my feet were like a Maasai warrior's! I could put a drawing pin through my calloused heels and toes, or walk across hot coals (something we do a lot of in Derbyshire) and still feel nowt.

The problem for me was at the tips of toes or in between; sore enough, but if properly treated certainly not debilitating. Once or twice on my journey, I would witness tearful submissions and premature ends to pilgrimages due to the scourge of crippling blisters. An issue not to be taken lightly, that's for sure.

Distance walked today - 20 kilometres (95)

SIX

Viana

to

Navarrete

I woke to a fine dawn chorus of twittering birds and a clear blue sky, auguring yet another hot and sunny day. The walk ahead today didn't look too severe, just one stiffish climb in front of Logroño in the region of the provincial border. No problem.

All set and away from Viana at 7.15am, my first task was to tackle a slight climb and short descent leading my way out of the town. Striding along nicely on a narrow dusty track, it was easy-going and very pleasant walking as I wound my way slowly down the hill, and through the vineyards and orchards of the surrounding fields.

The sun had risen initially into an empty azure, but by 8.30 it had completely clouded over, with a pleasant breeze coming in off the northern mountains. It was perfect walking weather, and I was determined to make the most of it.

Moving smartly along an even track and in good conditions for a brisk pace, the trail amidst forest and field, gradually merged onto the busy main road to Logroño. Spurred on by my steady progress, I soon came upon the sign announcing that I was passing from Navarre and into the province of La Rioja and its famous, luscious wines. Pushing on up the last steep climb and having made short work of the 10k or so from Viana, the clock had just ticked past 11.00am when I tramped past the city marker for Logroño.

From the top of a rise looking down on the large expanse of the city, I could make out a protective cordon, as it were, of industrial and commercial estates lying in front of the city centre. From that distance, Logroño looked like any other modern urban sprawl, but on walking into the city and crossing the large stone bridge over the mighty Río Ebro, I found there was a really nice feel and buzz about the place. It was certainly a busy and prosperous looking town, bustling energetically with businesspeople, shoppers and tourists, as I made my way through.

Walking along the hectic streets, keeping an eye out for yellow arrows infrequently daubed on pillars and posts, I found that all the activity and bustle felt strange and a little overwhelming, especially after the previous days spent in the peaceful countryside. It made for a nice and interesting change nonetheless, and I really enjoyed being amongst the sights and sounds of this pleasant city.

Logroño is the provincial capital of La Rioja, and appeared to embrace all the characteristics and presence of a large and important city. I would have liked to have explored its historic streets and plazas further, alas, I was only passing through and quickly at that. Stopping only briefly to replenish my supplies of snacks and water from a large supermarket on the high street on my way through.

Once beyond the city centre I rested for a while in an open space by the river, and whilst sat on a bench studying my maps, I was joined by a very nice and friendly old chap. Having ascertained I was a Camino pilgrim, he enthusiastically gave me a detailed and informative run down of the route immediately ahead, and for which I was most grateful. He was a Logroño man, and he had walked the Camino several times down the years, holding with great warmth how he envied my journey ahead. "Vaya con Dios" (God go with you) was his cheery fair well as I bade him goodbye, turning myself back onto the trail and towards the nearby railway track.

Crossing the lines over an iron footbridge, I joined a man-made path leading into what would turn out to be a very large and attractive country park. The 'Parque de la Grajera' extended over a wide area, and carried the Camino through and beyond the city limits of Logroño.

Pushing on through this stretch of pleasant and tranquil greenery, I came across a leisure facility and café in the middle of the woods by a large lake. I paused briefly here to admire the quiet and restful views over the water, enjoying the antics of the many different types of birds, playfully disporting themselves on and around the mere. The park trail continued its long meanderings out into the country, and it wasn't until about six kilometres out of the city that it eventually gave way onto a gravel path, and the road leading to Navarrete.

A steady, rolling and not too taxing walk amongst the vineyards and orchards, took me along the last five or six kilometres and within sight of Navarrete. It was an easy walk down the winding paved road, and for a short distance alongside a wire fence, closely stitched through with small crosses made from twigs and branches. I wasn't quite sure what their purpose was, but like the little stone cairns from the other day, once someone starts these things people are only too willing to contribute their little offering, even if they are not quite sure why.

You see a lot of this kind of thing on the Camino. I reckon if I sellotaped a toothbrush to a drinking fountain on the trail, I could come back in a month and find it festooned with dental paraphernalia from around the world, with lots of little notes saying things like: "In fond memory of Carlito's teeth, sadly lost on the Camino". Hark, do I hear the sound of bleating sheep?

Not bothering to add my own artwork to the display I moved on, and was soon into the outskirts of the village and at 3.30pm, the end of my walking day. How splendid.

Feeling the least tired of any day so far (I think my body was getting used to the demanding routine and the weight was dropping off!) it had just started to drizzle as I entered Navarrete, and by the time I had located my albergue it was raining quite heavily. Thankfully, I had no problem securing my bed for the night in the very nice and centrally located 'El Cantaro', another superbly appointed and inexpensive hostel.

I was becoming increasingly impressed with the standard and consistency of the albergues in which I had been lodging, and up to that point at least, I had found no cause for complaint whatsoever.

As I was one of the earlier arrivals I had my pick of the bunks, and took my time cleaning up and stowing my stuff in the locker provided. Feeling very hungry by now, I decided to finish off the snacks I had bought earlier and headed for the large dining room/kitchen towards the rear, in the hope of making a nice brew to go with my late lunch. It was there, I had the great and good fortune to meet up with three lively Mexican gentlemen, who at that time were tucking heartily into a sizeable picnic spread chaotically over the large kitchen table.

These guys were in their early/mid-sixties, all wearing that unmistakable Latin-American look. They greeted me with great warmth and kindly invited me to join them in their buffet. Comparing my meager rations with their sumptuous feast it was a no brainer, so I gratefully and greedily tucked in. I'm glad I did, it was bloody marvelous!

They were an intriguing trio. Alejandro, who seemed to be the group leader, was tall and slim, mustachioed, bespectacled and professional looking. I liked to think he may have been a school headmaster or bank manager, cool calmness personified. Alfredo was short and serious looking; limp, dark hair reaching over his ears 70's style. He had the look of a musician in a jazz band or a struggling artist maybe, shy and reticent but with an intellectual bearing. Fernando was built like a pocket battleship; small but very muscular and stocky with a seemingly permanent, mischievous smile playing across his face. I thought he could have been a retired footballer of the mid-field dynamo type, or a wrestler perhaps.

Strangely enough and despite my playful conjecture, I never did get to find out what any them did back home in Mexico City. I did learn early on however, that they were all now retired.

By combining my stuttering Spanish and their dodgy English we communicated very well, and soon teamed up for a stroll around the village. What nice chaps they were, and how I would embrace and enjoy their company over the coming weeks.

Shortly after leaving the hostel we met up with a Swedish couple, Charles and Ulla, with whom the Mexicans had been walking these past days. Once again around my age and both speaking perfect English, they were a very nice and friendly pair. As an added bonus, Charles also spoke pretty good Spanish, so he was able to fill in any gaps in communication between myself and my new Mexican friends. Perfect. Not yet known then of course, but the six of us would have many memorable and enjoyable moments together on the journey ahead.

Our little group now complete we decided to get out of the rain for a while, and found a nice traditional bar on the plaza in which to settle. It was a cracking little place with a wonderfully warm atmosphere, all presided over by a portly and very welcoming *posadero.*

 Well it was just brilliant. We had a very pleasant getting-to know-you chat over a few beers and amidst much laughter. It was a superb, heart-warming afternoon, and I felt very lucky to find myself in such good company.

Navarrete is a small village; medieval at its heart with an eccentric maze of winding narrow streets and alleyways, lending it real character. It had on its main plaza, one of the most beautiful and spectacular church interiors I had ever seen, resplendent with a gleaming baroque reredos stretching from floor to ceiling. It was absolutely stunning. The 'Iglesia de la Asuncion' was more like the inside of a miniature cathedral such was its glory. The photos I had taken, I feared, would not even come close to doing it justice, it was a real 'wow' moment. What a lovely little place Navarrete is, a sparkling jewel on the Camino.

Earlier in the afternoon, I had spotted several posters announcing a party taking place in the village that evening, and as part of the weeklong *Fiesta del Asuncion*. It looked as if it might be a lot of fun, and I thought, would be a very pleasant way to spend the evening. Unfortunately, none of my new friends seemed interested in this idea; it appeared they had already made plans for the night, none of which included me! This puzzled me a little. Having spent a couple of hours in my company and discovering what a brilliant bloke I am, did they really think they would have a better time without me? Very strange.

Alone then, but not at all lonely, I sat in the plaza sipping on Rioja waiting patiently for the live music to begin. However, as is often the way with these affairs in Spain, it was only due to get going around 9.00pm and that would be getting very close to my bedtime. I loitered for another half hour or so, the square and surrounding streets by now very lively, but the band were still tuning up on the stage, no live action yet. I couldn't delay any longer, I really was ready to sleep. Once again then and very reluctantly I cut my evening short, realising ruefully that I would be missing out on all the fun.

Twenty years ago I would have been the last to leave, helping the band pack their gear away no doubt. Not these days I'm afraid, I'm knocking on a bit now!

On the walk back to the albergue, I reflected once more on what wonderfully kind, family and community-oriented people the Spanish are, and none more so than in this region. Always extremely polite and respectful, their villages are spotlessly clean and safe, and all put out the very warmest of welcomes.

How fine it must be to live your life in these close knit and easy living communities, content with whatever life puts before you, simple and undemanding.

Nájera would be my destination tomorrow, and with quite a big climb to negotiate early on by the looks of it. So, even though it was not yet 10.00pm, I was heading for the land of Nod.

Incidentally, despite my earlier stated intentions, I had decided not to have a rest day after all, waving two fingers at my blisters and damnation to them! I couldn't wait to get started in the morning, I had the bit between my teeth now.

Whilst I've got your attention, I'll deal at this point with a question I'm sure all five of my readers are asking. "Why is this idiot describing his journey in kilometres and not miles?" Easy. All my maps were in kilometres, all the way posts and road signs displayed kilometres, I was drinking beer and wine in kilometres (need to check that one) I was in a metric land!

Quite simply, I couldn't be bothered and didn't feel it necessary to do any conversions. Also, at the time of writing at least and to paraphrase Basil Faulty, the UK was still 'On the continent'. Please feel free to do the math's, if you so wish!

Distance walked today 22 Kilometres (117) or about 1.32 million pints of beer if laid end to end.

SEVEN

Navarrete

to

Najera

I was wide-awake before six o'clock, but ignoring the early hour I lay on my bunk for a while, listening to the rustling and whispers of early leavers. Despite the close proximity nobody makes too much noise really. The mutual respect my fellow pilgrims had for each other's privacy and peace in the albergues was unvarying during this journey. This I know was always very much appreciated.

Feeling very comfortable and in no mad rush, I lazed for another 30 mins before getting myself ready for the day. I hadn't eaten since my picnic with the Mexican boys the previous afternoon and unusually for me, I felt hungry of a morning. Packed and all set, I wandered down to a small cafe I had spotted the previous evening, and as advertised, knocking out bacon, eggs, toast and coffee at just four euros. It was an idea shared by quite a few others too, for within minutes the place was packed. The breakfast was great and I wolfed it down, I really was hungry! Happily sated and fueled for the day ahead, I bade my fellow diners a 'Bon Camino' and hit the trail.

From Navarrete to Nájera is just 18 kilometres. Pretty straight forward on the face of it, other than one tasty looking climb in the early part of the trek. It was just fine, I ate up the distance and tackled the ascent up through Ventosa over the red clay path with no difficulty. I felt I was really getting into my stride now; the discomfort of the first few days, particularly the issue with my backpack, had all but disappeared.

Before moving on, I took a little detour and had a quick look at the 'Alvía' winery on the edge of the village. The giant silos, presses and tanks were silent and still today. There were several weeks to go yet, before they would be gorging on the plump, sun drenched Tempranillo and Garnacha grapes, currently maturing in their own sweet time in the surrounding vineyard, patiently awaiting the day they would undergo the miraculous transformation into Rioja wine.

I was doing really well for time too, so I took the opportunity for a short break opposite the church of San Saturnino, re-grouping before the last push to the top of the hill.

The trail really was quite beautiful today; winding and climbing gently through acre upon acre of the great and famous Rioja vineyards, their grapes ripening and getting fatter with their precious liquid as the summer wore on. It was all extremely captivating, and once again, I could easily imagine a simple life for myself in these quiet, sun kissed hills. Steady on now lad, lets crack on shall we?

From the peak of Alto de San Antón, I was treated to tremendous views of the Nájerilla valley and surrounding hills. It was a joy to be up here on this beautiful day; quiet and peaceful, basking in the warmth of the sun, transfixed by the wonderful scenery.

Eventually I dragged myself away, and it was a gentle and uneventful descent of just another 8 or 9 kilometres to the conclusion of the days hike. It was by far the easiest walking I'd had to that point, and I arrived at the outskirts of Nájera just after 1.00pm and feeling very chipper too, thanks for asking.

The next significant town was around 15k down the trail at Cirueña. I thought about it, but somehow I didn't really fancy taking on those extra kilometres today. Settled with my decision and looking forward to a nice relaxing afternoon, I strode through the extensive suburbs of the town in search of my chosen albergue, which I knew was close to the river. Nájera was a decent sized municipality, and I was a little surprised at how empty and quiet the town was as I trawled through its near deserted streets.

It's very hard to describe Nájera and give it any merit. The brochures say it was founded in the 10th century; but apart from the church, the monastery and odd bits of old walls, there was no real indication that this was anything other than a fairly modern and modest town. Coming in through the closely built up outskirts, I was quickly amongst block after block of standard, modern Spanish developments of 5 and 6 story apartment buildings, each of them with a hodgepodge of shops occupying the ground floors. It certainly wasn't shouting 'historic' to me.

I crossed the Río Nájerilla over a bridge built by San Juan de Ortega (of whom more later) and there things looked a little better and brighter. Several nice bars and restaurants hugged the gently shelving riverbank and there was a lovely esplanade running alongside it, offering the promise of a pleasant stroll later.

I was very pleased to meet up once more with my new Mexican friends, who happily had arrived in town shortly after me. Exchanging back slapping hugs and handshakes, we sat in the hot sunshine for a while on a low wall by the river, chatting amiably about our respective days walking and waiting patiently for the albergue to open at 2.00pm. Having now realised just what they had missed by not having me in their company the previous evening, the boys were desperately keen to meet up for a beer and a bite to eat later. They soon learn.

The albergue, needless to say by now, was just great. Bright, clean and airy and as always, inexpensive. The 'Turistico Puerta de Nájera' was a modern building occupying a corner block, the interior conversely, being of a more traditional wood themed design. A spacious dormitory and very nice shower rooms were on the first floor, brightly lit by large windows opening up onto small balconies. On the ground floor was a comfortable lounge with a small dining room, kitchen and laundry facilities. It was a very nice set-up, and an excellent place to spend the night.

Nájera is built on opposite embankments of a shallow stretch of river. The side on which my albergue sat was dominated by massive sandstone cliffs, which would have provided perfect shelter and protection back in the day. Indeed, the name *Nájera* is derived from the Moorish 'Between Cliffs'.

This side of the river was much more attractive, with lots of narrow streets packed with comely bars, restaurants and shops. I couldn't help but feel however, that the whole town was fighting a rearguard action just to stay on the right side of shabby, and probably just about managing it.

Although It didn't look or feel like a wealthy town, this Saturday evening saw plenty of people out and about filling the bars and restaurants, bringing a nice, lively atmosphere to its streets. Several of these hostelries were conscientiously sampled by Alejandro, Alfredo, Fernando and myself as we wandered casually around the town. We carefully selected one of them in which to have a bite to eat, a traditional *taberna* tucked away in a shady corner. From a lengthy menu, we all chose a fish dish with some shared vegetables, washed down, naturally, with a couple of bottles of superb Rioja. It was all extremely enjoyable.

An after dinner stroll found us crossing back over the bridge to the other side of the town. The principle feature on this bank of the river was the main plaza. This consisted of a church of no special merit, to my eye at least, dominating one side, with several little shop's located opposite. A handful of bars, a small bus station and a section of the old walls combined to complete the quadrant. It wasn't fantastic by any means, but it was ok.

My one regret, was that I didn't make time to visit the monastery and church of Santa María, which I was told later was beautiful and a real treasure house of art and architecture. Sadly, on a journey such as this, there just wasn't time to see everything one would like to.

Saying good night to my departing *amigos*, I finished my own evening off with another very large and very pleasant glass of Rioja, agreeably priced at one euro. Sipping my wine contentedly I deliberated upon the following days walk, which would now have to be taken on feet slowly filling up with blisters. Thankfully, they weren't that sore or troublesome as yet and I was able to walk unhindered. Still, not ideal by any means. I was very conscious and fearful of any infection getting to my feet. That would certainly mean the end of *this* particular pilgrims journey.

With that cheery thought, and in the crepuscular light of a very warm evening, I walked the short distance back along the riverbank to the albergue. In my absence during the afternoon and early evening, the place had really filled up. Pilgrims were crammed into the small dining area and spilling out onto the street, all chatting happily and noisily, chomping and quaffing on late suppers.

I spotted a few familier faces and stopped for moment or two to for a quick chat and very nice it was too. I wasn't to be delayed long though, I was feeling really tired and ready for a rest. Without any further fuss or bother then and following the most perfunctory ablutions, I drew the curtain down on a most satisfying and very pleasant day.

Distance walked today – 17 Kilometres (134)

EIGHT

Najera

to

Santo Domingo
de la Calzada

E arly to rise once again I was packed, on the road and absorbing myself into the swiftly changing colours of the early morning light.

On leaving the confines of the town I directly encountered my first climb, but nothing surprises by now and I was more than ready for it. It was neither a severe or long ascent, and in the still and cool morning air, I was soon up and over the Pico de Nájera and onto the tarmac road that would continue on to Azofra. All being well, I intended to make that my first rest point of the day.

My objective today was Santo Domingo de la Calzada, a trek of about 22 kilometres, but firstly, I was going to enjoy the extremely pleasant walk to Azofra. It was wonderful to be striding out in the glorious sunshine and through the vast hectares of vineyards that covered every visible inch of hill and dale, interrupted only occasionally by the odd fruit orchard popping up amongst the vines. The morning was warm and pleasant, the surrounding countryside superb and it really was the most agreeable walking.

The trail continued on in this lazy, comfortable way snaking through the grapes, with just an occasional little climb breaking up my mornings progress on the Camino. An undemanding and gentle rise finally brought me into Azofra where as planned I rested for a while; propped up on my pack, taking in a drink and a snack on the flood bank hard by the Río Tuerto.

I was eating up the distance today. It had become my practice to try and complete as many kilometres as I could in the first three or four hours, certainly before the sun and heat of the afternoon could get about its energy sapping work. I was definitely ahead of the game this morning.

Making probably my best time to date and feeling pretty good, (no problems so far with my blisters) I ploughed on up the long, steep climb to Cirueña. It was very hot and thirsty going now, and I was already thinking about another break. With time in my pocket, I decided to have a rest and a drink at the very next café or bar I came upon.

Pursuing the long, steady climb up to the town, it topped out quite surprisingly to a new and trendy looking housing development. The main feature of the area was a golf course and driving range, the whole complex parading under the title of 'Alta de la Rioja'. It all felt a little incongruous out here on the trail to be honest, but I have to say, it did look very nice. Just as I hoped, there was a fine looking bar attached to the golf course and open to the public, so I took the opportunity for a few minutes rest and a refreshing pot of green tea. Marvelous.

Checking my progress on the map, I saw that I was already over two thirds of the way to my destination and it was still only 11.00am. Well done that man. Cheered on by my good work, I started out on the last 6 or 7 kilometres of gentle descent.

From that point onwards, the surrounding vineyards began to thin out somewhat, gradually being replaced by a growing expanse of wheat fields. An ominous foreboding of things to come, but I didn't realise that yet, did I?

Still full of energy I tackled the last small climb of the day, and at the crest of the hill espied the distant town of Santo Domingo de la Calzada laid out on the plain below me. This first view, revealed a sprawl of industry clinging messily to the edge of the town. Behind that oily smudge though there was a more promising looking centre, and it was to there that I was headed.

Upon reaching the outskirts and perusing a map of the town posted there, it appeared it was going to be a long and dreary walk into the centre and to my albergue for the evening. On the road in, I found this part of Santo Domingo was principally made up of the now familiar 5 and 6 story apartment blocks, all huddled closely together and a little austere looking. Every building appeared to be more or less the same height, with only the bell tower of the cathedral jutting importantly above the rest of the skyline.

Battling my way primarily through a mix of industrial units, dilapidated buildings and petrol stations, the ugliness eventually gave way to a neat, tidy and venerable town centre. It was very busy on this sunny Sunday afternoon too, packed with families crowding the narrow streets, or squeezing into the many bars and restaurants that decorated the broad, tree lined boulevard through the town.

This is an excellent and enduring Spanish tradition, where Sunday is a special day set aside for families. It's wonderful to see grandparents, mums, dads and kids all tricked out in their Sunday best, promenading along the *paseos* or dining together happily and noisily in restaurants and cafes. Families really are the heartbeat of Spanish social life; a laudable example to the rest of us, who perhaps, may have less time and respect for our older relatives and lack patience with the younger.

We all have our place on the moving staircase of time don't we? It's easy to forget we were once young, and easier still to ignore the reality that the young too, will one day be grandparents. And so the world turns, but not on a moving staircase, obviously. I can't think of a suitable metaphor for a turning world, so I'll leave a gap; you can write your own in...
All done?

I found my albergue situated right in the centre of town, squeezed amidst an assortment of narrow streets and alleyways, each I knew, packed with beckoning bars and ice cold beers. I was one of the first to check in that afternoon, having completed todays journey in just over 5 hours. I really was getting quite good at this walking game now! As often happens though and having now stopped, a weariness began to creep up on me, so I was happy to shower and rest up for a while in this large and comfortable hostel.

The 'Albergue Confradia del Santo', is operated by the Brotherhood of that name, an old and distinguished religious order dedicated to St James. This was a very modern conversion of existing buildings, and a fantastic job they had made of it too. It was large and spacious, with three floors containing dormitories, shower block and library, with an ample dining room and kitchen on the first floor. Without doubt, this was a very impressive albergue.

The old Brother who checked me in couldn't speak any English at all, which for me was no problem. My fast-improving Spanish would do nicely and he very generously congratulated me on its excellence. Flattery indeed, and I felt even more buoyant, when the kindly Brother informed me that just 7 euros would be sufficient for my accommodation this evening. I'll take that!

Cleaned up and rested, I headed out for a mooch around this very nice-looking town. Its network of narrow streets was really delightful and interesting, with the houses and buildings drawn from a variety of architectural styles spanning the centuries. The effect was very random and a little quirky in places, but nonetheless, extremely pleasing on the eye. Santo Domingo (St Dominic) is himself famed for his building works in this region the 12th century, and I'm sure he would be more than pleased with the town that bears his name today.

The ancient heart of the town is centred around the cathedral of Santo Domingo. It had a very impressive exterior, alas, I can't offer a comment on the glories of its interior; the church is closed during the middle hours on Sundays, such is my luck.

The brochures tell of the legend of the 'Hanged Innocent', in which a medieval pilgrim who was wrongly accused of theft called upon two chickens as his witnesses, both of whom were not only headless but recently roasted! It's a long and very odd little tale and I believe there are many versions. But none the less and to this day, two live chickens are kept in the choir loft of the cathedral in celebration and honour of this 'miracle'.

Domingo, according to history at least, was a very kindly, generous and humble man. He could not however, have better staged managed his memorial himself. Not only did he help build the cathedral, it was named after him, and he is interred there as a beatified Saint, all in the town bearing his name.

Other noteworthy buildings on the plaza were the old pilgrim hostel, now a very nice hotel, and the convent of San Francisco. Both adding style and nobility to the stately presence of their surroundings. What a lovely little town.

I found a very colourful and lively back street *taberna* close by, and ordered an enormous plate of pasta, sauce and bread alongside a carafe of wine. Total bill, 7 euros 90 cents and it was delicious.

I spent the next couple of hours trying to track Manchester Utd on my phone in their away match at Brighton, gulping down many glasses of Rioja for both comfort and compensation.

The Rioja was superb, Utd were shit, stumbling to a 3-2 defeat. It would appear my team were in need of miraculous interventions too, if their season were to have any hope. 'headless chickens' were referenced more than once in the match commentary!

As the evening crept past 9.00pm, the days walking along with the food and wine began to catch up with me. Sensibly refusing the waiters offer of *una para la carretera* (one for the road) I called it a day, and made my weary eyed way back to the albergue for yet another early night.It had been a most enjoyable day on the trail, gilded by a really pleasant evening. It had been a long time since I had felt as happy, contented and purposeful as this.

◆ ◆ ◆

At the end of my first week on the Camino, I looked back with great satisfaction on what had been a very hectic but incredibly rewarding few days. The first two or three days had passed in a blur really, as I got used to the strains and demands of the trail. It had felt, naturally enough I suppose, that I had just been walking, eating and sleeping and not absorbing the ambiance and beauty of my surrounds. At that point it almost felt I was carrying out an onerous task without purpose or reward. These last few days however, had been very different.

I had developed a rhythm and routine that had placed the demands and rigours of the walking almost in the background, and I was now able to fully appreciate the stunning scenery I was blessed with each day, deriving such inspiration from it. I could now properly value the little glories of all the places I had passed through or stayed in, drawing from each of them a very special feeling, of being in a very special place.

I felt at this point that I was now truly part of the Camino; absorbed in it mentally, physically and emotionally, and I was beginning to mold my own shape and thinking to the patterns and contours of this ancient trail. Little by little, kilometre by kilometre, I was putting distance between myself and the 'other me' back home. My thoughts at last, were beginning to centre and coalesce around my journey and my reason for being here.

Everything was working out very nicely. My decision to take on this great pilgrimage to Santiago was proving to be a very good one indeed.

Distance walked today – 21 Kilometres (156)

NINE

Santo Domingo
de la Calzada

to

Belorado

Another up-with-the-birds start, and I was heading out of Santo Domingo, just as the first hesitant stain of light began bleeding softly into still darkened skies. It would be a day of steady, but not overly severe climbing that would carry me to my destination today, Belorado; a large town 24 kilometres in the distance.

I left the town over a long, impressively arched bridge. The original crossing over the Río Oja was built by Santo Domingo in the 12th century, the road element however, was clearly a more modern construction and capable of carrying motor traffic. At this early hour though, it was carrying only sleepy eyed pilgrims, shuffling noiselessly and undisturbed along its length.

The first moderate climb took me through the village of Grañón, the trail running parallel with the road here and there, and a bit boring too. Grañón would be the last town on the Camino in the region of La Rioja, placing me just 4 kilometres from Redicilla del Camino and where I had planned to have my first break.

Just before Redicilla, I made the crossing from La Rioja into *La Junta* of Castilla y León. This was another milestone to check off and the third province on my journey so far. Immediately before the border stood a large and detailed vertical map of the Camino, depicting its long journey across the Castilian plain. Standing in front of this very thorough representation and tracing the trail slowly up the map's length, it was clear that that this was a huge stretch of territory. At once daunting, but equally exciting.

I didn't realise it then of course, but it would be the last time I would use the word 'exciting' in context of the trail for the next two weeks!

With my mind reeling a little at the detail on the map and the journey it promised, I adjusted my pack, bent to re-tie my boot laces and inexplicably fell over, sprawling clumsily to the floor. Slowly picking myself up, embarrassed and covered in dust, I quickly exclaimed: "I always do that" in explanation to the bemused onlookers, "it's a long standing tradition of mine, to eat the dirt when crossing into a new province".

And so, with as much dignity as I could muster and cursing under my breath, I crossed the border into new lands, and more opportunities to make a fool of myself.

The landscape seemed to undergo a dramatic change as I took my first look at this new region. The green hills, vineyards and orchards of La Rioja, were now replaced by vast hectares of wheat fields, all recently cropped and parched looking. It vividly recalled my long-ago journeying through the cereal plains of the American mid-west.

The only relief from this desolate panorama, was to be found in occasional fields of sunflowers springing up here and there, their giant and colourful heads nodding in the light breeze. After the sumptuous diversity of the mountains and valleys of recent days, it all looked a bit drab and empty. I was soon to learn however, that this was but a harbinger of the bleakness to come.

On passing through Redicilla, I stopped briefly to equip myself with a few brochures of Castilla Y León from the tourist office, and purchase some more plasters for my fast breeding colony of blisters. Freshly bandaged, I stepped back on to the flat and endless terrain that would soon become monotonously familiar. With the Camino now and for some distance ahead running parallel with the N-120, I was once again making really good time as the trail continued its easy and steady progress along the contours of these pale, shallow and silent hills.

Slipping quickly through Castildelgado then onto Viloria de Rioja, the hiking was getting a bit tiresome now as the trail continued its attraction to the roadside. I was to experience that long sections of the Camino closely tracked the main roads through Castilla Y León, and it was rarely anything other than wearisome walking. Villamayor del Río too, quickly came and went. No reason to stop, nothing to see. Just keep on going son.

None of these small and nondescript villages had either a shop from which to buy water, nor a water fountain that was safe to use. Ominous placards shouting, 'Non Potable' (not drinkable) hanging from useless spouts. I had to carefully nurse my last bottle along the hot, dusty and empty trail, and the last few kilometres to Belorado.

Surely, only things like let's say, having to share an office with Donald Trump or even Piers Morgan come to that, could possibly be worse than running out of water on the Camino. Morgan, supercilious prat that he is, was almost beaten to his selection by the arch Tory tosser and 'Lord Snooty' impersonator, Jacob Rees-Mogg. The 'Beano' cartoon character of Snooty, of course, having significantly more depth of character and personality than his mincing mimic. Rees-Mogg, the buffoon, is the only man remaining who continues to wear double-breasted suits and *still* expects to be taken seriously as a politician. Ridiculous. I've been waiting for a chance to get that off my chest, I really enjoyed it too!

Unlike yesterday, where I had a long walk through the suburbs before finding my albergue, the one in Belorado was practically the first building I came upon and right on the edge of town. The 'Albergue a Santiago' had more of the look and feel of a holiday campsite than a hostel, it even had a small swimming pool. I think I was first to check in I could see no one else about, so I settled into one of a number of very nice rooms that were arranged inside a long, single story building.

This was a nice hostel. The sleeping area as I have indicated, was split up into several smaller rooms, each accommodating either four, eight or twelve people, the nightly rate becoming cheaper as the rooms got larger, if you get my meaning. The spacious, modern and gleaming shower blocks were situated on the opposite side of the corridor to the rooms. By the entrance to the grounds there was a large restaurant and bar, with a nice terrace to the front and a good sized pool to the rear. It was excellent, and I was once again very happy to have found such a good spot.

I was told later by the Manager that the restaurant and pool were open to the public, and both were very popular with the local townsfolk. It was easy enough to see why.

I took advantage of the unusually empty laundry room, indulging in a full wash of all my kit. Without venturing too far into the dark woods of political incorrectness, it needs to be said; if you didn't get to the laundry facilities at any Camino albergue before the ladies, you could forget it! For within minutes of their arrival, the *lavandería* would have been overwhelmed by hordes of jabbering and excitable women, staggering under the weight of arms full of clothes.

Having now been commandeered, the machines would soon be whirring non-stop. Washing lines, like yachts at a regatta, would be swiftly and colourfully adorned by acres of knickers. Oh, and try and make just the *tiniest* bit of room for your own meagre array of socks and undies if you dared. By touching even the merest hem or gusset of a lady garment, you would be rendered stone dead. The looks alone would kill.

Having then, triumphantly beaten the as yet to arrive manic washerwomen to the laundry room, I deliberately and smugly hung out my clothes across 5 metres of empty line, rubbing my hands together with glee as I did so. I always carry a pot with me in anticipation of such happy occasions.

Basking in my small victory, I treated myself to a nice cold beer from the bar and sat happily watching my gear dry in the hot afternoon sun; steam rising lazily from my tattered underpants. And at that, with plenty of time on my hands, I had a short siesta in the cool-dark of the empty bunkroom. Soap scented bliss.

Needless to say, when I returned after my rest to retrieve my stuff, every stitch of clothing was on the ground. Attached to a stray sock was pinned a crude drawing of a man swinging by his neck from a tree, knotted vests as his noose. I think somebody was trying to tell me something.

Feeling much better after my rest and freshly spruced, I took the short walk down the hill into Belorado. It wasn't much of a place to get excited about to be honest, certainly not compared to other towns I'd visited along *The Way*. There was a nice little church, a few interesting features dotted about and a pleasant enough main square, porticoed intermittently around its perimeter with a tree encircled bandstand at its centre. To complete this rather bare picture, several bars and restaurants were sprinkled around the plaza in a game attempt to add some colour and life. That was it really.

A little brochure I had picked up earlier, featuring more adverts than information incidentally, described Belorado as once being famous for its fur trade. Apart from dozens of feral and mangy cats sprawled around the streets however, I could detect precious little evidence of the towns pelted pedigree.

To pass the time as much as anything else, I had a cursory wander around the town in a vain search for points of interest. Unearthing little more than disappointment however, I returned to the Plaza Mayor, settling outside one of the better-looking bars for a welcome cold beer. I was joined shortly afterwards by my Swedish friends, Charles and Ulla. The Mexicans weren't with them, but were around somewhere and indeed they joined us a little later, providing an excuse for more drinks and lots of laughs, as if in truth, an excuse was needed. It was a pleasant little *intervalo,* exchanging war stories from the days march and comparing blisters. It was all very nice and comradely, and the beer was excellent too.

After an entertaining couple of hours we went our separate ways and with nothing much else to do, I went back to my albergue for a nightcap or two of Rioja. It was a real treat to be drinking a wonderful wine that would cost six quid a glass in a pub back home, whereas here I was paying just one euro. Very acceptable. I sat for this final daylight hour on the near empty terrace, sipping contentedly on my wine in the gathering gloom, casting my thoughts back over another great day on the Camino. After a while, the air began to turn chilly as the night closed in. It was definitely time to be indoors.

Taking no chances, I made sure to check that none of my clothes had been slashed or burned in my absence by a vengeful launderess. Reassured, I turned in at exactly 9.00pm. I never once had a problem with all these early nights, mostly in fact I needed them, and I always slept like a dead man.

A study of my map before retiring, showed that two thirds of the following day would be of steady climbing, all this before a steep descent into San Juan de Ortega, my planned destination. I also noted that there are no villages *at all,* from halfway up the hill to the end of the journey, a distance of over 12 kilometres.

Having had my fingers (and feet) burned previously, I must make sure I'm well provisioned for that. "A bird in the hand is worth a stitch in time, nor iron bars a cage in glass houses " My trusted and unfailing motto for survival. Oh yes.

Distance walked today – 23 Kilometres(180)

TEN

Belorado

to

San Juan de Ortega

I was making my way out of Belorado just as the clock ticked 7.00am. The first glistening blades of the new day, were already slicing into the dark canopy of the swiftly dying night.

If the general theme of yesterday's walk was of gradual descent, todays would be the opposite. There would be some tough looking climbing to negotiate, particularly during the middle third of the day. Come on then me owd cocker, let's get moving.

My destination today is San Juan de Ortega, and a tad over 24 kilometres along the Camino. Moving quietly through the empty, lamp lit streets, I was soon out into the open trail and a sweeping vista of wheat fields consuming the land.

Passing quickly through Tosantos, a village still sleeping, I pushed on up the hill to Villambistia. Here I took my own advice of the previous evening, stocking up on water and snacks from a little cafe in the centre of the village. Another short burst took me to Espinosa del Camino, where I halted for a brief rest just beyond its outskirts. Munching on bananas amongst the ruins of the Monastery of San Felices I checked my map, noting with some satisfaction that I had clocked over 10k already. Almost half of today's journey completed before midday. Good lad.

Almost from the get-go this morning, the trail had been rising steadily and getting steeper, and there were one or two very tough sections still to negotiate. The Camino from Belorado up to this point had closely followed the N-120 highway, but at Villafranca Montes de Oca the trail deviated sharply to the onset of a long, steep and energy sapping climb. To add spice to the mix; it was also becoming very hot.

The landscape changed too as I climbed higher. The wheat fields, temporarily at least, were being left behind, giving way to the deep forests that covered every hillside for miles around.

This region of Montes de Oca was once, according to the guidebook, notorious bandit country, with danger lurking behind every bush. It all seemed pretty quiet now though; I sincerely hoped. The bonus of these woodland tracts was their gift of long stretches under the shade of the closely packed trees, making it just a little cooler and more comfortable for walking.

After what seemed hours and hours, but in reality just a couple, the trail slowly began to level out and open up, but without ever losing the dense forestry that continued to crowd the route. It was clear after all the climbing that I was on some kind of high, wide ridge, but it was impossible to get any sense of it due to the impenetrability of the surrounding woods.

A little further on, the track opened even further to resemble a dirt-strip airfield runway, a very long airfield runway at that. Clearly man made, this must have been cut as an access road for the forestry industry of these parts, it was certainly wide enough to allow any kind of machine through. As straight as an arrow and with the sun lasering the back of my neck, the trail continued in this fashion for several kilometres, until at last, the path began to narrow again and begin the long, slow descent that would carry me to San Juan de Ortega.

Just at the point where the trail began to fall more steeply, I encountered a stark and moving reminder of Spain's bloody and not too distant history. In a quiet clearing at the side of the Camino stood a simple granite obelisk, with the legend '1936' inscribed on each of its four sides.

On the monument itself and in more detail on a plaque to one side was a description of its memorial. It was erected in honour and remembrance of the 300 people who were brought up here from the villages below, and shot by forces of General Franco during the Spanish Civil War. A little further back was the sight of the mass grave where the bodies had been dumped; I didn't quite have the stomach for that. It was a harrowing thought but nonetheless true, that this was just one amongst thousands of commemoratives to the many atrocities committed by both sides in that bloodiest of conflicts, and one that still evokes a lot of bitter and painful memories for Spaniards today.

I considered carefully about whether I should leave my comment on the Spanish conflict at that short paragraph. On reflection, I thought I would devote a couple of pages or so on a bit of background, and if you will allow, my own understanding of the history of the war. It was such an important period in modern Spanish history, and the regions I would walk through on this pilgrimage were as blood soaked and as horrifically scarred as any. Hold on then.

Perhaps not unsurprisingly, I found that of the many people I asked, most new very little of the Spanish civil war. More surprisingly, plenty more had never even heard of it. With that in mind and in the context of my journey, also in respect of my visit to the memorial I have described, I felt genuinely beholden to the memory of those innocent fallen to add these words.

As I have suggested, the Spanish civil war for many is a forgotten conflict, occurring as it did at the fading end of the short, twenty year peace between the two great world wars, and the monstrous loss of life and devastation that so dominates the history of the first half of the twentieth century. There are some observers who champion the theory that the Spanish war actually heralded the start of WW2; most modern historians however, view this as too simplistic.

Following José Sanjurjos partially failed coup in July 1936 (Franco would emerge as leader of the Nationalists after Sanjurjos early death in a plane crash) which was planned to sweep away the Republican government in one devastating action, conflict between the left leaning Republican government and its supporters, and the right wing Nationalist revolutionaries and its cohorts, soon broke out. The failure of the Nationalists to take over the entire country immediately, left Spain both politically and militarily divided. Civil war was the inevitable outcome.

Franco was not a fanatical Fascist in the mold of Hitler and Mussolini, he didn't have any hard line expansionist policies for instance. But he was most certainly an ardent devotee of the ultra-conservative right and held extreme authoritarian views. There is no doubt however, that the murderous brutality and totalitarian suppression he inflicted on the Spanish people during and after the war, would have got approving nods from his peers in blood-thirstiness; Hitler and Stalin. His philosophy was built on his unshakeable belief in traditional Spanish values and way of life: Monarchy, Catholic church, a strong military and a powerful, centralist government. The whole underpinned by the sacred values and customs of Spanish home life.

The democratically elected government were 'left' leaning and by exiling them, had rid themselves of the Monarchy some years previously. Its support was drawn from every hue of the colour red: Hard line Marxist-Leninists, other communistic adherents, traditional socialists of the labour unions and a peculiar mixture of anarchists and anarcho-syndicalists.

This clear division between left and right, soon attracted backing and support from the obvious quarters. Franco's 'Government' was heavily backed, financially and militarily, by Hitler's Germany and Mussolini's Italy. Both countries providing military advisors, troops, armaments, tanks and aircraft etc.

The Republicans main ally was Stalin's Soviet Russia. Whilst the Russians piled in with 'Advisors' troops and weaponry, these were neither of the same quantity or superiority as supplied by the Nationalists supporters. Much has been written about the 'International Brigades' flocking to the Republican cause, but these volunteers never amounted to more than 20,000 men. The Brigades attracted many prominent personalities of the time such as Ernest Hemingway and George Orwell. Many fought and died bravely, but their overall impact was minimal, at least as a military force. Their usefulness as a propaganda tool was crucially more important to the Republicans, as they sought to gain world recognition for their cause. It was these interventionist policies of the Fascist and Communist powers, that characterised the civil war as an ideological struggle between totalitarian dictatorship and democracy.

In every sense, the two sides could not have been further apart. The next two and a half years would not only be a true battle for the hearts and minds of the people, but also for the political and social future of Spain. It would be a merciless, bloody conflict with no quarter given. Ruthless massacres of civilians in their tens of thousands, would become a feature of both sides determination to enforce their own objectives. The monument I have described above San Juan de Ortega, being just one amongst thousands spread throughout Spain, commemorating such needless slaughter.

The bitter irony of course, was that for both Hitler and Stalin, the campaign was seen as opportunist and expedient, rather than as carefully planned strategic policy. There was little altruism either, in the despots backing of their chosen cause, both had their grubby hands out from the beginning.

Hitler was handsomely recompensed for his commitments, through the large quantities of raw materials such as coal and iron ore he received from Franco as 'payment' for his military backing. Stalin was rewarded for his support from the Republican governments gold stocks, some $500 million worth at late 1930s values. This was almost two thirds of the total Spanish government reserves at that time.

Hitler found Franco a tedious and unimaginative man, unwilling to embrace his world view of Fascist hegemony and racial purity. The Fuhrer however, was very amenable to use the conflict to test his new armaments and air force in battle conditions, fine tuning his revolutionary infantry tactics via the Condor Legions.

In the grand scheme of things, Stalin was even less interested and was more than a match for Hitler's cynicism. He would of course have been very happy to see a hard left, indebted (to him) Spanish government in power, as long as it was tied to the apron strings of 'Mother Russia'. Once Stalin realised the Republicans were headed for defeat however, he too turned his back on Spain.

Without the intervention of these great powers, the civil war would have been fought very differently and very possibly with a different outcome. The thought of a Stalinist-Communist leaning socialist government as dictators of a post 1938 Spain, doesn't encourage the possibility that the sufferings and deprivations experienced under the Francoist regime, would have been any less bearable to the ordinary Spaniard.

The superior forces and armaments of Francisco Franco's Nationalists eventually brought him victory, and the beginning of a Dictatorship that was to last almost 40 years. The loss of life during the conflict is still not determined to this day, and most historians are reluctant to give anything other than flexible approximations. 250,000 to a million deaths are often cited, but not validated.

Franco seized Spain in an iron grip, and the next few years of power enabled him to isolate and slaughter thousands more, either in acts of vengeance or removal of potential threats. Spain's recovery after the civil war was slow and painful, its economy staggering under the weight of the effects of war and a constantly failing economy. It wasn't until the financial liberation of the 1950s and 60s, and the ensuing 'Spanish Miracle' that things began to improve.

During that period with the endgame in sight, Franco had the young prince Juan Carlos brought back to Spain, tutored under his direction and groomed as his successor. On Franco's death in 1975, Juan Carlos was crowned King and he immediately announced a return to liberal democracy, with full and free elections forming the platform for a new Spain. A Spain that nowadays sadly and to my surprise, many people have always thought had existed.

Modern Europe, especially Britain, look at Spain as the country of the Costas and holidays, sangria and sun, which helped characterise and shape our contemporary view of the nation. The darkness of that terrible war, now mostly unknown and hidden behind the bright, sunlit beaches and bars of the popular resorts is still there; a piercing wound in Spanish history and on its people.

When I look around me now, in the villages, towns and cities I am so honoured to visit on my pilgrimage, and I see the warmth, joy and vitality of the Spanish people going about their daily lives, it is almost impossible to imagine their forefathers waging such a brutal and bloody war just 80 years ago. But that is the reality. As I remarked earlier, the civil war is still a subject of much anguish amongst the Spanish people. To this day the lost graves of war dead, many in large sites such as the one in this story are being revealed, the remains exhumed and reburied. It's a war that won't quite go away for the Spanish people, and probably won't be consigned to history for some time to come.

In the immediate years after Franco's death, the newly democratised Spanish Parliament in a desperate attempt to draw a huge black line under the past regime, passed laws that were basically designed to forgive, forget and bury the past as quickly as possible. A futile attempt to inflict a sort of collective amnesia on the Spanish people.

These shallow and shameless acts still haunt the corridors and policies of modern Spanish governments, as they continue to refuse to engage with this dark period of Spain's recent history and find real closure. This, despite the growing clamour for these laws to be repealed and for justice, finally, to have its day.

The war, its history and influence on modern Spain, was graphically described to me by a young Spaniard later on my journey. "It is a like a sinister and forbidding attic at the top of an ancient but very familiar house. You know it's there, and you know it's full of important things. But only go up into that dark place if you have to my friend".

I hope these last pages haven't been too much of too much. I felt it was important for me to write them, if only for the memory of those murdered innocents above San Juan de Ortega and the countless thousands like them, buried in lost graves throughout Spain.

Advancing swiftly down the steep, pebbly path, trying unsuccessfully to shrug off the ghosts of the past, I scuffed and picked my way through the last kilometres to San Juan de Ortega, easing into that little *pueblo* just before 2.30pm. The village was indeed tiny, with just a few houses sprinkled around its edge, overshadowed by the now disused monastery and adjacent church. I wondered without too much hope, what delights if any would keep me entertained during the hot afternoon and evening in this quiet, lonely little outpost.

San Juan de Ortega was a follower and student of Santo Domingo, (encountered earlier in the town bearing his name) and he too was a great builder in this region of Burgos, many of his creations still standing these long centuries later. It is understood that San Juan himself had a part in the construction of the cathedral, although I read later that this is called into question in some histories of the village.

Part of the monastery itself had been converted into an albergue, and it was here I would spend the night. Very pleasant it was too, to be amongst the cloisters and former cells of those long-ago monks. These buildings dated back over 800 years, and you could sense the history oozing out of the stonework.

The church was small and dark, with a few side altars and chapels placed along its walls. Prominent amongst them was the tomb of San Juan himself. In one of the chapels there is a window and so placed, that it lets sunlight through on the equinox days of March 20th and September 22nd, to illuminate a stone sculpture of the Annunciation of the Virgin Mary. A touch of pagan ritual finding its way into the fabric of a church dedicated to the teachings of St Augustine? Well I never!

The albergue, as befits a monastery I suppose, was the most basic so far, but still very clean and comfortable and complete with all the necessary facilities. The whole place was redolent of its ecclesiastical past. You could almost hear the chants of the cowled monks shuffling their sleepy way to morning prayer, the resonance of their lonely hymns, trapped forever within these ancient walls.

Having showered and changed I discovered, unsurprisingly, that there was absolutely nothing to do or see in this quiet little spot. To pass the time, I made a repeat tour of the cathedral and took a stroll along the back lanes, all done in twenty minutes.

I ambled across to the one small bar in the village for a couple of drinks, sitting outside in the hot sunshine to write up my notes. My Mexican *amigos* had arrived later that afternoon, and having just emerged from the pilgrims service in the church, they joined me for a quick drink and to catch up. They didn't stay long though, they had organised another of their famous picnics and had very kindly invited me to join them, but somehow, I didn't quite feel up to a feast that evening.

I'll take this opportunity to dip my toe once again, into the murky waters of political incorrectness! In the first couple of days after leaving Pamplona, I had been introduced to a lady of a certain age and size, who was "thrilled" to meet a fellow Englishman. I told her I was Irish, but it didn't put her off and she tagged along for a couple of days.

She was one of those people who talk constantly and never listen, and I soon tired of her. Not only did she talk non-stop, but she was her own principal subject and her stories were, shall we say to be generous, a little fanciful. A trail of donkeys hind legs scattering in her wake, would be the tell-tale sign of her whereabouts on the Camino. If, in a rare moment, she wasn't giving vent to some convoluted tale or other, this would be because she was eating. Man, could she eat. On this particular evening the lady of the hour was also staying in San Juan, currently ensconced in the bar outside of which I was sitting, demolishing a three-course dinner. I could hear her incessant babbling through the open window as she ate, the only voice I did hear in fact.

Approaching the bar to order a last drink our friend was also stood there; gravy dripping down her chin onto her ample chest, as she clutched bars of chocolate and packets of cake in her meaty fists, all presumably to sustain her through the long night. The last words I heard, and I swear this is all true, were these pleadings to the barman: ".... but if I order and pay now, would it be possible for you to leave something out for my breakfast in the morning?...."

She was the only person I met on the entire pilgrimage, who actually *gained* weight on the long road to Santiago! She asked me a day or so later why I had taken an instant dislike to her? I told her it was to save time.

Not a story told in the true and generous spirit of the Camino I appreciate. I probably wouldn't have shared it if after leaving the bar, she hadn't bumped into my table knocking over glasses, spilling beer and wine over everyone *and* without either a word of acknowledgement or apology. Do what you like but don't mess with my wine, or you'll end up as a 'baddie' in one of my books!

I decided to check in on Alex, Alfredo and Fernando before I called it a day, and to see what damage they had done to their banquet. They were still in full flight; gradually working through a wonderful array of tapas, breads and pastries. Stood to attention at the side guarding the feast, were the ubiquitous two or three bottles of wine.

Unable to resist their pleadings I joined in for a nibble and a glass or two, and it was of course, delicious. It occurred to me at that point, that they must have carried all this food and drink with them, there were no shops in San Juan. It transpired they had stocked up at Villafranca on the way through, knowing in advance there would be nothing of substance in this little village. That still meant carrying bags of food and drink for over 12 kilometres. These lads really were dedicated *gourmands*! They were happy to endure any and all hardships of the trail, as long as they could eat and drink their fill along the way. Tremendous stuff.

We chatted for a while longer, picking at the last crumbs and finishing off the wine. Between us we concocted a loose plan to meet up the following day in Burgos, although at that point none of us knew where we would be staying, nor times of arrival. At the finalé to our little fiesta, there was only bed and an early night to bring the curtain down on another fantastic, although a somewhat emotional and moving day. My closing thought was that this moment marked exactly two weeks, and I just have to say it, several pounds lighter since I had left England. Karma.

Distance walked today – 25 Kilometres (205)

ELEVEN

San Juan de Ortega

to

Burgos

I was up and running, well walking, towards a night sky beating a fast retreat from the irresistible onslaught of the new day emerging behind me.

Today I would be heading to the great medieval metropolis of Burgos, 25 kilometres from San Juan. Burgos is a large and important city with a long and famous history. It is also of course, the ancestral home of one Rodrigo Díaz de Vivar; better known to history and film lovers as 'El Cid'.

Most of the trail today would be of a gentle descent, but firstly there would be a significant climb leading the way out from San Juan. I wanted to get this little challenge out of the way as early in the day as possible, and certainly before the sun got cracking. Afternoon temperatures today were forecast at between 31-35oC, and I hoped to be well on my way to the finishing line before it got anywhere near that hot.

From San Juan de Ortega then, it was just a short hop along the main road before I was diverted onto rough track, and out into the recurring terrain of endless wheat.

A short, steep descent down a pine-tree shrouded path brought me to the pretty little *aldea* of Agés, with its lovely half-timbered buildings and ancient looking streets. A little further on, I crossed a stone bridge over a narrow river and onto the road to Atapuerca. This small town is an archaeological heritage site of some importance, due to significant pre-historic finds in local caves. I would have liked to have checked this out, but the caves were some distance off the Camino and regrettably, I just didn't have that kind of time to spare.

Once through Atapuerca, the ground began to rise markedly and I was immediately straining against the ascent. In the ever growing heat, I climbed mulishly up the steep and unforgiving slope for about 1.5k, eventually and triumphantly cresting the peak of Matagrande.

That was my first objective achieved. I had arrived hot and sweating at dead on 9.00am, just as the sun was starting to roll up its sleeves and lick its lips! Perfect.

From Matagrande, it was to be gently downhill for the rest of the way to Burgos and I soon settled in to a steady, untroubled rhythm. I was making great time too, stopping only briefly for a drink and a rest by the shady ruins of a church at Villalval.

Revived and refreshed I was racing along now, soon passing through Cardeñuela Ríopico, followed in short order by the lonely and seemingly deserted Orbaneja Ríopico. Once through Orbaneja, I caught a first sight of the great city of Burgos, looming large and impressively in the distance.

Descending comfortably along quiet country lanes, it came as something of a shock to be confronted by Burgos Airport. A smallish one for sure, but covering a lot of acres. The trail, almost reluctantly it felt, skirted the airfield, doggedly following the perimeter fencing and there was a lot of it. I cut my way through a small industrial area at the edge of the airport, heading for the long section of trail that would take me through a large country park and into Burgos. This entailed a hot and leg stretching hike of 6 or 7 kilometres, but it would eventually deliver me right into the heart of the city.

With the heat building steadily by the minute and energy beginning to drain from stiffening legs, this last stretch of trail seemed to drag on and on. It was pleasant enough walking though, I have to say. The path wove its languid way through the leafy and shade-a-plenty park, hugging the meandering banks of the Río Arlanzón, until at last, the buildings of the city hove into view, nearing with each aching step.

At length I crossed the river over a very ornate bridge, the 'Puente del Cid', once again feeling overwhelmed by the sudden presence of traffic and people. Just a few paces on and I was into the busy streets of Burgos.

Not having a detailed map of the city, I had no real idea as to where any of the many listed albergues were situated, so I simply tracked the Camino signs of the shell and yellow arrows, trusting I would eventually find something. Following a long and taxing trek through the streets of the very busy city centre, I found I couldn't get into either the first or second albergues I came across, both being full. Feeling very tired and hot by now and I have to say a little dispirited, I fortuitously bumped into my Mexican friend Fernando, and help at hand.

It transpired the three of them had arrived only a short time before me, and had just managed to get the last bunks in one of the albergues I had unsuccessfully tried. Fernando had been dispatched by the others to empty the shelves of a nearby supermarket in preparation for their evening banquet, and he had excellent intelligence to impart. He advised me that there was a very good, if slightly more expensive albergue across the river by the station and I should try there. Just a five minute walk led me to its doors and thankfully, there was plenty of room.

It was just a little dearer at 16 euros, but the large and imposing 'Hostel Burgos' was very nice and I didn't object to the extra few bob, especially given all the very inexpensive stays I had enjoyed on previous nights. It took an absolute age to check in though.

There were only a handful of people queuing in front of me at the desk, but it took forever for the clerk to process each one, as she painstakingly completed reems of paperwork and carefully scrutinised documents. Eventually it was my turn, and having been issued with folded sheets and towels I rode up the lift, and once inside the main body of the hostel found it to be excellent. It was modern, large and spacious with terrific facilities, each floor being neatly divided into smaller bunkrooms, one of which was to be mine. I quickly cleaned up, threw my gear in the locker and was out again within the hour.

Burgos is a grand and lovely city, clearly proud of its ancient past, its place in Spanish history and not least its most famous personage, El Cid. The central area was home to a collection of fine stately buildings and spacious plazas, all interconnecting with either narrow streets or wide boulevards. The nicest of these has to be the beautiful, tree lined Paseo de Espolón, stretching elegantly alongside the broad Río Arlanzón which cuts benignly and slowly through the city centre.

I liked Burgos very much indeed. It was vibrant and busy with tourists yes, but in a very attractive way. There was nothing tacky or cheap about the city, having a nice, relaxed and welcoming feel to it. I was very impressed, and I immersed myself expectantly into its busy streets.

Observing the very large crowds milling about filling the plazas, bars and shops, there was obviously plenty of money sloshing around. Burgos was not only an important place on the Camino, but also benefited from a wider tourist market independent of this. The city of course, was also the provincial capital and centre of administration, bringing all the commercial benefits associated with those civic and governmental affairs.

I really enjoyed wandering along these bright, sunlit streets and plazas, soaking up the atmosphere. Pausing occasionally here and there to admire the many splendid buildings and beautiful statuary. It was quite fabulous.

Burgos is a city of substance and character and a place in which I would have liked to have spent much more time, but as is the nature of the Camino that was not to be. I was however, determined to make the most of my brief stay, and I wasn't going to miss out on a visit to the famous cathedral.

I stopped for a bite to eat and a beer at one of the many bars and restaurants situated in and around the busy cathedral plaza, and very acceptable it was too. Nicely fed and watered I strolled across the square, drawn by the irresistible spectacle and grandeur of the great church itself.

The cathedral of Santa Maria is simply beautiful, its outstanding Gothic façade matched by an equally magnificent and massive interior. The original structure dates back to 1221, with significant alterations in the 15th and 16th centuries. It is not only an architectural work of art, but houses many treasures within. El Cid is interred here alongside his wife Jimena, their tombs clearly a major attraction.

Why are we so drawn to the vaults and resting places of the long dead and famous? What is it we expect from visiting these musty crypts? These ancient worthies are not going to rise up and speak to us are they? Why, for instance, is there so much kudos attached to announcing: "I visited and admired the tomb of William the Conqueror at L'Abbey-aux-Hommes"? When perhaps, your friends might be much more interested and impressed to here you report, that you had: "Visited and admired the arse of Rita Ora at the Glastonbury Festival". I know my friends would.

It would be easy to fill the pages of a large book in describing the many glories of Burgos cathedral, unfortunately, I can only offer a brief glimpse here through these few unworthy words.

It has to be said straight away that the church is huge, taking many minutes just to skirt its perimeter. Although principally of Gothic style; due to the countless additions and alterations to the structure down the centuries, several other architectural vogues can be discerned both externally and internally, all mightily impressive. The carvings and moldings on the exterior walls are a riot of many forms, and it is almost impossible to let your eyes rest on a single part but for a few moments. The massive towers and steepling spires, mostly added in the 15th century, are incredibly ornate and reach up spectacularly towards the sky.

The interior is almost beyond description, it is so lavish and decorative. There is almost too much to see and take in at one viewing, and I certainly felt as I had seen but a fraction on my short visit. The church is packed with stunning altarpieces, side chapels and fabulous statuary. There are endless little corners and alcoves, each holding a little gem of its own, it really is magnificent. Of the hundreds of spectacles, the stand-out must be the Constable Chapel, with its huge skylit dome, arched stained glass windows and guilt altarpiece.

Just before the resting place of El Cid, is set the most stunning example of wood carving my tired old eyes have seen! These outrageous choir stalls are a visual opera in themselves, incredible. Lastly, but by no means least of all, is the *Escalera Dorada*, or Golden Staircase. Italian Renaissance in style, it could easily be the original 'Stairway to Heaven'.

I could go on and on, alas, these few short sentences must suffice. If you ever get the chance to visit the cathedral of Santa Maria in Burgos, then you must do so. It really is a most memorable place.

Worn out and visually frazzled, I sought instant resuscitation in a smashing little bar in a shaded alley to the side of the plaza. Forced reluctantly by the fearsome *mesera* to order a large beer, I sat very contentedly watching the world go by, thinking how splendid life can be sometimes. Unbidden, the wickedly cruel waitress ordered me to have another beer. I couldn't believe it, honestly.

The growing and ever nearing fanfare of drums and trumpets, heralded an evening procession of armed and costumed musicians, knights and their pages, large flags and heraldry waving aloft. This was *I think*, a reproduction of the ancient ceremony of the rounds of the night watchmen and locking of the city gates. Whatever it was, it was all very colourful and noisy, and a magnet for hundreds of sightseers and their clicking cameras. Well, maybe not so much clicking as humming in these digital days.

Don't you miss that wonderful feeling and satisfying sound of the proper click of a camera button and ratchet of the film spool as you wound it on? You couldn't instantly check your results then of course, and would be mildly worried that you might have cocked-up the shot. Wondering two weeks later when your film had been developed, why you had a photo of the front wheel of a moped instead of your granny eating an ice cream! Nowadays there is no real skill to everyday photography is there? It's just point and push. Everybody is an instant David Bailey, assuming I'm sure, that film negatives are just bad reviews for movies.

It was impossible to travel too far without bumping into a reminder of Burgos' most famous son, El Cid, (splendidly and memorably portrayed by Charlton Heston and beautifully supported by the stunning Sophia Loren, in the famous 1961 film) his name and face appearing everywhere. The statue of him near the cathedral in full armour mounted on his rearing steed is superb, and he is certainly worth a brief mention here.

Born in 1043 into a family of lower nobility, El Cid was raised and tutored in the court of King Ferdinand and would eventually go on to serve his son, King Sancho the second. Rodrigo rose through the ranks as a young man and soon became a commander of the armies of Castile, leading several campaigns on Sancho's behalf.

By various twists of fortune and the vagaries of royal patronage, El Cid (Moorish for 'Lord') ended up fighting for both the Muslim rulers who then occupied that region of Spain *and* the Christian forces of various kings, managing to be proclaimed as a great hero by both. No mean feat in 11th century Spain.

Through great victories and exploits, El Cid and his beautiful wife Jimena eventually became rulers of Valencia, with both Muslims and Christians living side by side as loyal and peaceful subjects. El Cid continued fighting his various enemies right up to his death in 1099, his legend built throughout his life and still enduring today in his home city of Burgos and beyond. What a great story! Somebody should make it into a film.

Feeling very content at the end of another hard but extremely rewarding day, and thoroughly enjoying my brief tour of Burgos, I returned to my swish albergue. Before arriving though I decided on a whim (they're every 10 minutes from the bus station) that a brief diversion and a last glass of wine at a nearby bar was called for, ambidextrously writing up *mis aventuras del día* with my non-drinking hand.

At around 3.00am, my half dozen or so room companions and I were suddenly and rudely woken by the drunken stumbling, crashing and swearing of another resident returning from a night out. When politely reminded by one of his Spanish compatriots that we all had to be up in three hours, I was told later in translation of his pissed-up response. Apparently our drunken friend cared not a solitary shit for his rudeness, as he was "not a fucking pilgrim" but was on his way to Madrid to get pissed again with his mates, and was only "stopping off in this fucking dump" as it was cheap, near to the train station and he didn't have to get up until 10.00am, so "bollocks to you all" his apparent diminuendo. I thank you and good night.

Burgos is a large and multi-ethnic city, carrying all the problems associated with immigration and poverty typical of most large European cities, I realise. There was a lot of begging on the streets, seemingly ignored by the authorities either in its cause, effect or provision of a solution. It was a pitiful sight to see these weary looking people, young and old, desperately in need and struggling for a few pennies to survive, especially in a prosperous city such as Burgos *and* in the heartland of the Camino.

All to be expected I suppose in these modern times. The 'establishment' would no doubt leap to the cities defence in claiming that they were doing their best, and that the problem was much worse in other towns across Spain. Very true I'm sure, but that doesn't make life any easier for the desperate and disenfranchised folk of Burgos, living below the sight line and care of the more prosperous majority.

But, let me say this without any fear or hesitation. Neither this issue or any other dark cloud, could detract from my view that Burgos is a very, very fine city indeed, and I would be more than happy to revisit its many wonders in the future.

The one truly significant downside for me however, was that despite a thorough search, I could find neither Charlton Heston nor Sophia Loren. I wasn't all that bothered about finding Charlton Heston to be honest.

Distance walked today – 27 kilometres (232)

TWELVE

Burgos

to

Hornillos del Camino

I had decided upon a later start this morning, not checking out of the albergue until 8.00am. My re-drawn plan was to have a little rest today, maybe have half a day in Burgos for more sightseeing, then walk for just a couple of hours to a mid-point town with accommodation. On rising however, I went straight into 'Ready' mode and hit the trail as normal, full of beans and all set for a good day's walk.

To be honest, I'm not sure how much control I had of these events. The Camino robot in charge of my head seemed to just take over, ordering me into action! A bit scary that.

The journey out of the city took well over an hour, pursuing the long N-120 main road past the University complex and bringing nothing to liven up this dull and overcast morning. For quite a distance, the path either followed or crisscrossed the busy roads out of Burgos, traffic whizzing variously above and around me. It wasn't until I finally reached Villalbilla de Burgos that the Camino once more escaped the tarmac and re-joined the open countryside.

It was from this point and with a weary slump of shoulders, that I gazed despondently over a sprawling landscape of wheat, stretching interminably across the gentle hills and plain. The narrow trail sliced a clear, sharp and meandering swathe through the grain, as if cut by a large, out of control lawn mower.

Pressing on regardless, it wasn't long before I was joined in yet further battles with the local road system. The trail once again, was obliged to swerve around or duck under the inter-secting highways that acted as a by-pass to the west of Burgos. It was all extremely noisy and unpleasant, and I was very pleased to escape the mayhem and settle once again into the relative quietness of the Camino, as it re-acquainted itself with the N-120 highway.

At Tardajos I stopped briefly for a break, encouraged by espy-ing my Mexican and Swedish friends breakfasting at a roadside cafe. After a quick chat and an agreement to meet up later, I headed off up slowly rising ground which, almost inevitably, would become sharper and more severe over the next two or three kilometres.

On I marched, by means of the little village of Rabé de las Calzadas, clambering up and along the undulating hills for several kilometers, until finally gaining the heights just beyond Fuente de Praotorre. Here, I surveyed another stark expanse of stubby cereal fields, understanding perfectly now, that this would be the dominant and continuing feature of this endless stretch of the Castilian *meseta*. Below me on the plain and just a few kilometres in the distance lay my destination for the day, the little *pueblo* of Hornillos del Camino.

I set off cautiously down the long rocky path, picking my way carefully between the stony, ankle twisting obstacles as the trail continued its descent. The way softened and became easier going as it neared its destination, and immediately on crossing a bridge over a little river I was entering the village. Luckily, I managed to grab the last bed at the first albergue I came upon. And a nice, homely place it was too.

The 'Sol de Sol' was but a large, converted house really. It consisted of a nicely furnished lounge cum dining room and a well equipped kitchen downstairs, in turn opening out to a large garden to the rear. There was a small accommodation area upstairs, and a little dorm with bunks for just four people on the ground floor, into which I was shown by the very friendly and welcoming owner. It was very nice and comfortable and was equipped with a superb private shower room, in which I was soon disporting myself in a carnival of soap-suds and steam.

On completion of my ablutions and whilst getting settled and sorting my pack, a strange but very humorous scene unfolded.

A very tall German gentleman, well into in his seventies I should say, burst into the room and announced in broken English that he too was bunking here. Without any obvious humour, he apologised in advance for his loud snoring and then proceeded to upend his pack, emptying the entire contents into the middle of the floor. Great, I thought, this is just what I needed.

A moment or two later, a much younger couple entered and I assumed by their familiarity, related in some way to the old boy. Some anxious Teutonic chatter and much gesticulating ensued between the three of them. The albergue owner was called for and before you knew it, the old chap was happily set up in a bed in the garden with his kit. He seemed absolutely delighted with it!

The nights were very warm, and with a bug net he would be just fine. The bonus for me of course, would be no snoring and a peaceful night. How on earth they managed to persuade him that this would be for the best, I have no idea.

My kit sorted and having exchanged introductions with my two remaining roommates, I set about some urgently needed sock washing. My chore completed, it was time for a nice relaxing sit down in the neatly trimmed back garden, under the spreading shade of a large apple tree. Wonderful.

Sipping on an ice-cold beer purchased from the shop opposite and whilst writing up my journal, I spotted my Mexicans and Swedes through the open doorway. What great timing.

Delighted that they had arrived so soon after me, I rushed on to the street to greet them and another group of pilgrims I was friendly with. It transpired that Charles and Ulla had pre-booked one of the small rooms in my albergue; the boys however, were staying at another hostel just a little way down the street.

After settling in our little band soon reconvened. What followed was the most fun filled couple of hours: drinking beer, playing music and dancing in the street, it was superb!

There didn't appear to be a bar close by, but the solitary shop had a seemingly endless supply of large cans of ice-cold San Miguel, and after a few of those we were all getting quite lively and I have to say, a bit noisy too. A young mum emerged from one of the nearby houses and cautiously came amongst us, hand-in-hand with two goggle eyed little 'uns, bursting to see what was going on from the looks on their upturned faces. A couple of the girls in our group swept up the kids and soon had them dancing, they loved it! Not to be outdone, mum was soon boogying too. It was absolutely joyous.

Surprisingly, I might add, none of the girls had asked me to dance yet. I think they were just playing it cool.

I hadn't really socialised that much with my fellow pilgrims so far; my only regular companions being Alex and Fernando, Alfredo, Ulla and Charles. I knew on some level that I probably should be mixing a bit more, especially in the evenings, but I didn't think it was a big deal. I was perfectly happy doing my own thing to be honest, allowing myself all the time I felt I needed for the contemplation and brain scrubbing that had become my *raison d'etre* on this trip.

I really was very happy in my own skin, never in need of constant companionship nor desperately seeking it. There were plenty I met on the Camino who couldn't bear to be alone for five minutes. Me? I loved it! There was no need to over analyse it; I simply preferred walking on my own and having some time in the evening just to myself. To a large extent, I think you *have* to walk the Camino on your own, or at least have plenty of your own space. You can be in a group, but without being immersed in it, if you understand my meaning. I had never once felt alone or lonely and there was company enough when I needed it. I felt comfortable in all of that and it was definitely having a positive effect.

Consequent with the time I had been on the Camino, I had acquired a growing and palpable feeling of wellbeing and contentment and I had been lifted by it. I realise life on the Camino is a forced and to some extent unreal environment, living in a bubble if you like, but the generosity of spirit I found amongst my fellow pilgrims was tangible enough. There was a real sense of brotherhood and belonging, all sharing happily and without ego, yet everyone appreciated and respected ones need for privacy and quiet. For me, that was essential.

There was a tremendous amount of goodwill and kindness amongst the walkers, and I could give many examples of it. Nothing was ever too much trouble, people were always pleased to help and share. Everyone was drawn together by the mutual challenges, the aches and pains, the extremes of joy and often desperation that the Camino experience offered.

You quickly learned to draw on your own strengths, you had to, but help of all kinds was generously available amongst fellow pilgrims if and when needed. Each day you would find out a little bit more about yourself, you coped, adjusted and moved on, because on the Camino it's what you do. It was a truly inspiring place to be and to experience and I was immensely proud and happy to be part of it, and to have the opportunity to share this wonderful journey with these fine people.

Most pilgrims had by now been on the trail for over two weeks, and of those I had spoken with there was an acknowledgement of a real feeling of change within. One chap said he felt as if he was building a quiet place inside himself as he walked, a place only for his 'Camino-self', as he described it. I could especially empathise with that. There appeared to be a gradual shedding of problems and worries that in another environment would lead you to question it; out here on the trail though, it seemed just right.

It was a unique congregation of emotions and thoughts and unlike anything I had experienced before. But, I wasn't fazed or concerned, nor did I feel the need to ignore or suppress these feelings in anyway.

I was here on the Camino de Santiago, deliberately and purposefully on a journey of exploration and discovery; not just of new places but also of self, however that may be defined. Any and all new experiences or thoughts generated by this special and enlightening journey were to be welcomed and embraced, without fear or overburdened with expectation. *Que sera, sera.* What will be, will be, as the lovely Doris Day once wisely sang. Not here in Hornillos though obviously, she sang it in a film. Somewhere else.

Our little street party went on into the early evening, new arrivals joining in as others left. All good things come to an end though and gradually the fiesta began to wane, the street reverting to its quiet anonymity as the revelers drifted away.

It had been another brilliant day on the Camino, and a superbly enjoyable beer softened afternoon and evening, but I was feeling pretty whacked now. Saying my final good nights, I accompanied my idiot grin back into the albergue, looking forward to a long nights rest.

With the old gentleman banished to the garden and a peaceful night beckoning, I crept quietly into the bunk room. My two remaining German companions and fellow party goers were already tucked up in bed, and of course, they were both snoring like jackhammers! What was that bit about *que sera, sera* again?

Distance walked today – 20 Kilometres (252)

THIRTEEN

Hornillos del Camino

to

Castrojeriz

Well rested following a good night's sleep, I rose bright and early to greet the new day and was once again ready to leave by 7.00am.

Creeping quietly from the fug of the small bunk room, I left my still-sleeping companions to their window rattling snores. I decided this morning to grab a quick brew to help me on my way, tip-toeing across the dining room into the dark and deserted kitchen to put the kettle on. I knew that this hostel was full last night so either everyone else had left or were still in bed, either way it was like being aboard the *Marie Celeste*. There was not another soul to be seen or heard.

My journey today would be to Castrojeriz and 18 kilometres of good, hard walking. I should really try and make it to Itero del Castillo, which was the next town after Castrojeriz with accommodation. That, however, would entail an additional 10 or 12k hike and somehow, I didn't feel quite up to that today. "Listen to your body" a lesson quickly learned on the Camino.

Trundling unaccompanied through the silent and empty streets of Hornillos I was soon onto the open trail, where I was greeted once more by horizonless oceans of cereal crops. It's all getting a bit monotonous to be truthful, each day replaying the same film over and over. Don't misunderstand I enjoyed the walking, loved it in fact, and welcomed the various challenges each day brought. Out here on the vastness of the *meseta* though, your eyes and mind become battered by the emptiness. You find yourself constantly scanning the distance, desperate for any diversion or sign of life.

Still, at least I was having some fantastic conversations with myself, quite often serious arguments too. I fell out with myself so badly one night, I got up and slept in another bunk. No really.

There would be a little bit of climbing to tackle this morning, and in advance of the long hike that would take me to Castrojeriz. There was a pretty tough if short ascent immediately on leaving Hornillo, descending unsurprisingly onto to another wide agricultural plain. The haul up to the heights above the village of San Bol wasn't too bad really, other than for the last steep section which peaked onto an expanse of? yes, your right! nothing but bloody crop fields in every direction.

After giving my legs and lungs a short rest, I allowed a little smile to crease my face. That last ascent had announced the end of the serious climbing for the day. I would like to say the view from here was a spectacle of mountains, valleys and forests, alas no, just more of the same. I'm running out of ways to describe wheat fields, so please bear with me.

Having reached the highest point of today's walk, the trail began its gradual descent down the ancient and rough cart track to the village of Hontanas. It was very pleasant hiking now, with the day warming up nicely. A welcome, gentle breeze was fanning my face and teasing cotton bud clouds across bright-blue skies. It was very, very quiet too. Looking back up the trail, I could just make out one lone walker on the peak, and ahead of me; there was not a soul.

It's amazing how the Camino appears to gobble up its walkers. When you arrive at your nightly stopover, most places are invariably busy with pilgrims, both in the albergues and towns. Yet out on the trail, you might only see a dozen or so people all day. I'm sure it's a lot different at the height of the season, but today it was eerily quiet.

Hontanas is a tiny and attractive hamlet of stone buildings and pantile slated roofs, all huddled together in a bundle of narrow streets. The domed tower of the church could be seen from quite a distance, and close up, seemed to completely dwarf the rest of the village. The whole place was clearly reliant on the Camino and its pilgrims, the main thoroughfare being almost completely made up of bars and albergues. God knows what they do for a living in the winter? I'm sure many of these small villages along *The Way* have the same problem, but they all seem to survive somehow.

Following a short rest I pressed on. The trail out of the village firstly crossed the main road, then climbed steadily up and into a broad valley that folded around the narrow stream of Arroyo de Garbanzuelo, the well-worn path cut neatly into its far side. It was all very absorbing and picturesque, a welcome change in scenery from the endless grasslands, that's for sure.

The Camino wandered on in this way for several kilometres, faithfully following the gentle contours of this really pretty vale, descending almost imperceptibly as I journeyed on. After a while, the track reached the bottom of the valley, intersecting sharply with the main road into Castrojeriz. Here at the junction of trail and road and parked in his little red hatchback, I came across an enterprising chap selling Camino trinkets and the like, literally from his car boot. I hope he had another means of income. Other than myself there wasn't a solitary person to be seen, and I bought bugger all!

It had become much hotter as noon passed, with the sun climbing irresistibly higher and gaining in intensity. I didn't have too far to go now though, thank you very much. I would be very happy to get out of the heat today, that's for certain.

The last of today's stages was to be five or six kilometres of tedious trudging along a straight tarmac road, enlivened only briefly by the ruins of the 15th century convent of San Antón. Nothing else was to catch my eye or turn my head as I completed the final, sunbaked stretch into Castrojeriz.

Down to my last few euros I needed cash before doing anything else, so I headed straight for the centre of town in search of a bank. My wallet replenished, I had a quick and very welcome cold beer at a just-opening bar in the middle of a small municipal park. I had a brief chat with the young *mesera*, asking if there was anything interesting happening in town. There wasn't, she replied a little sheepishly, only at weekends or fiestas, it was a very quiet town otherwise she observed.

Well, that was ok by me. Tempted to have another cold one but resisting, I dragged my pack on to my shoulders, heading back up the steep hill to seek out my albergue for the evening.

At the foot of the hill, I was accosted by two surly looking young lads in a beat up old car, clanking away and spewing dark smoke from its exhaust. Leaning from the window, one of the youths shouted "eh senor, peregrino? (pilgrim)" "Si" I replied warily. "You English?" he said "you want a lift? I give you a lift, get in car" A good pummeling in a dark alley and relief of my wallet, no doubt their true intention. I explained to him that I didn't need a lift as I didn't live on the top floor of a block of flats, quickly making my escape whilst leaving a car full of puzzled frowns behind me. What fools these evil hearted boys were to joust with me and my razor sharp wit!

I knew that the Camino was relatively crime free, but I had also read that there were many opportunists lying in wait to take advantage of weary travelers. Pickpocketing and theft of clothing, believe it or not, being prime examples. They would have to get up very early to catch me unawares though; what, with my eyes peeled, ears pinned back, chin up, lips sealed, nose to the grindstone, shoulder to the wheel, back to the wall, finger on the pulse, elbows greased and feet on the floor. Oh yes.

I soon settled upon another lovely and welcoming little hostel. The 'Albergue Ultreia' was set on an ancient main street part way up the hill, and running straight through the centre of the old town. It was a long, narrow building with the dormitories set on the right and the shower rooms to the rear. There was a nice two-tiered patio on the left side of the corridor, complete with tables and chairs, laundry facilities and a barbeque range. For those interested, there was also a tiny pre-fab pool on the top terrace, it was spot on.

There were two decent sized dormitories, separated into male and female sections in this hostel. I shared my little quarters with just one other guy, a very nice German chap, Berndt (I was tempted to ask him if his surname was Toast!) who after introductions and a brief chat, seemed happily content with his own company.

Down the hall there was a long dining room and kitchen, and a *menú del día* was on offer for dinner later in the evening. I just didn't have much appetite today though, so I declined. I could always grab a snack later if needed.

Castrojeriz is another very old town, founded in 882AD and settled around the base and curves of a large, steep hill. At its top, stood the ruins of the ancient Castillo de Castrojeriz, which all visitors were encouraged to visit. There was zero chance of me scrambling up the crag in this heat though, just to have a look at a pile of crumbling ruins. I was enough of a crumbled ruin myself! It wouldn't be long before tourists would be queuing to have a look at me!

Castrojeriz was a well-appointed town although quiet on this hot afternoon, siesta being strictly observed. It had a good range of small supermarkets and shops, although many of the latter appeared to be solely for agricultural supplies. There were a few bars and restaurants dotted around and it had three banks, a rarity in these parts, signifying the towns importance as a commercial centre for the numerous surrounding villages.

I had another little tour round in the late afternoon and early evening, but couldn't find very much to divert or interest me. There were a couple of nice-looking churches, and I had a poke around those. I do like a good poke in an old church. One of them, the Iglesia de Santo Domingo, was described as being constructed in the 'Plateresque style'. Look it up, I had to.

Some days on the Camino were eventful and full of interest, others were quiet and plodding. This had definitely been one of the latter and very welcome it was too. There being nothing else on offer to entertain, I had a tasty sandwich and a couple of glasses of superb Rioja at a small, traditional *taberna* along the street. Nice and quiet and relaxing.

The evening was winding down now, as indeed was I, and it wasn't long before I was wending my sleepy way back to the albergue. It was still daylight, but I was very pleased to be pulling myself gently under the sheets.

Can I say that?

With only two of us occupying a dormitory for twelve it promised to be a nice peaceful night, and this time with no Germanic snoring. Hang on a minute though, I wonder if I snored?

Distance walked today – 21 Kilometres (273)

FOURTEEN

Castrojeriz

to

Boadilla del Camino

I had a little lie in this morning, but I was still nicely away at 7.45am and into the embrace of another bright, sunlit day.

Today I should be heading for Fromista, but from looking at my map the previous evening, I thought that I might stop just a few kilometres shy of there at Boadilla del Camino. I didn't really fancy doing battle with a large town today, and the brochure of the region suggested that although Boadilla was a small and quiet *pueblo*, it did have a couple of very nice albergues. That would do nicely then.

A short walk down the hill led me out of the town and I was soon back on the trail. This first section stretched out towards a very large peak, looming ominously about 3k in the distance. This, I knew I would have to climb. The only consolation being that after conquering this prominence, I would be rewarded with much easier walking for the rest of the day.

I wound my way across the meadows to the foot of the mount, steeling myself for the climb ahead. Immediately on crossing a small wooden bridge over the Río Odrilla the ground began to rise very quickly, and looking up, I could see the distant shapes of a handful of fellow walkers, inching their way upwards. This, I ventured to myself, could be a very tough gig.

It proved to be a relentlessly long and winding climb, seriously steep in places. I had to pause for a rest on several occasions, trying my best to admire the spectacular views whilst desperately sucking air into gasping lungs. Head down, with a slow and steady gait, I eventually crested the peak of Alto de Mostelares, which in turn looked out over a vast plain of scrubland and crop fields. This was the Tierra de Campos; exposed, bleak and whipped about by a strong, swirling wind that had a real chill with it too, way up here on this high plateau.

A small wooden *refugio* stood close by, so I took the opportunity for a rest and a drink before commencing the long climb down. That last ascent was a real sinew stretcher. I calculated later that the peak I had just gained, although just under one and a half Kilometres in length, constituted almost 800 metres in height. The *average* degree of incline along its length was 11%. No wonder I was knackered.

I shared a bench with an achingly beautiful, dark eyed Senora. In her early forties I would guess, with long, jet black hair tied in a braid. She had the most magnetic almond shaped eyes and Hollywood-white teeth. Most alluringly, she also had a small birthmark in the shape of Italy in the cleavage of her heaving chest, which I stared at for a few minutes. The heaving chest, not the birthmark.

I decided, in an ill-advised moment of bravado, to risk a little Spanish banter. But, before a word had formed on my slavering lips, she fired at me one of those withering 'Don't even think about it' glares, that I'm getting so used to receiving these days.

Giving her my best 'it's your loss kido' look in return, I made to get up, turned and tripped over my pack, stumbling to the ground and banging my head painfully on the cabin wall. Falling over it would appear, was one of the challenges of the Camino I seemed to have mastered with little difficulty. Expecting a helping hand and, perhaps, the offer of a comforting sit on her knee, all I got was a face full of dust as she swept soundlessly past. I have got feelings you know.

On with the grind then, I dragged myself back to the head of the trail where my battered spirits took a further knock. Spilling out before me was yet another gigantic prairie of wheat, with not a single structure of any kind visible. The only feature breaking the monotony was the trail itself; a strip of chalky gravel ploughing through the parched brown fields, pointing the way like a long, white, bony finger to distant and longed for mountains. I could have wept.

With as much positivity as I could muster, I pushed on. It was easy enough walking now at least, and the kilometres ticked over quickly. After crossing a bridge over the broad and fast flowing Río Pisuerga, my mind-numbing march carried me through the village of Itero de la Vega. A nothing kind of place really, yet the only visually exciting thing I had seen all day. I should have erected a statue to mark the occasion.

I had a quick look round the deserted streets in search of what, I don't know, then turned wearily back on to the gravel track. I endured 7 more foot baking, heart breaking kilometres before, thank you God! I saw the first signs of Boadilla del Camino. It's few modest buildings appearing to my eye like the Las Vegas skyline, after the emptiness of the day.

This would *have* to be my stop for tonight. My brain had been frazzled with the boredom and heat, and I needed a bit of stimulation, cold beer and a good dinner. In that respect, I had made a wonderful choice.

Boadilla, although small boasted three albergues, and I chose the one close to the church of *Nuestra Señora de la Asunción*. The 'En El Camino' was the best albergue I had stayed in to date, and that was amongst stiff competition. Set in a walled garden overlooked by the large church, the accommodation itself was in a ranch-style long barn, fitted out with great facilities. It was very nice indeed and I quickly got settled, picking out a bottom bunk for myself by an open window.

It was a busy hostel, and whilst not full it wasn't far off and there was a really nice buzz about the place. As always with these albergues it was spotlessly clean, with great showers and toilets and a homely, comfortable lounge area and well stocked library to the front.

The 'barn' looked out onto a beautiful garden, grassed throughout with a small, kidney shaped pool by the opposite wall. Placed around the grounds were several works of art: A large and funky modern mural along one wall, a couple of ex-cellent metal sculptures of *'Peregrinos del Camino'* in an abstract style, and several interesting stonework pieces strewn around. The whole effect was superb, very welcome and enlivening to the eye after today's blank canvas.

To my everlasting joy, I discovered a small bar/ restaurant tucked into one corner, sheltered by the branches of the biggest apple tree I had ever seen. The entire set up was absolutely delightful.After a couple of cold beers I felt much better. What fine, restorative powers are contained in a simple glass of ale, no wonder I doted on the stuff! I had seen from my journey in that there was nothing at all of interest in the village, so I took the opportunity for a nice lie down and to rest my feet for a while, soon dropping into a pleasant, dreamless snooze.

A little later and by now quite hungry, I indulged in a bowl of lamb estafado with crusty bread at one of the outside tables close to the bar. It was mouthwateringly delicious, and I honoured the meal by helping it down with a carafe of fine Rioja. All was now well with my little world

I sat day-dreaming for a while, letting the spirit of the wine relax my weary bones and spending a few minutes writing up my journal. With the night closing in, the chill wind that had been prevalent all day was now turning cold as the sun dropped away. That was my cue to retire.

Heading back to the bunk house and to my surprise, I saw the frosty faced Spanish lady from earlier sat alone and forlorn looking at a nearby table. 'Serves you right, misery arse', I mumbled uncharitably. Looking straight at me and with a beaming smile, she waved and said: "Hola! I see you made it, it was a hard day wasn't it?" her dazzling smile broadening, whilst her heaving chest, er, heaved in my general direction.

Too stunned to reply, I offered a hesitant wave and walked quickly past. I will never, NEVER do you hear? understand women!

Distance walked today – 21 Kilometres (294)

FIFTEEN

Boadilla del Camino

to

Carrion de los Condes

As the end of August approached, daylight was noticeably breaking later and later. I didn´t set off until 7.30am, yet the night sky was only just beginning to fracture, like bonfire toffee under the gentle hammer-taps of first light.

Leaving behind the few rickety looking buildings on the edge of Boadilla, I was quickly out of the village and onto the trail. Today I would be heading for Carrión de los Condes, a steady walk of around 24 kilometres. Or so I thought.

The footpath leading from the outskirts of the village soon merged alongside a broad canal that would take me towards Frómista. The Canal de Castilla, still navigable on this stretch by pleasure craft, was once an important trade route, carrying grain from the great bread basket of the Castilian plains to the Atlantic ports on the Bay of Biscay. Its principle purpose these days however, is as a source of irrigation to the region's agriculture. Reasonably maintained with a wide towpath running alongside, it was nice to be walking by the water; reminiscent of many similar hikes back home along the Peak Forest and Cheshire Ring canals.

A pleasant and untaxing walk brought me to the turn off to Frómista. Here I crossed over the now disused locks on the canal, taking the short walk past the railway station and into the town.

With the day by now bright and sunny, I decided to swap into my sunglasses. Frantic searching led quickly to panic, and a dawning horror that they were not in my pack. This, I realised, was because I had left them on the window shelf by my bunk back in Boadilla. Fuck, fuck, fuck!! These were no ordinary sunglasses that I could have just abandoned and written off, they were expensive prescription lenses. I had no choice but to return and rescue them.

Fuck, fuck, fuck part two!! Having just walked 6 kilometres, I now had to walk the same distance back to the albergue to retrieve my specs. Bugger. Back at Boadilla, I was relieved to discover my glasses had been found and kept safe. I took a 5-minute break to weep and curse and drink coffee, then took the same journey back along the canal to Frómista.

So, by that time, I had already walked 18 kilometres and my day had hardly started. I knew that if I was to get to Carrión today, I would have to walk an additional 18k, making 36 in total. Please God, let this be a dream. Too late, it was already a nightmare.

To make the day worse, if that was at all possible, the rest of the trail was to be along an arrow straight paved road, and across what must surely be the biggest, flattest, agricultural prairie on the planet: the Tierra de Campos.

A peculiarity of this stretch and possibly the only talking point along its entire length, was that every half kilometre or so, the small stone pillars that carried the Camino way signs were set in pairs, like gate posts on the path. I never did find out why, and I don't think I ever saw this feature again. That was fascinating wasn't it?

Almost driven mental with boredom, I decided to liven things up by composing Limericks apropos of the region. I offer for your delectation, a selection of the least offensive and printable:-

There once was a farmer from Spain
who was cursed with a very small brain
he was always in doubt
and could never work out
why the fuck he had grown all this grain

A pilgrim grown mad in the sun
had a brilliant idea whereupon
with combustible material
he would burn all the cereal
that grew in Castilla y Leon

On the road from Burgos in the heat
a walker was dead on his feet
as he lay down to die
his last mortal cry
was "thank God, no more fucking wheat!"

Keeping up a good pace to try and recover some time, I was at least able to gobble up the kilometres, desperate to get off this section of the trail and see something, *anything* of interest.

Even the names of the lonely, empty villages I passed through gave a hint as to the desolation of the place. After Frómista it was Población de Campos, literally translated as 'People of the Fields', oh really? On I tramped through Revenga de Campos, 'Regain the Fields', Ha, no kidding? Next up, Villarmentero de Campos, named after the first bloke to commit suicide there I expect.

By this time, I was even finding the ever-present swarm of flies interesting company. I was fairly certain that I had picked up my group of flies just outside Pamplona, and they had been with me ever since. I had even given some of them names, such was our familiarity. No amount of swatting made a difference. A second after you thought you had killed the lot in one deadly swipe, they were back, hovering six inches in front of your face, immovable, indestructible.

Feeling in need of some refreshment and relief from the sun, at Villalcázar de Sirga I ducked into the shade of a nice little bar, bumping into Berndt, my sole bunk room companion from Castrojeriz. He acknowledged me with a wave of his hand, unable to speak through bulging cheeks as he was in the process of demolishing a huge plate of food. He indicated I should join him at his table, and after swallowing the baby horse he was evidently eating, we enjoyed a few minutes of chatter about our respective walks since Castrojeriz and plans for the next few days.

Being very hot and thirsty and in need of something more exciting than water, I treated myself to a couple of small bottles of the local dry cider. They were ice cold and nectar. Resisting the temptation of more drinks and feeling much refreshed, I wished Berndt a comradely Bon Camino and set my smoldering boots back onto the trail.

Finally and almost desperately, I arrived at Carrión de los Condes at 5.00pm. I checked immediately into the parish operated and very large 'Albergue Paroquial de Santa María', 5 euros for the night, bargain. The hostel was very busy and I reckoned almost full, but I was led gently by the Hospitalier to a little corner as yet unoccupied. It was an almighty effort to resist the temptation to collapse immediately on to my bunk, I can tell you that.

Los Mexicano's arrived shortly after me, and after our ablutions we joined several other pilgrims gathering on the patio at the back of the Albergue. It was to be one of those squirm inducing 'Let's all introduce ourselves' meetings, followed inexplicably by a sort of Boy Scout jamboree singalong! It was a game and sincere attempt by the lay Brothers and Sisters I suppose, to entice atheists, heretics and any wavering Glasgow Rangers supporters into Roman Catholic ways.

I grew up with all that kind of stuff, I knew the script by heart, so I just sat quietly in the corner absent mindedly picking at my blisters. It was all a bit disconcerting really and I didn't enjoy it all, particularly as it was delaying my rendezvous with a couple of pre-blessed and sanctified cold beers. Amen.

Following this religious interlude and as inducement or payment, I'm not sure which, for enduring the preaching and singalong, some food had been laid out in a small refectory for the congregation. A line was forming out of the door, which put me too much in mind of a scene from the pages of *'Oliver Twist'*, so I gave it a miss. The Mexicans, I was amused to note, were numbers one, two and three at the head of the queue!

On very unsteady legs then, I wobbled, boggle eyed and possibly drooling into the town in search of food and drink of my own choosing. I picked out the first likely looking bar, ordering and consuming a completely unremembered dinner on automatic pilot, struggling gamely to stay awake as I forked food robotically into my mouth.

Returning shattered to the albergue, I eased my burning feet out of my sandals and into bed before 9.00pm. I only had a cursory look around the town, not enough to get an impression of or feel for it that's for sure. I was so tired, I just couldn't summon up the energy or enthusiasm for anything else. I wouldn't forget *anything* again on this journey, I promised myself that much. If I did, it could bloody well stay forgotten!

This would be my last day as a 50 something. Tomorrow I would reach the crumbling milestone of 60. I suppose I should have rested my chin between thumb and finger, furrowed my brow and thought deeply about the years of my life passed. Sod that! I was far too tired for all that nonsense.

What a day! And one I wouldn't forget in a hurry. I collapsed onto my bunk, still clothed I recall, thinking that at some point I would look back on this day and have a good laugh about it. I think that day was a little way off yet.

Distance walked today – 36 Kilometres (330)

SIXTEEN

Carrion de los Condes

to

Terradillos de los Templarios

Today I am 60!! "Happy birthday to me", I sang melodiously to myself.

A couple of months back, I had been enjoying a gentle stroll around the Pavilion Gardens in the Peak District town of Buxton. It had been another stunning day in that rarest of gifts; a beautifully hot English summer.

In the middle of the park stands a miniature railway that trundles kids and adults along on a short circular tour, and which is very popular. I was ambling alongside the long queue for the ride, when my attention was drawn by the antics of a young boy of around three or four, jumping up and down excitedly in anticipation of his train trip. I heard the little fellow ask of his Dad how much longer he would have to wait? In reply, Pa said he thought it would be about ten minutes. "Ten minutes!" exclaimed the boy, a look of deep concern clouding his little face, "Is that a long time Daddy?"

I remember smiling to myself at his innocent question, thinking that at his age, when you are *desperate* for something to happen, ten minutes is a lifetime. You can hear the creak of every minute, as it grinds its way with agonising slowness around the clock, your treat is *never* going to arrive. Ten minutes is well....forever!!

Now having arrived at the once unimaginable of age of sixty, those same ten minutes have taken on the characteristics of a nano-second; blink and its gone. An hour seems like a minute, a week gone in an hour. Months and years overlap each other so quickly, I'm often unsure in which of either I am currently visiting.

My own earliest memories would be from when I was around that little boys age, and here I am decades later wondering where the time has gone. The years and memories have just bled into each other, and I often struggle to accurately recall just what happened and when. I find I can be years out in accurately remembering the timing of events, or how old people are:

"That must have been about ten years ago wasn't it?" " No, it's nearer twenty!". "So, you must be about 25 now?" "Err, actually, I'm 37 next". Anybody in their middle years will know where I'm coming from!

As each year passes my memories have become increasingly treasured, more frequently recalled and spoken of. I think it's because the present can be so traumatic and draining and the future so uncertain, that I find the past so comforting and reassuring, and I am progressively drawn to my recollections of years gone by.

I know everyone says the same as you get older, but I guess you never really mentally prepare for your later years. I've never been dulled or restricted by the advance of time, indeed, I've always thought of myself as being younger than I am. Well, the bad news of course is I'm not, the big six-oh is here, ready or not! Well, I'd best crack on with it then.

In the absence of any other gifts, this anniversary has presented me with a cold, a cough, sore feet and aches and pains all over. I felt so run down you could see the tyre marks. Great, thanks, much appreciated. I tried to buck myself up with the thought that in two more days I should be in León, with over half of the kilometres to Santiago completed. It didn't work.

My destination today is Terradillos de los Templarios. My map showed that this would be 26 kilometres of pretty flat terrain, so at least the walking shouldn't be too bad. The last 2/3rds of the Camino on this section once again appeared to be completely devoid of life; so I stocked up on water, snacks, tissues for my snotty nose and birthday candles; just in case.

Stealing away in the feeble post-dawn light, I left Carrión through silent morning streets, the only irritating noise issuing from my racking cough. I crossed a bridge over the wide Río Carrión and stepped onto the main N-120 road heading out of town. This stretch of highway would also double as the early section of today's trail.

On the edge of town I diverted off the road back onto a gravel path, and the next four hours can be encapsulated thus: "Nothing happened, there was nothing to see. Six billion brain cells shriveled, died and were ejected through my festering nose".

If the days prior to this had been boring, today would surpass them all. Kilometre after kilometre of agricultural wilderness, with the trail as flat and as straight as a yard stick running through it.

The only point of interest this morning, and I say 'interest' heavily burdened with irony, was walking for a while on an exposed section of original Roman road. This was the *Via Aquitana*, which I read later once stretched from Bordeaux to Astorga, a distance of almost 700 kilometres. Fancy having to paint the road markings on that!

It would have been done by slaves of course. Imagine been hauled from the dark depths of a Roman galley thinking you'd been freed, only to be handed a bucket of whitewash and a paint brush. "Oy, Whiptus Dogus, start painting the lines on this bleedin' road" the Centurion would say "and don't even *think* about stopping off in Biarritz for a fortnights holiday, you miserable, idle bastard". I couldn't see any markings now of course. I expect they've worn off.

Even this interlude lost its appeal after a while. As one would expect after a couple of millennia, the cobbled road had deteriorated into a rugged unevenness, making for very uncomfortable walking. *Senatus Populus Que Romanusa*? That was that then.

Apart from the odd pop-up bar along the route, there was absolutely nothing to break the monotony, certainly nothing of any interest to set down here. Although a little disheartening and energy sapping, there was naught to do but press on, and about 10k from Terradillos the village of Calzadilla de la Cueza emerged out of the fields. A little way into the village I spotted a bar and found myself strangely drawn towards it. Thankfully it was open, so I stopped to rest up for a while and empty my pockets of snotty tissues. The cough seemed to be getting worse too. Not good, not good at all.

Even though it was not yet noon it was after all my birthday, and having made excellent time I decided I would treat myself to a beer. Toasting my own good health, the beer was ice cold, wonderfully refreshing and it cheered me up no end. "Happy birthday to me", I sang to myself once more, and to the wide-eyed bemusement of the *camarero de taberna*.

Feeling much brighter I pushed on, and at long last the scenery began to change and break up a little. A few wooded hills began to close in, with the trail weaving its serpentine way through their pleasantly leafy glades. The noise of traffic drifting through the trees however, was a constant reminder that I would never be too far from the main road on this section. A further 5 or 6k down a gently undulating slope brought me to the village of Ledigos, and oh look! Another bar. Why not?

With only another 3 kilometres or so to Terradillos, I sat thoughtfully sipping my beer, pondering on what an extraordinarily dull life it must be, to live in one of the many small and remote farming villages I had passed through in recent days. I realised of course, it was what the older generations were born into and would not expect or even want anything different, but how do you keep the young people there? With seemingly nothing to do apart from hang about the streets, and with no entertainment at all for miles around, it must drive them crazy with boredom.

Surely these kids must yearn for a better life, or at least a more exciting and interesting one? They travel miles every day to the bigger towns for school and also, I assume, at weekends and holidays to grab whatever entertainment is on offer. From an early age then, they are exposed to different lifestyles and opportunities and must think: "I've got to have some of that".

The population of these places must fall with each passing year too, as the elderly die and the young leave. The average age rising inexorably in the process and squeezing even more life out of the community. It doesn't even look as if the agro-economy pays well either. There is no evidence of booming towns, big houses or flash cars; just modest little villages, with graveyards of rusting farm machinery acting as monuments to a dying way of life.

But life there was, of that there is no doubt. And clearly enough people willing and happy to tend those vast hectares of crops and get them to market, eking out what ever living they could. Sincerely, good luck to them I say, and the greatest of respect to those folk and their lives of dedicated toil.

I deliberated further as another beer appeared (Gracias Carlos). A constant feature of all these villages, was the extraordinary collection of farm implements seemingly dumped at random everywhere one looked. These tools and accessories, clearly designed to be attached to a tractor or some such, were the most lethal looking objects. They were resplendent with forks and knives, prongs, blades and shovels and any number of peculiar looking utensils whose use and purpose was beyond me. All this technology and mechanics, clearly replacing what was once done by hand.

This brought to mind a book I had picked up in the library at the albergue back at Boadilla. It was one of a series gathering dust on the bookshelf, and seemed interesting enough. Well, at least when compared to a 30 kilometre hike through fields of parched wheat stubble.

It was a detailed report on the region of Castilla Y León, its future plans and developments and so on. Like all government chronicles the world over, it was replete with graphs and tables highlighting even the most obscure statistics. One graph that struck me, was of labour employed on the land in the region since 1970. Astonishingly, to me at least, in that one year of 1970 and only in this region mind, there were over 400,000 people directly employed in agricultural works. In the year of this report, 2010 if I recall, there were less than 100,000 souls working the land. God alone knows how many more people have been lopped off that figure in the intervening years. I asked him, he confessed he didn't know and wasn't remotely interested either. Charming.

Victory for those versatile implements and their manufacturers clearly, also an indication of how much Spain has changed and developed in the post Franco decades, especially in its agricultural regions. This is not of course, a gauge of the falling importance of agriculture to the Spanish economy, far from it. It is simply a reflection of the radical change of emphasis from labour intensive, to machinery-based farming.

On researching this later (I did honestly!), I discovered that of all EU countries, Spain is second only to France in terms of land deployed for agriculture. It has almost a million farms of one type or another and employs 750,000 people. Agri-business is worth around 3% of Spain's GDP, generating around 40 BILLION euros in revenue! Definitely not small potatoes. Now, where was I?

Beer and musings finished and conscious that I may well have been talking to myself, I picked up the trail and completed the last few kilometres along the tarmac road to Terradillos de los Templarios. This was said to be a village steeped in the traditions of the ancient Knights Templar. I very nearly said 'exciting' then.

The very first building I encountered on entering Terradillos was an albergue run by the Brotherhood of those same Knights Templar, superb and very Dan Brown! The albergue 'De Los Templarios' was a very modern building, large and spacious and with plenty of room for me, my germs and backpack at 8 euros. Three-for-one, I couldn't fault it. Scrubbed shiny clean and dressed in my birthday finest (shorts, t-shirt, sandals), it was once again time to attack my laundry.

Making use of the hand-wash facilities in the spacious garden to the rear; the washing machines having been taken over at gun point by marauding, forward patrols of W.A.L.K (Women's Army for Laundered Knickers) I discovered a young couple from South Korea, getting stuck into their own *dhobie* in the traditional way.

The young lad with his shoes and socks off, was stomping up and down in a tub of suds, soapy clothes tangling around his legs, whilst his tiny young partner did the same in the 'rinse' barrel, as it were. Both were dreamy eyed and holding hands as they gave their togs a good kicking, a real soap opera love scene. Brilliant. It was certainly a leap of imagination, to envisage spoiled British teenagers setting about their own laundry in this way. Of that, I am very certain.

It was now just on 6.00pm and time for a little look at the village. I also hoped I would bump into the Mexicano's and er Swedeeno's, as we had made an earlier arrangement to celebrate my birthday together. Alas, they must have stayed in another village, for they were not to be found at the only other albergue in Terradillos. They couldn't possibly be avoiding me....could they?

This second albergue was named after Jacques de Molay; a famous Knight of the Templar order and its last Grand Master. He was one of the Templars who were infamously rounded up, tortured and killed on the orders of King Philip IV of France.

The king, not uncoincidentally, was in serious debt to the Knights and not at all keen on paying back what he owed. Philip had Molay and scores of other Knights arrested on trumped up charges and imprisoned. Once under lock and key, the King then subjected these blameless men to hideous torture in order to force false confessions from them, thereby justifying his actions. Most of the captives, including Molay, were later brutally put to death by burning, and with that, the Order of the Knights Templar was effectively finished. Molays arrest and the coordinated round up of the other knights happened in October 1307. Friday the 13th to be exact. Get it?

The village itself was dead with not even a solitary bar, none that I could see anyway, just a clutter of old houses peppered around, all shuttered up and closed on deserted streets. A little frustrated I returned sulkily to my albergue, there was nothing to do but dine alone.

With a huge plate of spaghetti and a bottle of wine, I once more wished myself a happy birthday and lots more to come. It would have been nice to have had some company I guess, but I wasn't too bothered, in my own way I'd had a really enjoyable day. It would have been even more agreeable without this increasingly persistent and bloody annoying cough. Shocking.

Tomorrow I would be walking over 30 kilometres, so I planned on the earliest possible start. The weather had been getting hotter and hotter, and the forecast was indicating 35oC by the afternoon. With that joyful news filed away, I determined to get my walking day over as soon as I could on the morrow. And so, following a very pleasant and alcohol enlivened day; it was another early night, goodbye to my 60th birthday and hello to my 61st year!

Distance walked today – 27 Kilometres (357)

SEVENTEEN

Terradillos de los Templarios

to

El Burgo Ranero

On perusing my map the previous night, I discovered that today's route did not promise any significant improvement on recent days. It looked to be a long, straight trail, empty and flat. And so it proved.

I have to say though, the last few days have been paradise when compared to today. Without any doubt, the most boring, mind destroying, energy sapping 31 kilometres imaginable. It was absolutely heart breaking.

The early segment of the trail today once again clung closely to the N.120, as it cleaved its way through the surrounding, lifeless fields. The first village I encountered today was Moratinos; a charming *pueblo* of adobe houses, its lovely little plaza adorned with brightly coloured beads, hung or fixed on what appeared to be every available surface. I have no idea why.

Beyond Moratinos I found myself in San Nicholás del Real Camino, where I replenished my water supply and had a short break. Soon after departing San Nicholás, my internal level detector eagerly signaled a slight rise in the ground, and what would probably be described as a mountain in these parts. The elation derived from this little hump in the road was brief however, as the Camino from that point turned into a long, wearisome trek. The trail was as straight and flat and about as exciting, as a Geoffrey Boycott forward defensive stroke when on 99 not out, and leading all the way to El Burgo Ranero some 20k in the distance.

With precious few diversions or redeeming features to be found along the route and feeling pretty sickly too, I could feel my brain boiling and evaporating through my skull as I pounded the dusty trail. All that remained, was a residue of steaming emptiness swirling around my brain pan, perfectly mirroring the surrounding scenery.

Just before Sahagún, I crossed a Roman stone bridge over the Río Valderaduey and into the grounds of a small, brick built church; La Ermita de la Virgin del Puente. I hadn't seen a church built in this style previously. I later read it was constructed in the Romanesque Mudejar style, which as far as I can gather means they used brick instead of stone. So what? Who cares? Not me on that day.

It wouldn't have mattered to me if it had been built of straw to be honest, I fell on this little visual feast as I would a nugget of gold on the path. At least it was something to break up the monotony.

Picking up the trail once more, I followed the empty footpath into Sahagún. I didn't stop to take notice of anything really, I had eyes only for the way ahead. Once through the town, the Camino carried a long line of evenly spaced trees, each throwing out a patch of shadow onto the path. An annoying incantation grew like a pecking bird in my head: "....In the shade, in the sun, in the shade, in the sun....." as I stepped between shadow and light. I really thought I was going crazy!

Al Calzada del Coto came and went in a blur. Bercianos del Real Camino? I don't remember travelling through it at all, such was the addled and sun fried state of my mind today. Amidst all this superheated drudgery and misery, my discomfort was further amplified by an unstoppable streaming nose and chest crippling cough. I think it's fair to say I'd had better days.

At last! I reached El Burgo Ranero at 3.00pm, thoroughly barbequed, hot, thirsty and exhausted. I trudged wearily along the main street, desperate for some relief from the heat and in search of some accommodation to provide it. In a zombie like trance, coughing and sneezing, driveling and chunnering to myself, I tracked the yellow arrows through the streets, eventually stumbling into the comforting arms of an albergue on the edge of town. I must have looked like one of the characters staggering out of the desert in the film, 'Ice Cold in Alex'. But not the one played by Sylvia Sims, obviously.

The albergue 'La Laguna', was set in a high walled, gated compound with low outbuildings surrounding a spacious lawn area. This barely registered on me however as I signed in, (with a scrawled 'X' if I remember) pathetically begging cold water from the hostel manager. After being shown to the dormitory, I dropped my pack to the floor, collapsed on my bunk and slept as though in a deep coma for two hours.

A good sleep and a shower perked me up no end. I was now feeling very thirsty and hungry and looking forward to being lavishly entertained, as was my just reward. Checking I had spectacles, testicles, wallet and watch, I eagerly headed out to see what excitement the town had to offer. Nothing, it was a dump! A village falling to pieces with derelict or soon to be derelict buildings, with adobe walls and battered roofs pitifully collapsing in on themselves. Even the streets that were whole looked downtrodden and empty; save only for the skulking dogs and mean looking feral cats that littered the footpaths wherever one looked.

The town itself was surrounded by the paraphernalia of agriculture: Huge barns and grain silos, gigantic stacks of hay bales, many carrying the scorch marks of recent fires. Farm implements and battered vehicles littered every corner. It was a grim prospect to behold, especially at the end of a day that had carried enough bleakness of its own.

In search of some consolation after a withering day and my enthusiasm for its dregs waning, I picked out a decent enough looking bar for a drink and a bite to eat. I gulped down a large cold beer followed immediately by a second, accompanied, I have to say, by a very excellent and extremely tasty homemade cheeseburger and fries. All this was efficiently and enthusiastically served by two very nice young *señoritas*, both desperate to practice their broken English on a significantly more broken

English man!

It was a busy little bar, with a nice terrace to the rear where I sat, and everyone seemed to be enjoying their food and drinks in a very agreeable, friendly atmosphere.

It was quite pleasant really, and I began to think I had maybe been a bit premature in my judgement of the town. It was all too easy to make these snap appraisals when tired, unwell and not in the best of moods. On sauntering out into the fading light, it really *did* appear a little softer and easier on the eye. Mind you, by that time I'd had several restorative libations and I would have been enamoured with Beirut.

I decided to move on to one last bar and a nightcap or two of wine. I soon fell into a difficult, but nonetheless pleasant chat with two French ladies whom I had seen from time to time along *The Way*. I had no French, they spoke no Spanish and just a little English, but somehow, as is the way of these things we communicated.

The elder of the two was 73, 5ft tall and built as if from twigs. She and her companion were walking the entire Camino Francés, from St Jean-Pied-de-Port on the French side of the Pyrenees all the way to Santiago, an incredible effort. The older *madame*, was having her pack transported from albergue to albergue by the excellent Camino courier service, but she was doing all the walking. Her younger friend I was informed, was carrying her own pack. She was only 65 however!

I could not but admire these fine ladies and their tremendous endeavor. I determined there and then to stop complaining, given that that these two had experienced and endured exactly the same route and conditions as I had. In saying that though, I was no spring chicken myself now at 60.

With the effects of the days walking and subsequent lubrication beginning to tell, I could feel my engines running out of steam and needing to be switched off. Bidding the ladies a good night and bon Camino, I limped back to the albergue at the end of what had been a very trying day indeed. But it's all part of the challenges of the Camino, and you most certainly had to take the occasional rough with the plentiful smooth.

Tomorrow, León will be in theoretical striking distance at 37 kilometers. I didn't think I would attempt it in one day though, probably better to cover it in two. Given my current unhealthy state, it wouldn't do to plan too far ahead.

Distance walked today – 31 Kilometres (388)

EIGHTEEN

El Burgo Ranero

to

Puente Villarente

I closely questioned myself again. Did I want to go all out and try and march the 37 kilometres to León? I knew I could do it physically, for by now I was a righteous and beaudacious top walking dude, but was it necessary? The best thing I thought, given my current wobbliness, was to set out with León as a target and suck it and see as I went along.

The walk today can be summarised thus: rewind, play, repeat. I think you get the picture by now, of what it was like out here. So, with my chin firmly set and guided by the steely gaze of an intrepid traveler, I set my feet to the trail, striding manfully and purposefully out of El Burgo Ranero in the delicate and ethereal light of a new day..... Returning 10 minutes later to retrieve my one and only towel that I had left drying on the line. Dear me.

Needing only to stand on tiptoes to see for miles, I stood, slack jawed and staring through disbelieving eyes at the white gravel path, as it disappeared into the distance in a Euclidian straight line. A study of my map earlier had illustrated a terrain with hardly a bump in the road ahead. Even at this distance, if I could have stood on a milk crate, I felt certain I would be able to see León.

With a heavyweight sigh and a racking cough, doubling me up at times it was so severe, I headed out. There was nothing more on my mind right now, than getting through the day with as many intact brain cells as I started out with. That wouldn't be very many then.

As I walked resolutely on, I began to discern the outline of a large and substantial mountain range, looming menacingly and forbidding in the far distance. I wondered, not without a frisson of excitement, if these prominences would play any part in my journey ahead? Please God, I hoped so.

About 5 kilometres out from El Burgo, I came across a small airfield set just to the side of the Camino and close to the village of Villamarco. It looked like it was a base for crop dusting airplanes and the like, it was certainly in the right place. The aerodrome also advertised extremely inexpensive flying lessons. Also on offer, was a more discreet airborne service for anyone wishing to throw themselves from a highflying aircraft, thereby relieving themselves of the mind destroying tedium of life on the prairie. There was a very long queue for this.

I had stuck to my now well-established routine of blitzing the early mornings, and I had completed 13k before 10.30am. Pleased with my progress, I stopped for a breather and a brew in Reliegos, a dusty little nowhere in the middle of the plain. It did have an attractive cluster of large electricity pylons though, so as my treat for the morning I looked at those for a while. It was er, electrifying.

Recharged (sorry) and back on the trail, it was really just a question of head down and hoovering up the relentlessly dull kilometres on the road to León. Grasping at any straw that signaled a change of scenery, I clasped myself with joy as the wheat fields slowly gave way to corn; a much neater arrangement in well irrigated plots.

That was about as interesting as it got, but trust me, you take your entertainment anyway you can get it on this part of the Camino. Even more stirringly, the far distant mountain range from earlier suddenly seemed an awful lot nearer and bigger. I clutched myself again to deepen the moment.

Hiking on, I passed through Mansilla de las Mulas, crossed the bridge over the Río Esla, then turned sharply onto a footpath running parallel with the road. The Camino clung to the N-601 for the next couple of hours, passing traffic providing the only amusement on that hot, dusty trail. Awakened from my walking stupor by the onset of the village of Villamoros, I perked up with the happy realisation I was closing in on the end of today's march.

I had decided a little earlier, that I was definitely *not* going to go all out for León. I couldn't possibly have countenanced the extra hours on this mentally punishing and enervating section of the trail. I now planned to stop off a few kilometres short and pass through León the next day, perhaps spend an hour or so in the city and then press on to a destination as yet to be decided.

I had settled on Puente Villarente for the night about 12 kilometres this side of León, a brochure I had of the area recommending a good albergue there. I must have lost the thread a little at that point, what with the sun broiling my head. I stopped for a few minutes at a bijou rest station; an unmanned little refuge in a shady corner and fitted out nicely with tables, chairs and vending machines.

Sloshing down some ice-cold water and munching on a chocolate bar, I calculated I had about another 5k hike to Puente Villarente. With that in mind I set off, winding through a nice little meadow, the path taking me over a wooden slatted bridge and a clear, sparkling river.

Rising up an embankment the roofs of buildings began to emerge, and puzzlingly, I could hear the sound of nearby traffic. Seconds later, I was on a busy main road on the edge of a town where a sign greeted me: 'PUENTE VILLARENTE'. The 5k I expected to walk after my little rest, had turned into just 5 minutes. I wasn't complaining. It had been a heavy day, as tough on my mind as on my body and I was happy to call it quits.

Set on my right was a modern motel, looking very respectable and tidy too. Peering through the fence, I could see it had a large terrace leading on to a good-sized pool, all set in a nicely grassed garden. Thrown a little, I thought this was where my albergue should be, and so it was; tucked away in a corner behind and to the side of the motel.

The ´El Delfín Verde´ was a small annex to the main building and it was, as expected, clean and tidy, well equipped and most welcoming. The very eccentric albergue manager, a caricature of a sixties dropout hippy, gave me the grand tour, asking just 5 euros for my night's stay. Incredible. More so, as these few euros included full use of all the motels facilities, comprising restaurant, bar, terrace and pool.

The bar and terrace I would most certainly make use of, and after showering and changing, I got a cold beer from the former and sat under the shade on the latter to write up my notes. It really was very, very nice.

Desperately in need of something to tackle my increasingly nasty and debilitating cough, I walked into the nearby town centre to locate a chemist. The long central road slicing through the town was a classic 'strip'; lined with bars, restaurants and shops of all kinds with parking roadside. With León just a few kilometres away it must be a tough place to run a business, but those I walked past certainly seemed to be busy enough.

I found the chemist shop, and the smiling assistant observed sympathetically: "Ooh you've got a chesty-cough there". "Yes", I replied, "I've got all his books, he's my favourite Russian author". Laughing hysterically at my world class wit, she recovered sufficiently to inform me that relief for my cough was at hand, but would necessitate relieving my wallet of 7 euros 50 cents. I would have paid double that to get shut of the fucking thing to be honest. I was really, really suffering with it.

Whilst out and about, I had a delicious mixed plate of pastries and nibbles in a lovely little bakery on the main street. There was a tremendous selection of bread and cakes, sweets and savories, all baked on the premises and clearly very popular with the locals too.

Filled up with fine food and brushing crumbs from my shirt, I made my way back to the motel bar. The ones on the high street were either completely empty, or not very appealing. The hot day had, by this time, developed into an even hotter evening. The sun was beating down fiercely from a cloudless sky, and it was so nice to sit in the shade on the terrace enjoying a lovely Rioja, pondering pleasantly on the journey completed so far, and that which was yet to come.

When I set out from Pamplona, I had only a sketchy idea of what lay ahead. I was really uncertain of how I would cope with the distances and difficulties of daily life on the trail, and also, just how far would I get? Initially, I had it in my mind that I should at least get to Burgos and with that city now successfully negotiated and behind me, thought of León as an achievable target. Now on the doorstep of that city, I had already convinced myself that I would be able to complete the pilgrimage to Santiago, and was genuinely excited by the prospect.

There was no way I could have quit at that point, not having travelled so far and achieving so much. I felt increasingly determined, and despite being plague ridden, very capable of finishing this great expedition.

I was so buzzed in anticipation of the second half of the journey, I was very tempted to squeeze myself again such was my elation. I decided, however, that perhaps such exuberance three times in one day was maybe a little excessive. Not to be denied, I celebrated instead with another 'fishbowl' of Rioja. Well, it was literally as cheap as the bottled water and a whole lot tastier, and enlivened my weary particles in a much more satisfactory manner.

Happy just to sit for a while watching the fading light cast shadows across the terrace, the combined warmth of sun and wine slowly worked on my eyes, and I could feel myself nodding off. Reluctant to drag myself away from this pleasant little spot, I nevertheless caved in to my drowsiness and retired to my little *dormitorio*.

Despite the heat of the evening I felt a bit cold on entering the bunk house, no doubt my festering ague amplifying the chill. Thankfully, there were several soft, chunky blankets folded and stored in couple of tall cabinets and I grabbed one for my own bunk. I cocooned myself in the warmth of the sheets, closing my eyes on what had been a particularly difficult and in some respects unrewarding day, but most certainly a very pleasant afternoon and evening.

The sands of my day had run out, and without offering even the slightest defence sleep charged in, claiming victory immediately.

Distance walked today – 27 Kilometres (415)

NINETEEN

Puente Villarente

to

Valverde de la Virgen

I was a lot later getting underway today. I felt terrible upon waking; coughing up my lungs with a pint of phlegm, and all this before I'd even put my boots on. It was 8.00am before I finally got away; coughing and spluttering like an emphysemic coal miner, eyes streaming, nose running. I think I must have been born upside down; my nose runs and my feet smell.

The first section of today's walk would comprise of the 12 kilometres I needed to complete to reach León. I was really hoping that the scenery and milieu after León would be different. The last few days had been nothing but a routine of knocking off the daily stages through the most tedious, mind numbing countryside imaginable.

Since Santo Domingo, I had been mostly passing through uninspiring little villages with little to offer, hoping for just a crumb of comfort or variety in passing. My mindset each morning was to grind out the kilometres, and hope that there would be some relief or compensation at the end of the day. To be fair, I usually found something to reward myself with, even if it was only in the solace of strong drink!

I'm trying not to over exaggerate the monotony of recent days, although I'm sure my mordant observations may not help with this. It almost certainly won't seem as bad on reflection as it had in real time, I'm sure. As I've commented previously, I truly loved the walking and welcomed the daily challenges, but all too often it had been so relentlessly mind numbing. After all I have said about walking alone, maybe this would have been a good time to have had a walking companion? Kismet.

The sprawl of big cities usually have a long reach, and it appeared that Puente Villarente was to all intents a suburb of León. The route from here seemed an unbroken jumble of warehouses and repair shops, with a riot of tatty looking apartment blocks dropped randomly in between. Carbuncles of shiny glassed car showrooms and agricultural equipment yards, provided the finishing touches to this avenue of industry and commerce; the gateway to one of the great medieval cities of Europe. It made the A.4 into London look like the Appian Way.

After adhering to the busy A.60 road for a couple of kilometres, the Camino veered off and wound its way up through a rare and welcome wooded area. Soon after turning sharply onto a rise at Puente Castro, I paused to catch a first glimpse through the trees of the suburbs and city of León. A sprawling urban mass, stretching out like spilt coffee onto the plain below. Even from this distance, it was possible to discern the huge cathedral standing out in brilliant, sunlit white. It was like a giant wedding cake, set imposingly amidst a table of much lesser fare.

I walked down the uneven and scrubby track towards the city, and after crossing a stretch of rough ground joined a paved road that led into the centre. This final approach into León picked its way languorously through the countless drab buildings of outer suburbia, each one anonymous and undistinguished.

Losing hope of things brightening up on the long walk in, I suddenly came upon a section of the old city wall; partly ruined but still high and impressive. Passing expectantly through an arched gateway, the atmosphere and architecture changed immediately as I stepped into a maze of narrow cobbled streets and alleys. Most of these avenues led on to lovely little squares or shady parks, all busy at this time of the day with locals and tourists. Familiar scenes and features by now, of course, of the many fabulous medieval towns and cities found on the Camino.

I cut my way through the bustling streets leading to the cathedral, carefully following the shell inlays and yellow arrows generously and helpfully dotted along the pavements. I had read a few pieces about the grandeur of Leon, and I was very much looking forward to my short visit.

On the way in, I noticed many old and imposing buildings and little spots of interest to catch the eye, but for me, there was something lacking. León, at this first view at least, didn't seem to have the drama or historic feel that Burgos, for example, had plenty of. Of course, it is impossible to get a proper impression during such a short visit, but I like to think I have an eye and feel for these places. As yet, however, León just wasn't reaching out to me in the way I had expected.

Having negotiated a tangle of busy roads through the commercial part of the city, I eventually came to a large bridge spanning the wide and stately Río Bernesga. I stopped here for a few moments, enjoying an informative chat with the helpful tourist officials thoughtfully stationed there. A very nice civic welcome indeed, at this impressive crossing into the old city.

Faithfully following the Camino markers, I emerged at length through a maze of small alleys and onto the main cathedral plaza. There the great church itself rose up massively, it's cream colored stone gleaming brightly in the midday sunshine.

As with many of the ancient buildings I had encountered on this journey, the edifice was partially under repair and hidden behind a protective covering, somewhat reducing its impact. There was no doubt however, that this was a magnificent structure.

The cathedral of Santa María de León was built principally in the 13th century in classic Gothic style, dazzling with acres of stained glass windows on all sides. The twin towers either side of the façade, guarded a huge circular window set over the main entrance. The enormous arches of the doorways appeared to be lifting the entire building from out of the ground. It was absolutely stunning.

The interior of the church is no less impressive, although on this day it was oppressively packed with tourists and difficult to get around, so I only lingered for a short while. The cathedral was absolutely dripping with works of art, exquisite architecture and statuary. The stunning stain glassed windows offered eye catching evidence as to why Santa María was also known as the 'House of Light'.

It would have taken hours to have seen all of the cathedrals many wonders, unfortunately, that sort of time wasn't available to me that day. The siren call of the Camino was luring me irresistibly on.

There were many more impressive buildings and grand plazas to admire as I made my way from the cathedral and across the city, but to revisit my earlier comments, I wasn't getting any special atmosphere about the place. Perhaps it was just me in a contrary mood, feeling unwell and unreceptive to the city's nuances. After all I had read about this grand city, I felt that my visit was too rushed, and I was tempted to stop here for the day and do proper justice to my visit. In truth, I felt drained of enthusiasm for anything today, so without much further thought, I decided I would just move on.

I departed the city through an uninspiring estate of warehouses and commercial units. The cheerlessness seemed endless, as I plodded on through the sharply rising streets of this industrialised suburb. It had also become very hot, and I was really beginning to feel the strain of the days walk.

Eventually, the trail broke away from this wearisome drabness, but only onto a bewildering series of underpasses, crossovers and interchanges of the surrounding road system. Turning first one way then another I would have been hopelessly lost, were it not for the wonderfully reassuring Camino markers and yellow arrows showing the way.

It was now past 2.00pm; the trail was grubby and very hot, and I was feeling drained and disheartened by the drudgery of today's walk, not helped of course, by the continuous coughing and snorting. I felt absolutely terrible to be honest, not even the brief interlude of León seemed to have given me a lift. I was functioning as nothing more than a pre-programmed walking machine today. By this time I had put León several kilometres behind me. But I had barely been registering my surroundings, or even having much idea as to where I was come to that, such was my discomfort. Still I slogged on, snotty and barking and feeling miserably sorry for myself. I really wasn't well at all. Please, don't upset yourself; by the time you read this I'll be just fine. But if you still insist on sending me a 'get well' card along with some money, that's ok. Cheques would be just fine too.

Without even bothering to check my map, I felt sure I was closing in on my days destination. Sure enough, after another 2 or 3 kilometres of road hogging trail, I emerged up a dusty slope to see the town marker for La Virgen del Camino. With great relief, I knew that just a short distance from here salvation was at hand, and in the shape of the longed for *pueblo* of Valverde de la Virgen.

The trail weaved its scrubby way through another bewildering and busy spaghetti of intersections and flyovers, terribly dusty and noisy with traffic. After passing under the massive concrete span of the AP-66 Autopista, I sensed the near presence of my final destination. And there it was; my albergue for the night, beckoning oasis like just across the busy N-120 highway on the edge of the town. My spirits were immediately lifted and my tiredness was swept away, as I very nearly was myself! In my addled state, I had momentarily forgotten the direction of traffic, and *just* avoided stepping under the wheels of a gigantic truck as I mindlessly crossed the road. Without doubt I was a deadly danger to myself, it was a miracle I was still alive!

The albergue 'La Casa Del Camino' was just brilliant, maybe my favorite so far and just pipping the one at Boadilla. It had only been opened a year or so, yet looked and felt well established.

The hostel was a low, stone built building with a front porch set in a lovely grassed and quirky garden. The lawn was busy with all manner of interesting features and different kinds places to sit and relax, it even had a foot spa. It appeared to be owned and operated by a mum and son, ably assisted by a couple of friends and it had a wonderfully comforting, family atmosphere about it.

The *dormatorio* was spacious, modern and bright, and offered wonderfully welcoming and comfy bunks. I was very pleased to be berthed opposite a young and very beautiful Hungarian lass, and with whom I had briefly chatted to earlier outside Leon cathedral. I could see the disappointment crumpling her face as I told her firmly, that nothing but sleep was on my agenda for tonight. I think it's only fair to be up front about these things, don't you?

I got myself cleaned up and felt a lot better. I was very tired though and feeling a bit sickly with it, and I knew I wouldn't be venturing far this evening. Whilst relaxing with a deliciously chilled beer and writing my notes in an easy chair in the garden, the young lad in charge asked if I would be having dinner in the albergue? I quickly agreed that I would, and I wasn't to be disappointed.

Cometh the hour, our host placed me regally at the head of the table. But I suspected this was to separate me and my germs from the others, rather than a nod to my seniority and magnificence. We sat down to a mammoth three course *menú del día* of salad, homemade meatballs in tomato sauce and pasta, followed by a bitter-sweet mousse dessert. All this washed down with copious, and I mean copious amounts of local red wine. I am proud to tell you that despite being proper poorly, I did my very best to drink my share. Such sacrifice.

It was a real treat; more so spent in the splendid company of my fellow and I have to say, much younger guests. The table was lively with chatter and laughter, adorned, it goes without saying, by my brilliant wit and badinage. It was one of the nicer evenings spent on the Camino, I think we all felt something like that. Our host brought the dinner to a close, by passing round shot glasses full of what I *think* he said was a homemade concoction. It tasted of nothing more than lightly flavoured raw alcohol, but we all drank it, *and* asked for refills!

Relaxing with yet more wine graciously served by our wonderful hosts, I dropped, nay, collapsed into a hammock in the garden. Full of bacchanalian spirit and goodwill to my fellow man, I watched the sun slowly setting behind the distant hills.

I don't think I had felt happier or more at peace with and within myself for many years. The Camino was reaching deeply into me now, and I felt at ease with and very committed to it. I was certain I had been experiencing a kind of 'emptying out' of a lot of unwanted and burdensome crap on this journey; the hard kilometres acting as a purge it seemed.

I had long felt I had been lugging around way too much of the world and its worries, as well as the burden of my own life's trials and tribulations, such a weight at times. It was a great relief to be able to drop some of it off for a while. It will still be there to pick up again on the other side. Of that, I had no doubt!

Distance walked today – 27 Kilometres (442)

TWENTY

Valverde de la Virgen

to

Astorga

Having wrestled through a night of wine steeped and restless dreams, I was wide awake at 6.00am, listening to the quiet-as-can-be rustlings of those already up and departing in the pitch dark. This, more than an hour before any sign of daylight. Not for me I'm afraid.

Despite an interrupted night I felt reasonably well rested and fit, notwithstanding of course, the persistence of my non-improving blight. I was on my way just before 7.30am, with daylight just insinuating itself into hitherto star spangled skies, heralding yet another sun-drenched, steamingly hot day.

The trail began where I had left it yesterday; immediately opposite on the N-120 road, and would continue faithfully along its route for several kilometres. The oncoming traffic, headlights still beaming in the gloom, was quite busy with commuters heading in the opposite direction and back towards León. With a terrible shudder, memories were evoked of all the years I too had spent killing myself in early morning commutes, solely to sacrifice irretrievable and unappreciated lumps of my life on the altar of commerce. Leave it lad.

Occasionally the path would spur away from the road, encouraging me into thinking I would be heading back into the countryside, alas no. Each diversion was quickly corrected, escorting me back to the roadside and kilometre after kilometre on the same path, and just the other side of the crash barrier. Hundreds of cars and lorries zoomed past at speed, creating both dust and din. Not very enjoyable really.

I continued on through Villadangos del Páramo, soon followed by a very smart looking San Martín del Camino, constantly hoping and looking for that long sought after change of setting, but it wasn't to be just yet. Remaining true to its course alongside the road, the trail sustained its predictable way for another 5k or so, until at long last, it broke off into open countryside and some welcome respite from the traffic.

The expanse surrounding and ahead was still of agricultural plain, but now dominated by neatly planted corn fields, all squared off and well maintained. The gurgling rush of the myriad irrigation channels along the way, had me feeling desperate for a dip in their cooling waters as the sun rose higher, the punishing heat growing inexorably with it.

Taking a welcome rest at the picturesque and charming village of Puente de Órbigo, I could see that I was at last reverting to the varied and more scenic trails of earlier weeks, well at least for a while. I knew of course that there was still plenty of the Castilian plateau yet to cross, so I wasn't getting too carried away. Still, it was nice for my eyes to settle on something different for a spell.

I crossed the superbly restored medieval bridge over the Río Órbigo, hurrying then through the *pueblo* of Hospital de Órbigo, small and neat and offering a choice of trail. I briefly weighed up my options and decided to stick to the main Camino; both routes would merge again anyway a little further along.

I was now back into the open countryside, and hallelujah! Onto a track that actually showed signs of rising a few feet. I strode eagerly onwards, and towards the ever-nearing higher ground at Villares de Órbigo. This was a very nice little town, with a simple monument on its plaza dedicated to all passing pilgrims.

On and on I plied the ever demanding Camino, across the fertile plain of the Órbigo and towards my terminus at Astorga, now less than 15 kilometres ahead. Re-invigorated somewhat by my new surroundings, I was quickly through Santibáñez de Valdeiglesias and onto the beginning of a long, hot and steady climb, that would ultimately bring me to the heights overlooking Astorga.

A long unbroken stretch of climbing ensued, such a change from the endless uniformity of the previous days, being both welcome and enjoyable. Onwards and upwards I trooped over the scorched red clay, until topping out at last onto a broad flat upland, with the Camino running straight ahead and through it. The surrounding views were superb. On this beautifully clear day, I could see for a great distance across an unbroken stretch of forests and hills, and beyond those to distant peaks, gradually disappearing into a shimmering haze.

It had become very hot by this point, and I was extremely thirsty. I was getting a little nervous actually, having almost finished my supply of water when a little miracle occurred. At the side of the trail and quite astonishingly, there appeared a long, sandstone building surrounded by an enclosed garden. To the front of the garden was a variety of benches and chairs, tree-slung hammocks, Arabian style banquettes and much more.

Set amongst these beckoning resting places was a fantastic selection of food and drinks, liberally spread around in pots and crates and on the counters and shelves of little shaded stalls. This great hoard, was generously provided by the kindly owner of the *finca* for the benefit of passing pilgrims, and all he asked was for a reasonable donation to be dropped in the honesty jar placed on one of the counters. There was a terrific choice of goodies, all absolutely superb. I tucked into a huge piece of melon and a couple of bananas, washed down with several glasses of the best, hand squeezed, home-made lemonade I had ever tasted. Utterly life-saving.

"God bless you sir, whoever you are" I exclaimed whilst raising my glass to a great and true friend of the Camino. I later learned that this wonderful refuge was owned and run by a Senõr David Vidal, and was known as 'La Casa de los diosos', or 'House of the Gods'. Under the circumstances, a perfect description!

Now quite refreshed and eager to finish my walking day, I filled my water bottles with some of that great lemonade and rejoined the trail for the last few kilometres to Astorga.

Up in the distance, I could just make out a large stone cross set on a plinth. This turned out to be El Cruceiro de Santo Toribio and upon reaching it, I found myself on the edge of a high ridge gazing over the ancient Roman city of Astorga; its cathedral clearly visible and standing prominently and proudly at its centre. A sharp plunge down the trail took me to the small *pueblo* of San Justo de la Vega. I paused here for a moment to admire an excellent bronze, depicting a travel weary pilgrim refreshing himself from his gourd at a water pump. It was a really impressive and evocative piece of work. Annoyingly, I have since lost the scrap of paper on which I had noted the sculptors name. I always like to acknowledge these wonderfully imaginative Camino artists where I can.

With Astorga now in site, I livened up a little and quickened my pace. I was desperate to get off my feet, take off my pack and sink several long dreamed of cold beers. I had walked almost 35k today and I was feeling every step. It had been a long, hot, tiring day to say the least but despite all, I promise you, I really was loving it!

To the toll of a distant church bell striking 4.00pm, I began the last distance over a zig-zagging metal bridge across the railway tracks. A final slog up a steep hill and there was my albergue, perfectly placed right at the edge of the city centre. Fantastic.

The 'Albergue de peregrinos Siervas de Maria' was very big, easily the largest I personally had stayed in to date. It was an old building, with an almost ecclesiastically styled exterior, topped by a small bell. The hostel was situated on a little plaza adjacent to a quiet, leafy park. Standing just outside was another superb large bronze. This one was of a pilgrim decked out in a broad brimmed hat and long coat, a bag slung over his shoulders. He stood as if in deep thought, brooding on the demanding kilometres ahead before reaching Santiago. I knew just how he felt.

The hostel interior had been nicely modernised and decorated and was spread over four or five floors, with a double basement opening on to a large rear yard. This was just the second hostel I had visited that separated the lads and lasses. Why bother? By this point on the journey, I don't think anyone notices or cares with whom they are sleeping with! It was very busy and filling up quickly, and I was thankful I had managed to get in. I wouldn't have enjoyed tramping round in search of an alternative, especially tonight. I felt completely shattered.

This was another albergue run by the 'Amigos del Camino'. I have mentioned previously that this is a terrific organisation of lay people, all volunteers, who do terrific work as Hospitaliers and on the Camino trail, and I was given a friendly greeting and guided tour by one of the brethren. Resisting the strong temptation to collapse immediately onto my bunk, I showered and changed, sorted out my kit and set off in search of those cold beers I had promised myself. By God, was I thirsty?

It was, thankfully, a very short stroll into the heart of the city center and I sat at the first bar I came across, pretty much collapsing into the nearest chair. Immediately on noticing my plight a lovely young *camarera* tended to my needs, swiftly furnishing me with a very large beer. I drained half of it in one gulp, signaled for another and settled down to write up my journal.

It was getting late and I was desperately tired, but at the very least I wanted to see the cathedral tonight before it got dark. The 15th century church of Santa María de Astorga is simply magnificent, and I had read a little about it prior to this visit. Sadly, it was just closing for the day by the time I got there so I was unable to see inside. The exterior was stunning however, and well worth the visit on its own merit.

Smaller than it appeared from a distance, it made up for it in sumptuousness. An amalgam of the Baroque and Gothic in style, with two mighty bell towers that would have been at home in Florence. It was simply a work of art in stone.

The cathedral was beautifully dressed with delicate, filigree style carvings around the portals and high on the façade, with fine statuary in high relief adorning the walls. it was impossible to take in all the exquisite detail, and to accurately discern the story those long-ago masons had picked out in the stonework.

The church itself had taken on a burnished-bronzed look, as the sandstone edifice glowed in the last of the evening sunshine. This for me was one of the great sights on the Camino, a real diamond in its crown. It was a great shame and a big disappointment that I couldn't take a look inside. The pictures posted on the friezes outside, strikingly portrayed the artwork, majesty and beauty of its interior. Maybe next time eh?

Another building of great interest to me was close to the cathedral and designed by the great Antoni Gaudí. Gaudí is perhaps most famous, to me at least, for his work in Barcelona, especially its magnificent cathedral. Here in Astorga, this building was a large, stone-built structure and difficult to catagorise. It appeared to be part church and part fairy-tale castle in style, with more than a hint of Moorish influence, and as you would of course expect from a Gaudí, it was very striking.

Originally it had been built as a bishop's palace, oddly enough though, no bishop had ever lived there. Happily, it had now been restored to the city as a museum and art gallery, alas, this too was closed to me that evening. Why did they keep doing this to me? It's as if there was a team of 'spoilers' constantly working just ahead and keeping a sharp lookout for my approach. "Here he comes now" they would shout, "shut the doors on the bastard before he arrives, that'll teach him". So unnecessary, don't you think?

If you have never seen any of Gaudí's work up close, I recommend you do so at the first opportunity, I promise you will never view architecture in the same way again. I was lucky enough to visit Barcelona a couple of years ago and saw a lot of his work, including of course, his breathtaking cathedral, still under construction. The man was a genius, his work beyond world class.

Chancing a brief look around the centre as the evening closed in, Astorga seemed to me to be a wonderful city. It was sturdy and prosperous looking, with imposing buildings set on fine avenues, and grand, decorous plazas and gardens located throughout. Everywhere was busy on this warm Friday night, with both locals and tourists mingling happily and having a fine old time.

There was plenty of money around clearly, with lots of Mercs, BMWs and Audis on display. I spotted quite a few snazzy looking sports cars cruising around too. Everybody looked smart and expensively dressed. Many of the ladies were lavishly bejeweled in the grand Spanish style, with the gentlemen sporting designer suits and shirts. Make no mistake; this place had a real swagger to it.

Astorga is famous for its chocolate, and is considered to be the European capital of this addictively sweet treat. This surprised me somewhat. I always thought this distinction was attributed to my sister's house in Scotland. Chocolate, in a carnival of varieties was on sale everywhere, some shops selling nothing else and a lot of it was ridiculously expensive too.

Not my thing really; I prefer my treats to be uncorked rather than unwrapped, and with a more relaxing effect on the knees. I do like a nice chocolate liqueur though, I have to say.

I lingered for a while on the main square, pulsating with night-life now and so full of atmosphere. I looked admiringly at the grand city hall, itself looking like a small cathedral, and the many other fine buildings adorning the plazas perimeter, each adding a touch of history and elegance to the scene. I thought about trying one of the many, very busy bars for a glass of wine, but not only would I have struggled to get a seat (I just couldn't have stood) I was pretty much done in, desperately in need of a rest.

Grudgingly then, as I didn't think I had seen anything like enough of this marvelous city, I scuffled on tired feet back to the albergue. It had been yet another fantastic day on the Camino, but one that had taken it out of me a little to be honest, but that's how it was. There are no hiding places out here my friend!

I clambered up the stairs to my little bunk room and found I had acquired a couple of room-mates in my absence, both were wrapped up in sleeping bags and fast asleep. Morpheus too, was crooking his anaesthetising finger beckoningly at my weary body.

Distance walked today – 35 Kilometres (477)

TWENTY ONE

Astorga

to

Rabanal del Camino

I was wakened at 6.00am to the sound of both my room companions packing and readying themselves for an early start. On you go boys. As I have observed previously, walking for long distances in the dark by torchlight never had any attraction for me. I took my time getting myself organised; re-checking my itinerary for the day ahead and patiently awaiting first light before setting off.

I knew from a few chats I had had along the trail, that some of my fellow pilgrims were knocking out enormous distances each day; never less than 40k and often more! Personally, this punishing routine of walk/run, eat, sleep and repeat would have killed me. I'm sure there was a sense of achievement in this endeavor, but where was the enjoyment?

You would see some of these Camino athletes from time to time, staggering into albergues late in the evening. You would never see them in the morning unless you got up for a pee at 3.00am, Just around the time they would be setting off again. If you did happen upon one of these possessed characters, you would be advised to stand well back.

You would first be drawn by a gaunt face and wide-eyed stare; motionless and piercing, transfixed on some far distant point way beyond the confines of the room. The sounds of indecipherable mutterings stumbling from dried and cracked lips could just be heard, peppered with manic laughter and an occasional sob. All this would be accompanied by twitching, jerking and random pointing, certain signs our marathon man was possessed. It was a most bizarre sight.

These characters could always be found rubbing a variety of creams, lotions and unguents over their bodies and feet, and throwing supplements down their scrawny necks as would a child with cheap sweets. None of them weighed more than 11 stone, but all sported bulging calves usually seen on rugby prop-forwards. Their back packs would be just big enough to carry spare shorts and socks and not a lot else. It appeared the only thing they ate and drank was the kind of things astronauts would take into space, or Everest climbers might find appetising. Forget it brother.

Today I was headed for Rabanal del Camino, and at 20 kilometres seemed to promise an easy enough hike compared to yesterday. Well, at least in terms of distance. The entire section I knew would be one of steady climbing, so it wouldn't be a day off by any means.

I emerged from the hostel at 7.30am exactly, by which time there was at least enough daylight to see the road without needing search lights strapped to my head.

Setting out from the albergue, I diligently followed the Camino signs that guided me around the cathedral and out of the city. Unlike most of the larger conurbations I had visited, the trail out of Astorga was quite short and I was soon into open country. After a short while, the path spurred off into a series of corn fields and steadily rising ground, and the beginning of a climb that would occupy me for the rest of the morning.

Quickly becoming fairly steep the trail rose up and up, providing fantastic views of the surrounding landscape as I continued climbing. This was La Maragatería; a region of unique landscape, architecture, culture and gastronomy that swept over the country west and south of Astorga. Swathes of dense forestry shrouded the adjoining hills and valleys, with a range of high, soft peaks in the mid-distance. Further away still were the outlines of more serious looking mountains, stabbing majestically through the early morning sky. It was absolutely breathtaking.

I pressed on through the sleepy village of Murias de Rechivaldo, continuing steadfastly up the obstinate climb, and let me tell you, I was thoroughly enjoying every single step. After days of monotonously flat trail and endless prairie, it was blissful to be once more straining against the slopes and enjoying these fantastic views. There wasn't a noisy road or bustling town in sight.

Despite the climbing I was making excellent time, so I stopped for a rest and a pot of green tea in the beautiful little village of Santa Catalina de Samoza, comely with its multi-coloured little houses. It was just 10.00am, and I wasn't far off halfway to my destination. I decided I could afford to drop down the gears a little.

A further 5k or so down the trail I came upon the *pueblo* of El Ganso, which translates literally into 'The Goose'. What an eccentric name for a village I thought, and I just had to have a little look-see.

Located in the center of the town, a couple of bars were sat next to each other. One of them was decked out as a sort of wild west saloon, with all kinds of cowboy paraphernalia decorating the place. This was worth closer inspection, so I ordered my tea and had a browse round whilst it was mashing.

Grabbing my camera to take some photos, a hysterical screech arose from behind the bar. This emanated from the frenziedly arm waving barman who was shouting, 'No fotografias, no fotagrafias', pointing frantically to signs posted outside making the same request. In my best Spanish, I tried to ask him where the harm was in taking a couple of snaps? his only reply being an increasingly animated and noisy 'No fotografias, no posible, no posible'. Quite extraordinary.

As is the way of these things in my world of course; whilst he was bollocking me for infringing his copyright or whatever, there was upwards of 350 people stood around taking pictures and videos, Steven Spielberg was setting up a film crew and a TV news helicopter was circling above. OK, I may have made some of that up. It was Tarantino, not Spielberg.

More amused than anything else, I left the barman chasing camera clicking and life-risking customers around his bar, the threats of lawsuits and life-long banishment pursuing them. It was only after I was several kilometres away that I remembered I hadn't paid the lad for my tea! Fuck him, peculiar person.

The climb was becoming steeper and much more taxing now as the day grew hotter, the sun blazing down relentlessly under piercing blue skies. It was becoming almost too hot to walk. I think yesterday's long hike was beginning to tell on me too, as even though it was still only mid-morning, the effort was really beginning to bite. On top of all that my cough seemed to be getting worse, accompanied by a river of glutinous snot dribbling uncontrollably from my nose. How nice.

After a few more kilometres of steady climbing I crossed the stone bridge over the Río de Rabanal at Puente de Panola, walking for a little while alongside yet another fence stitched through with little twig crosses. Well, I was getting seriously fed up with seeing these fiddling contraptions; what was the bloody point of them?

With a roguish sneer, I scooped up a collection of twigs, small branches and other woodland paraphernalia, and over the next few minutes constructed a perfect, miniaturised replica of Astorga cathedral, complete in every detail. I finished it off with a spray of gold paint and wedged it in the fence. "Let's see if you can follow *that* then!" I exclaimed. Well, it passes the time.

With the lure of imminent rest and cold beers urging me on I continued my battle against the slope, cheered now with the knowledge that I had only another hour or so of walking to complete. It was just before 1.30pm and still climbing, that I trudged heavy legged into the village of Rabanal del Camino. I felt tired, sickly and pretty knocked about as I staggered up the final meters. Nonetheless, I was also happy and satisfied with a decent mornings walking behind me, and in a pretty good time too.

Luckily, one of the first buildings I came upon was to be my albergue. It was small and neat, beautifully clean and presented and once again just 5 euros for the night. The albergue 'La Senda' was built from local stone and externally at least, heavily reminiscent of many little Derbyshire pubs of my frequent.

The hostel consisted of two floors: a smallish general dormitory on the lower, with a kitchen/dining area and some small private rooms on the next. It was very cozy indeed, and so far, it appeared only a couple of others had checked in.

With my pack sorted and stowed under my bunk, I showered and changed and felt much livelier. I was also delighted to note it wasn't much past 2.00pm. I was looking forward to a little half-day holiday and a restful afternoon and evening, a nice treat to myself. Something I definitely felt I more than deserved and needed.

Rabanal is a very handsome village, picture postcard. Built on a gently rising hill and centred on its long, narrow main street, it was a delight of small traditional houses, snug looking bars and surprisingly, a couple of swish looking restaurants along its length. A beautiful 17th century church and a more modest looking 15th century monastery sat either side of the street, definitely inviting closer inspection.

The Monesterio de San Salvador del Monte Irago was absolutely superb. Its chapel was tiny and simple, but had a quiet, restful beauty about it. Split either side of the aisle were wooden monks stalls, guarding the way to a small, plain altar, all set underneath a high vaulted ceiling. You could almost feel the weight of the centuries pressing on this wonderfully atmospheric church. It was dimly lit throughout, with the cloying smell of incense invoking memories of my own, now very distant altar boy days.

It was a perfect place to sit and contemplate, so I did just that. I settled myself in to the still quietness of this wonderful old building and closed my eyes, just for a while, on the clatter and din, the strains and uncertainties of life. I let my thoughts drift and wander back down the years, bitter-sweet and long forgotten memories were unlocked and brought unexpectedly to the present, causing a little choke of emotion, I readily confess.

This is how the Camino works its way deep inside. How it seeks for and eventually peels back, the complex and resistant carapaces of your life. Layer upon layer built up over a lifetime, in which I sincerely believed I may have given of my very best; yet deep down, knowing there was so much more I could have done and maybe should have done. I remembered a line from a song I had heard: "I try to live life eye to eye, but at times I find it far too tall". Life is a constant challenge, I know. Yet all too often, we fail to live up to the test.

I think I had begun to realise that we have to expose, or somehow be exposed to our true selves, in order to properly evaluate our achievements and recognise our failings. It's easy enough to wander through life saying, 'well, it is what it is', but I saw now that it's important to pause, to take stock, to look at oneself in the mirror and ask: 'Is this right? Is this enough? Could I do more? Can I be better?'

The Camino had provided me with the environment and opportunity to take a breath; to reflect and to ask those important questions. The biggest test now of course, is what I do with the answers!

After a long while, I emerged blinking into the bright sunlight, feeling very peaceful, contented and more than a little humbled amidst these ancient and historic surroundings. What stories these walls could tell! It would be nice to think, that by giving expression to my own recollections and contemplations, I had been able to add a little of my own life's story to them.

To my pleasant surprise, I discovered that this monastery was still inhabited and by monks of the Dominican order.

From the busy notice boards outside, it was clear that they were very active in the local community and beyond. Amongst the many services available, the monks offered residential retreats or private meditation sessions to pilgrims and others, I was told there were plenty of takers too. It was easy enough to understand why people would want to take shelter in the peace of a more reflective, quieter world; even if only for a short while.

Regardless of faith or beliefs, it was great to see these fine old buildings still lived in and put to good use for the benefit and enjoyment of others. The past connecting positively with the present, I liked to think. Perfect.

As lovely as this little village was, there was something scratching at my mind as I wandered its atmospheric streets; after a while it dawned on me. The whole place looked new! Built from old and original materials for sure, but on closer inspection, pretty much every building in the village had, in very recent times, undergone a major reconstruction. It was clear that the stonework had been rebuilt and or repointed and where necessary, completely replaced. The main street and adjacent ones too, had all been reset and recobbled. Almost everywhere I looked I could see evidence of repair and revitalisation; all done extremely professionally and in a most complimentary style.

It was all very pleasing on the eye, clearly done with the pilgrim and tourist euro in mind (nothing wrong with that at all) and it looked and felt just right. To confirm its success and on passing the monastery chapel later I could see it was absolutely packed, and just around the corner was parked a huge coach originating in León, almost 70 kilometers away. Sneaking a look at a couple of the more expensive restaurants later, these too were completely full. All in this little, middle-of-nowhere village.

Rabanal is just one of the many communities one comes across on the Camino, whose livelihood and often resurrection derives from the largesse of the Way of St James. Rabanal was once an important centre of trade in this region of La Maragatería. But, as in so many other ancient and rural areas of Europe, the encroachment of modern commerce and a drift away from traditional trades, left this particular village in near destitution and close to abandonment.

It was only in the early 1990s and through the direct intervention and restoration plans of the *Confradia* of St. James in London, that sparked Rabanal's revival, paving the way for its continuing prosperity today.

Hat's off then to those enlightened folk, who's vision and endeavor restored this modest little *pueblo* to its special place on the Camino. I am more than happy to say, that all these excellent and worthy restorations, only added to the pleasure I derived from being in such a lovely place and to the all too few, very enjoyable hours I was allowed to spend in it.

Around tea time and to my great joy, I spotted my Mexican *amigos* ambling into the village at the end of their own walking day. Having arranged to meet up as soon as they were refreshed, we got together for a bilingual chat, a few beers and a nice bite to eat in one of the several small bars that the village boasted. It was always a pleasure to meet up with these chaps; warm, friendly and funny and always cheery and positive. By now I can say that we had become good friends, and I was very proud to call them so.

After they had left, (they were staying in the same hostel as me) I had an idea to have a look in at one of the aforementioned restaurants. The one I had in mind had an annex with a bar and a few tables, and it was very nice indeed. Although entirely indoors, there was a canopy of vines overhead and so lit, that it gave the impression of being outside under a star studded night sky. It was absolutely charming.

I sat at a table with a large glass of local red wine and a complimentary bowl of olives, watching the bar quickly filling up. Word must have got round that I was in town. A little later, a Mum and Dad with two little kids bundled in, unsuccessfully scanning the room for a table and hanging around in that awkward, 'what shall we do now?' fashion. Being the gentleman I am, I chivalrously offered them my table and gathering my drink retired to the bar; admiring looks and glowing thanks following me as I went. I even thought I heard a small ripple of applause? Maybe not.

Whilst at the bar, I overheard a couple of guys talking. One said to his friend: "......I've got to show you this; I found it shoved in a fence back down the trail. It's a fabulous miniaturised model of the cathedral at Astorga made from twigs, sprayed in gold and perfect in every........." . Honestly, you couldn't make it up!

Feeling absolutely buzzing at the end of another wonderful and very special day on *The Way*, I returned to the albergue in the last of the daylight hugely contented and lifted by the day's events, and already looking forward to tomorrow.

My retirement was delayed a while however, as upon entering the albergue I heard some familiar chuckling and Latino banter coming from the dining room upstairs. The boys were sat round a table, groaning under the weight of one of their late-night feasts decorated, inevitably, by a couple of bottles of wine. Well, it would have been rude to have said no!

Distance walked today – 25 Kilometres (502)

TWENTY TWO

Rabanal del Camino

to

Molinaseca

Breaking my early morning rule just a little, I was back on the Camino in the inky darkness of 7.15am, with the first hint of daylight just beginning to tease the night skies. The Mexicans I knew, had planned to leave even earlier, confirmed by their squared away and empty bunks which I passed on my way out of the albergue.

The road up the hill and out of the village was a continuation of the trail from yesterday, and I was immediately into a stiff climb. I was headed this morning for what would be the highest point on the whole of the Camino Francés. From that landmark I would take on the long, steep descent, that would guide me to my objective today at Molinaseca.

The trail out from Rabanal was not to treat me gently this early morning, beginning with a sharp rise that rapidly became steeper with every passing step. I was very glad I had started out on this section nice and early this morning, and before the onset of the great heat of the day. Nonetheless, my early exertions had already left me drenched in sweat.

Hiking steadily up to the high sierra, the ground rose over 500 metres in just 10 kilometres. That's quite a climb under any circumstances, but immensely enjoyable nonetheless. Well, for a climbing wierdo like me anyway! The first section of the ascent alone accounted for 200m of height, rising up through densely wooded hills and on to the quaintly rustic village of Foncebadón.

I paused here to have my pic taken by the villages famous cross, deciding now was a good time for a little rest and refreshing brew.

A brochure I had picked up the previous day described that Foncebadón in the not too distant past, had almost fallen into complete ruination. And like Rabanal del Camino, was only rescued and revived by the ever-growing popularity of the

Camino. I was therefore, very pleased to be able to contribute a few euros to its continuing good health and prosperity.

I ambled up the hill to an already busy café at the top of the village, where I found my *amigos* already entrenched outside, tucking into large omelets and pots of coffee. Those boys certainly loved their food. A green tea and a croissant would do nicely for me, and after a brief rest and a chat with the lads I regained the trail for the last heave up to the top.

The exacting demands of the climb persisted over its steep course, not easing in severity at all as I pushed onwards and upwards towards the peak of Monte Irago. As I mentioned earlier, this would be the highest point (with respect to sea level) on the Camino Francés. Not the end of the climbing though, not by a bloody long chalk my friend!

Scrambling up to the top, bent almost double under my pack and on wobbly legs I was met by quite a crowd, all gathering on and around the 'Cruz de Ferro'; an iron cross atop a tall wooden pole and mounted on a rocky hillock. I *thought* I had read somewhere that this is a replica and that the original is in a museum somewhere. I'm not certain of that though. Either way, some kind of monument or other had been on this spot for thousands of years, a Christian cross originally being sited after the Roman era. This is a place of legend as well as one of the highlights of the Camino, and the views afforded around the compass from here were both dramatic and spectacular.

Not wanting to be delayed too long and conscious of more climbing ahead; I followed tradition and placed a small stone at the top of the mound by the foot of the cross. Stepping slowly backwards, as if retiring respectfully from an audience with the Queen.........well, everyone was very kind and helpful picking me up off the floor, dusting me down and asking me if I was OK, plasters and bandages sympathetically offered. "Is the old gentleman alright?" I heard a thoughtful soul ask. Fucking hell!

As a venerated spot on the Camino, the cross and its pebble strewn mound was an essential place for pause and reflection to many pilgrims. On closer inspection, a lot of the stones that made up the sizeable mound around the cross bore inscriptions of prayers or personal thoughts and the like. Some were wrapped in paper baring similar messages and pleadings. Many pilgrims carry a pebble with them from the start of their journey, solely for this solemn purpose.

It's easy enough to be cynical about this sort of thing, but in the context of the Camino, the purpose and status of the Cruz de Ferro has its rightful place. I observed several people just during my short visit, visibly moved by their presence at the cross and being able to place their unique stone and message alongside the countless others, each of them lost in their private contemplations.

Descending down the slope from the cross and just before Manjarín, I came across the famous cabins and lodge of a devotee of the Knights Templar. This was home to Tomás Martínez; Hospitalier and legend of the Camino who lives his life in honour of the Knights and has done so for many years. His dwelling is given over to flags, armour and all kinds of Templar memorabilia and is a sight to behold. Rough sign posts to destinations around the world, were nailed or strung around the property, evidence of its many international visitors down the years.

Everyone and anyone were free to have a look round, he even supplied refreshments and a bit of history for those interested. There is accommodation available also I believe, but the place looked deserted on this day as I passed by. I was told it is a terrific place to visit, and I regretted later not taking the time to do so properly.

That's the enduring frustration on the Camino. If you spent time visiting every attraction or point of interest, and there are thousands of them, it would take you three months or more to get to Santiago!

Above Manjarín, close to the large military communications transmission post at the summit, I at last broached the topmost part of the trail. I paused here for a while, taking in the incredible views of the surrounding peaks of Los Montes de León, and the plunging valleys that were guardians to the many mountain streams of the region. It was truly breathtaking and carried that 'on top of the world' feeling. It really was a very special, moving and memorable sight. I spent a few moments in deep admiration, lost in thought, absorbing the spectacle and taking unworthy photographs. It was completely captivating and unforgettable.

Dragging myself away and pocketing my memories, I began the long and steep descent to Molinaseca; the village I had decided upon earlier as my sojourn for the night. What an excellent choice that would turn out to be.

Anyone who has done bit of climbing will tell you; as tough as an ascent can be, the climb down is often even tougher, and this was pretty much the case here. It was an incredibly steep descent over rough and difficult terrain, and it was a challenge to keep my feet and balance. I was glad it was dry, it would have been a nightmare if not impossible to negotiate safely in the wet.

I stumbled onwards and irresistibly downwards over the jagged rocks and scree, carefully planting each step, anxious to avoid a painful fall, or worse. Every stride was murder on my leg muscles, I almost had to lean backwards at times to stop the weight of my pack and the sharpness of the descent pulling me over.

After 7 kilometres of this precipitous plunge, I arrived with much relief at the picturesque village of El Acebo; stood arms wide open on the mountainside and joy of joys, welcoming bars to collapse into.

With a huge sigh of relief and respite from my toils, I gratefully sat down outside a café with a pot of my beloved green tea, legs shaking with adrenaline and so glad of a rest. It was with a mixture of empathy and amusement that I watched my fellow walkers stagger around the corner of the trail, their faces turning from grimaces to grins at the wonderfully resuscitating sight of the village and its bars.

Amongst the intrepid were Alex, Alfredo and Fernando, grinning broadly as they strode towards me, seemingly unmoved and untroubled by the torrid descent. They didn't fool me for a second; each of them ordered and gulped down the largest beers available and were ordering re-enforcements within moments.

A brief chat with my mates and I was back on the trail, fearful of stiffening up after sitting too long. The severity of the incline was relentless, with no sign at all of it easing off. The only encouragement to be drawn at this point, was that the valley floor below appeared to be drawing ever closer.

I stumbled on down the rocky path and through the village of Riego de Ambros, shyly revealing its ancient timbered houses and jaunty, but rickety looking verandas. Beyond Riego, I at last found myself firmly in the lower reaches of the valleys that shaped and scarred the region, a check of my map confirming it was just a few more kilometers now to my destination.

Resting for just a moment and gazing up to where I had started the descent, the view beggared belief! It didn't seem possible, that just a short time ago I was atop that distant looking peak. It appeared to be many kilometres away and impossibly high. Turning back to face the medicine, I knew there was still plenty of walking below me too. Come on then old cock, I adjured myself, let's crack on.

The trail at long last began to lose some of its acuteness, whilst simultaneously closing in on the steep road that had been winding down the mountain and leading directly into the town. After another kilometre or so and with great relief, I joined that same road for the last stretch.

With the combined effects of the mountaineering and the terrific heat of the day, I was pretty well done in as I approached Molinaseca. I was desperate by now, to get off my feet and down a few cold beers. Have I said that before somewhere?

On the approach into Molinaseca, I was amused briefly by the escapades of a couple of cyclists at the side of the road. They were a mid-aged lady and gent and there was something about their demeanour that made me stop and observe. I guess I'm so attracted to the discomforts and pitfalls of others, as I seem to endure plenty enough of my own.

They had pulled up by a fenced-off old building, and it was clear by her agitation and finger pointing that the lady intended scaling the fence, presumably for a pee behind said building. Using his hands as stirrups, her man gamely tried to hoist the lass onto and over the barrier, and after many attempts and a lot of shouting and falling, finally succeeding. The poor girl by this time must have been desperate, for as soon as she landed she dropped her Lycra's and squatted down in full view of all who were passing, defeating of course, the objective of climbing over in the first place.

The *pièce de résistance* however, was that having restored her dignity, *madame* to her obvious horror, spotted and pointed to a gap in the fence that should have been obvious, slipping back through about four feet from where she had climbed over. The bewildered gentleman needless to say, received a mighty bollocking for the whole cock-up. As is the nature of these things of course, the whole debacle was clearly his fault. Superb!

My first view of the village was very impressive, as I dragged myself across the ancient stone bridge that straddled the broad but shallow Río Meruelo. Dozens of kids and adults were disporting themselves in the cool waters below, or sunbathing on its grassy banks. On this stiflingly hot afternoon, it all looked incredibly inviting.

On the other side of the bridge and close to the river sat several nice-looking bars and restaurants. They were assembled as if to form a welcoming gateway into the town's main street, and into which I now walked. Cool, dark and narrow and shaded from the blistering sun, it was heaven sent. With a sign pointing the way to my albergue on one side and a beckoning little bar on the other, I decided after a brief fight with myself to check in first, dump my pack, *then* return to dive into a vat of desperately needed cold beer.

The albergue 'San Blas' was solidly built of stone, nestling amidst a maze of ancient, narrow alleys. I checked in with the very friendly owner, after which she gave me the grand tour. Thankfully, this didn't take too long and she left me to my own devices in the dormitory block.

The bunk room and the restaurant were in opposite and separate halves of the building, occasioning the need to leave one to reach the other. Quite small, with room for less than thirty I surmised, the dormitory was split into several smaller rooms, each one very nice and comfortable. On finding mine I dumped my pack, quickly showered in the exceedingly smart washrooms, returning as fast as my shattered limbs could carry me to the bar I first spotted at the end of the alley.

A cold beer had never tasted as good; well, not since the last the last one anyway, and it soon disappeared to be replaced quickly by another. After relaxing for a good while and regaining a bit of strength, I decided to have a little look round and see what was on offer. I'm a very simple and undemanding soul really; a couple of beers in a nice bar can change my world in moments!

The best feature of Molinaseca was its long, narrow and very atmospheric main street. There was a larger town surrounding it I knew, but this was of no interest to me I'm afraid, on my short visit. Many bars and restaurants, tiny shops and houses lined the street, which on this late afternoon and mid-siesta was very quiet. I decided that I would have a proper look round later, but for now I would try one last beer - purely for medicinal and rehydration purposes you understand - then retire for my own well-earned rest.

Returning to the same table I had recently vacated, I sat looking down the street towards the bridge, there espying *los tres amigos* wobbling along on unsteady legs, looking parched, dusty and knackered. Spotting my waving arms, they joined me at my table and were soon downing large beers themselves. So pleased were they to see me after a gap of three hours they had also bought one for me, so before I knew it, a little drinking session was breaking out. Let me tell you; never was one so much deserved by the four of us, and we spent a pleasant hour or so exchanging stories and mishaps along the way, great guffaws of laughter renting the air. Deep joy.

Such wonderful, wonderful company are my dear Mexican friends. It is one of the glories of the Camino that brings people together and forges friendships like this. I felt so lucky that Alejandro, Alfredo and Fernando had come into my little world, especially on a journey such as this.

In between gulps of beer, they remembered they had yet to find accommodation for the night. I directed them to my albergue which was close by and I knew had plenty of room, so off they tottered to check in whilst I finished my own beer. Still plenty of time for that little nap, I thought.

A couple of hours later and feeling much revived after a good rest, I met up once again with the boys. The albergue was offering a very good deal on their *menú del día* that evening, so the four of us plus a few others, dined in the nice little restaurant attached on a marvelous Spanish chicken casserole; all washed down with bounteous amounts of the local wine. To be honest, I could just as easily have called it a night at that point and the boys felt the same. Not wanting to waste such a beautiful evening however, we wearily dragged ourselves into the now very busy main street for a little exploring.

Frustratingly and I don't know how, I almost immediately lost track of the lads and I couldn't spot them anywhere. Bugger. I had to be content then, to wander the darkening streets in my own company, taking in the sights and sounds of the village on this very warm, tranquil and flower scented evening.

There was plenty of evidence that this town too had enjoyed a very recent makeover, but I won't revisit my previous observations *vis* Rabanel del Camino. There was clearly a pattern here though, as so many of these wonderful little villages on the Camino, glowed with new life and prosperity under the aegis of the French Way.

I had come to really love and appreciate these old towns and villages on the Camino, each with their own personality, history and stories to tell. The people always appeared happy and content; drawn no doubt, from the sense of security and stability honed from a rich and ancient past, providing in turn, a steady bulwark against an unknowable and uncertain future. These fine folk seemed strengthened by the knowledge that whatever happens in the wider world, be it at home or abroad, their villages and culture would endure, secure and certain, bound by the unbreakable bonds of family, faith and community. Truly wonderful.

I Spotted a very basic and traditional bar tucked away in a corner and ordered a glass of the local red, and in honour of now being proudly placed in the 'Bierzo' wine region. A very large goblet came my way and it was superb. This wine was more mellow and fruitier than the Riojas I had been enjoying and it went down a treat. Deciding on another before retiring, a similarly generous measure was served up by my dark eyed and lovely *camarera*, and I took my time drinking it.

After the several large glasses of wine I had consumed with my dinner, added to the many beers I had slurped down earlier; I was beginning to feel very relaxed to say the least!

I sat outside for a while, striking up a hit-and-miss conversation with a handful of locals, many of whom were trying desperately and kindly, to offer advice and treatments to cure my hacking cough. If I understood correctly, most of these concoctions seemed to involve drinking enormous amounts of alcohol of one type or another. *Gracias mis amigos*; I've already got that prescription!

It was simply grand watching the townsfolk enjoying the evening and the company of their families and friends, and so heartwarming to see the children laughing and playing in these safe streets, pestering mums and dads for late night treats and begging for "Just a few more minutes, please papá!" as bedtime called. Unforgettable moments.

Lulled by the wine, the warmth of the night and the exertions of the day my race was run, so I went inside to settle my bill. "Uno euro" my *bonita amiga* asked of me. One euro for what must have been two thirds of a bottle of wine. I could get used to this!

I headed back through the still-busy streets, the Spanish really are night owls, thinking that I was so lucky to be experiencing this glimpse of another way of life, this window into a simpler, happier world. Reflecting on the experiences of recent weeks, I genuinely felt that the events I have been describing had really begun to reshape my way of thinking, and to influence how I viewed the future. It was almost as if I had walked from one room of my life into another and finding it so different, so new, and freshly furnished with great promise.

Nothing to do with the several glasses of wine I had imbibed, obviously, but I spent the next ten minutes cursing and swearing whilst trying to gain entry to the wrong building.

Eventually though, I was led gently by the hand by a kindly fellow resident and to the correct door. Heaving myself a little unsteadily into my bunk, tired but feeling ridiculously happy with my lot, I cast my thoughts to tomorrow and the 30 plus kilometres I would be walking. Goodnight.

Distance walked today – 26 Kilometres (528)

TWENTY THREE

Molinaseca

to

Villafranca del Bierzo

Question. What is a quag and why do you only find them in mires? I ask because on waking this morning, I felt my head to be painfully quagish and immersed in the deepest sludge. It was pitch black and I had no idea of the time. Please let it be about an hour after I had gone to bed, I certainly felt as if it was. I looked hopefully if not pleadingly at my watch but my worst fears were realised; it was just shy of 6.00am.

Dragging myself reluctantly from my bunk, I stumbled and lurched my way into the bathroom, ungluing my tongue from the roof of my mouth whilst trying to force open congealed and throbbing eyes. Carefully now lad; one lid at a time, one lid at a time.

I rarely suffer from hangovers, but I freely admit that I had, perhaps, supped rather too deeply from the fathomless depths of the booze well the previous afternoon and evening. Peering cautiously into the mirror through bloodshot slits of eyes, I risked a look at my tongue; not good. I pushed the blackened, swollen, furred up slug back into my mouth, attacking the contents with a couple of vigorous brushings. Staggering into the shower, I could feel my stomach roiling, lurching and bubbling threateningly....... And insistently.

And so my dear reader, as you accompany me on my short dash from the standing up cubicle to the sitting down cubicle, so to speak, I shall now strike a blow for authentic writing.

Think of all the books you've read down the years, the adventure novels, romances and crime stories etc. Think of all the heroes and heroines, lovers and scoundrels, villains and detectives that feature in these epic tales, and tell me, when do they ever go to the toilet? When do you ever read something like: 'The sniper steadied his sights on his target, spoke quietly into his throat mic and said 'Hello control, I'm going to have to postpone this kill, I'm desperate for a crap'. Never, it doesn't happen. What about: 'As she slipped out of her underwear, she turned to her lover and said, 'before you do that special thing to me darling, I really must go for a piddle, I'm absolutely bursting'. You've never read it!

I spoke to friend of mine who had read the steamy volume 'A whiter shade of pale grey at 50' or whatever it was called. She was able to confirm that whilst there was no mention of toilet performances, the couple in question had peed on each other, which I'm not quite sure is the same thing, but anyway. Widdles and craps hardly ever feature in novels, why so squeamish? It's perfectly natural. Ian Fleming first wrote about James Bond in 1953. Over 65 years later and the poor bugger still hasn't been for a piss.

So, here goes!!

Pursuing a panic-stricken, naked dash from shower to W.C, I collapsed onto the porcelain pedestal for an emergency discharge of all unwanted baggage. The hideous noise and smell created, I fear, can only be compared to that of a lorry carrying scaffolding poles and planks, crashing at high speed into another truck transporting live pigs. Thank God there was nobody else in the bathroom when I emerged from the stall. See, that wasn't too bad was it?

After another explosive burst of coughing, my sickliness still clinging on, I popped my throbbing eyes back into their sockets, risking a glimpse through the window at the lamp lit streets that lay in wait for me. My destination today was Villafranca del Bierzo; a hike of over 30 kilometres with a fair bit of climbing too, according to my map. God help me.

Following hard fought negotiations between my head, stomach and legs, agreement was finally reached allowing me to head out. But steadily, please! Steering myself delicately around the quiet outskirts of Molinaseca, I wound my way slowly up the gently steepening paved road out of the town. Each gulp of mountain-fresh air, was slowly lifting the fog from my befuddled brain and the dead hand of sluggishness from my body. I'm never ever drinking again! Well, not at least until this afternoon.

Daylight was slow in breaking through the overcast skies this morning, quite a change from the relentless sunshine of recent days. I was headed initially for Ponferrada; a large town 7k down the trail and where I hoped to find a desperately needed cash machine, there being none in Molinaseca. The concept of 'cash back' hadn't yet reached these parts either.

As I snaked through the tiny *aldea* of Campo, eccentrically adorned with shaky looking wooden verandas jutting out over its narrow streets, it started to rain. It was only 'teenage rain' to begin with, (just a few spots) but soon developed into a sharp, but short-lived heavy shower. I quite enjoyed splashing through the downpour and without bothering with my water-proofs, it was most invigorating too.

With the rain quickly passing over I strode on, soon sighting Ponferrada rising up on the opposite bank of the wide and fast flowing Río Boeza. I crossed the bridge over the Río Sil into the town, as yet quiet and with not much traffic about, proceeding up the steep hill towards the centre in search of a bank, wandering quite a way off the trail in doing so.

I eventually found a cash machine, somewhere in the next province it felt like, and quickly rejoined the route. At the top of the hill leading up from the town centre, I took a slow walk past and around the large, imposing and well-preserved 12th century Castle of the Templars; impressively and colourfully festooned with heraldic flags and bunting. In the shadow of the castle walls stood a large plaza, empty now, but just coming to life at the cessation of the rain, with pinafored *camareros* sweeping their frontages and setting out tables.

Picking up the yellow arrows of the trail I traced my way through a huddle of narrow streets, and at the onset of another short sharp shower, crossed into a park on the outskirts of the town. Ponferradas' history is built on coal, iron and steel. Whilst there still seemed to be some production, the skeletons of large foundries and factories could be seen peppered around, standing as grim evidence of industrial decline.

Striding across the aforementioned park, I spied *mis compañeros* a little way ahead, catching up with them just as another brief shower was abating; the sun now trying its very best to break through the stubborn clouds. I walked for a little while with the lads, but as I had often found on this journey they walked far too slowly for me! Following a quick brew of life restoring green tea in a little bar at Columbrianos, I bade them *bon Camino* and cracked on; gradually leaving both Mexicans and Ponferrada behind me.

The Camino at this point was fairly flat going, the surrounding fields now of a completely different nature than those of recent days. The agricultural theme here was mainly of allotments and smallholdings supporting a variety of crops, with expansive vineyards dominating the surrounding hills. A number of the smaller plots were neither productive nor well-maintained, with odd patches of fenced-off scrubland, clearly not harvesting any produce for quite some time.

The trail leaked out in this lazy, comfortable fashion for several more kilometres, passing through a series of small, unremarkable villages along its way. Vineyard rich Fuentas Nuevas and Camponaraya, being amongst the largest and noteworthy of them.

Vineyards were becoming more prevalent now, springing up on either side of the Camino and across the steepening hills that were quickly closing in, the trail climbing steadily with their onset. It really was very agreeable walking through this pleasant and undulating countryside, as the path squeezed itself carefully between the vines; their plump bunches of overhanging Mencía grapes, carefully nurturing their precious juices in anticipation of the coming harvest.

The sun was now beginning to win its battle against the slowly scattering clouds, with the day warming up significantly as a result. It was getting time I thought, for another short break. A few kilometres on I came to the town of Cacabelos, with a couple of large wineries and a visitor center standing at its gateway. I decided this would be a very nice spot to rest up for a while.

Cacabelos is a decent sized town standing at the heart of the 'Bierzo' region; a large wine producing area of the same name, which straddles the A-6 autopista from Albares to Villafranca del Bierzo. I was very much looking forward to sampling more of its produce later.

Hangover? What hangover?

For the umpteenth time then and having made excellent progress, I sat outside a nice bar in the centre of town, treating myself to a pleasant half hour with my feet up. I got to chatting with a German chap and fellow pilgrim, whom I had spotted from time to time at various points along the Camino. Usually I had seen him in the company of a younger guy whom, I had assumed, was his son. He wasn't. He was "a close friend from home", if you get my drift, and they had had a big fall out. Oooh er!

I decided against asking if it was a lover's tiff. Not only was he a big lad, he may well have been in search of an alternative and compensatory orifice. Bugger that. He was stopping over in Cacabelos this night, but not I. Rested, refreshed and *anus integrum*, as the ancient Roman Legionnaires of these parts would have once exclaimed, I pressed on to complete the last 7k or so to Villafranca.

◆ ◆ ◆

There are lots of Germans in this little tale I know; this is because they were absolutely everywhere. Far more representative in number than any other nationals I encountered on my particular journey.

Armed with this knowledge, I was on constant high alert for the throaty roar of Tiger tanks and troop carriers, or the smack of jackboots on the Camino cobbles. Well, you never know. Can we really trust out erstwhile foe? They used to shoot at my Dad you know!

It has long been obvious to me that being 2-0 down, as it were, in the World War Series, the Germans had decided on a change of strategy in their pursuit of global domination. Instead of storming the frontiers of Europe with steely eyed stormtroopers; it would now be corpulent, euro-laden businessmen and tourists in the vanguard, buying up commodities, companies and countries.

In place of tanks and motorised armour; it would be Mercedes, BMWs and for old time's sake, Herr Hitler's Volkswagens that would provide the wheels of action, rolling unstoppably into every Acacia Avenue driveway. If their plan was to conquer Europe through hard work, industrial and technical excellence and commercial might, they seem to be making a decent fist of it. As I am sure Frau Merkel would love to be able to say: "Put your rivet gun down Tommy (UK plc), for you, zer var is ofa". We'll call it 2-1 then, shall we?

After passing through Pieros, the trail began a steepish though undulating ascent, and I could see before me that I had a fair bit of climbing to complete before I reached my days end. At this point, I was faced with one of the trail options that the Camino occasionally offered. I couldn't tell from my map which would be the most preferable. It looked like a choice between a seemingly straightforward route adjacent to the road, or a more interesting and scenic diversion over the hills. It goes without saying that I chose the wrong option.

The route I settled on evolved into a hot, grueling slog over extremely rough and undulating terrain, weaving first one way then another through very elevated vineyards. It took me over two hours to complete this last section, and I was definitely feeling the strain when the last steep climb brought me mercifully to the municipal albergue overlooking the town of Villafranca del Bierzo.

The albergue 'Municipal de Peregrinos' was set high on a hill overlooking the town and was typical of the more basic style, municipal hostels. It was plain and functional but also of course, very clean and comfortable. Arranged over two floors; with the common rooms and kitchen on the first and bunk rooms on the second, it had the feel of a British youth hostel and like most of those always seem to be, it was virtually full.

I felt as if I could benefit from a little snooze and to rest my weary bones, that last slog had really taken it out of me. I fought against it however, fearing that if I was to fall asleep, I wouldn't wake up. Reluctantly then, I threw myself under an invigorating shower, changed into my Tuxedo and met the delectable and sexy Eva Green in the cocktail lounge for a couple of gins before dinner. Oh, I'm so sorry, I must have fallen asleep after all.

My dream popped; and in the absence of sultry and beguiling film stars, I sat on the porch of the albergue instead, sipping on a can of beer bought from a vending machine thoughtfully provided in the absence of a bar. Lest I should forget, I took this opportunity to write up the notes of my day's adventures so far. Right, where was I? "..... Throwing off her Armani rucksack and Jimmy Choo hiking boots and slipping casually out of her sheer silk anorak, Eva beckoned me alluringly towards the creaking bunk......"

In the meantime, the skies had become seriously leaden and were darkening by the minute. Anticipating a downpour at any moment, I decided to have a look around the town whilst the going was good.

Villafranca del Bierzo was hard to work out. The part I was able to explore, albeit briefly, was built on a concertina of rugged hills, with narrow streets tumbling down into a small plaza containing the usual mix of bars, restaurants and shops. Looking further afield though, I could see the surrounding peaks were dotted with smaller hamlets and clusters of buildings, and I couldn't decipher if they were separate from or belonging to a Greater Villafranca, as it were.

The town centre was really attractive. Quiet on this early Monday evening it had a real alpine feel, nestling as it did comfortably amongst the encroaching mountains. The surrounding streets were quaint, homely and inviting and a pleasure to stroll around. There were also several interesting looking churches and stately buildings in and around the centre, and which I hoped to be able to investigate. The Convento de Padres Paules in particular, looked well worth a visit.

Sadly, I would get to see none of these. For soon after, as if unable to hold off a moment longer, the skies burst open to a tremendous downpour, causing rivers of rainwater to rush through the streets almost immediately.

Grabbing some victuals from a supermarket just off the square, I sprinted (oh yes) back to the shelter of the albergue and after toweling myself dry, settled down to a little indoor picnic and a bottle of inexpensive local wine. It was most enjoyable and I scoffed and supped the lot. My hangover from this morning was now consigned to history and the pages of this book, my disavowal of strong drink, flung from my memory. I could feel another mantra developing here.

As I ate and drank and relaxed, it suddenly dawned on me that for the first time since my birthday over a week ago, it felt as if my seemingly constant companions of cough and cold, were at last packing their bags and showing every indication of leaving. Shares in pharmaceutical and tissue paper companies must have tumbled with the onset of this savage blow to their incomes.

I had hoped to see the Mexicans boys by now, but there was no sign as yet. I discovered the next day that they too, like my German friend earlier, had decided to stop over in Cacabelos.

In the absence of any worthwhile diversions and with the rain still teaming down, I browsed desultorily through a couple of books in the small library for a while. Soon tiring of this, I decided it would be more profitable to get some rest and sleep. So I did.

Distance walked today – 32 Kilometres (560)

TWENTY FOUR

Villafranca del Bierzo

to

Las Herrerias
de Valcarce

S hock,horror! I didn't wake up until 7.10am, I had slept for almost 10 hours! I guess I needed that, and I felt much better for it I can tell you. As an added bonus, I could feel straight away that my hideous cold was definitely in its death throws. A slightly later start wasn't a huge problem really; I had only 23 kilometres to negotiate today so on the road by 8.00am was just fine.

This day, I would be heading for Las Herrerias del Valcarce, a small *pueblo* at the head of a very long and deep valley. The itinerary actually called for me to get to O Cebreiro; however, as this was a place of legend on the Camino, I knew well that to reach it would entail climbing in excess of 600m over a steep and very tough 8 kilometres. Sensibly, I thought I would be better off tackling this challenge in the cool of early morning rather than in the heat of the afternoon, thus my decision to stop short in Las Herrerias. Brilliant eh?

Just think how differently Captain R.F. Scott's Antarctic expedition of 1910-13 would have turned out, if he'd have had my fantastic expeditionary planning skills to draw on? Answers on a postcard please.

The route escaping Villafranca involved a long yet shallowish climb, passing through many of the little outposts I had wondered about the previous day. Yes, they were all part of Villafranca! Although quite misty on the climb out, it was still possible to admire the spectacular scenery of the surrounding peaks as they emerged occasionally through the gloom.

For long stretches on my way up the valley, I was boxed in by the towering, incredibly steep and wooded slopes that crowded the trail and it was a really impressive sight. The northern slopes were the Sierra del Caldeiron, and I would walk in the looming shadows of these heights for the rest of the morning.

I continued my steady walk up through the gorge, with the Camino closely following the mostly hidden, but gurgling and fast flowing Río Valcarce. It was so hard to believe, that this modest watercourse had gouged and cut this huge ravine from the rocks towering above me. And you know what? it was still at it!

The route was punctuated at regular intervals by a series of unpresuming little villages, each hosting at least one bar or café, so it was easy enough to take a rest and keep supplied. I pressed on up the valley; initially through Pareje and 5k further on into Trabadelo, and with the day now warming up nicely, I decided this would be a good time and place for a break and a refreshing brew.

I settled myself outside a nice little café and ordered some green tea. The *camarera* quickly obliged, simultaneously attracting my attention by pointing animatedly at a pair of expensive looking walking poles by a deserted table opposite. She managed to convey in a potage of Spanish and English, that the couple recently departed had unwittingly left them. Not 'recently departed' as in dead of course, but as in 'just left', you see. Come on, try and keep up.

Knowing exactly who she meant, I picked up the poles and rushed up the hill on my errand, only to find both parties punting along nicely with a set of sticks each. 'Not ours' was the obvious reply to my redundant question. Returning to the cafe somewhat puzzled, it turned out the poles belonged to a young girl, who, unseen by either the owner or myself had just nipped inside for a pee, emerging just in time to see me legging it up the street with her designer equipment. Apologies and explanations provided I finished my tea, shaking my head in wonderment at the frequency these things happened to me.

A few years ago, Manchester City FC fielded for a short time, shall I say, a rather emotionally challenged footballer; Mario Balotelli. His angst ridden demeanour and chest beating tantrums, once led him to displaying a T-shirt under his kit with the slogan, 'Why Always Me?' writ large across it. I was beginning to understanding how he felt.

Just to be certain it wasn't a nasty trick, I had a quick look round to see if the cycling, peeing pair from Molinaseca, weren't looking over the fence and enjoying a revenge laugh. It was all clear.

I was making excellent time, and delighting in the superb scenery as I continued the steady climb up the narrow pass. The gradient had hardly changed since I started the ascent and was quite comfortable going really; just nice and steady. The skies now were of the deepest, clearest blue, but the sun would not properly clear the tops of these towering heights until well after midday, which, I can assure you was just fine by me.

As it made its steady progress up the ravine, the Camino frequently passed under the A-6 mountain road, precariously threading itself here and there across impossibly high overpasses and bridges. It was quite an impressive sight too, in these lofty sierras.

I could only imagine though, the carnage and disruption that building these gigantic structures must have brought to the quiet little villages they crisscrossed. La Portella de Valcarce, Ambasmestas, Vega de Valcarce and Ruitelán, all standing stoically under their massive shadows, as I made my way through this chain of tiny hamlets.

Despite the long climb I must have zoomed along, for at just 1.15pm I found myself on the heights overlooking my destination of Las Herrerias de Valcarce. A short walk down through the meadows and across a little bridge, and I was soon ambling into that quiet and pretty little *pueblo*.

As far as I could make out, there were just two albergues in the village and I checked into the nearest one, the 'Albergue Miriam'. This hostel was staffed by volunteers I believe, and I was greeted by a couple of young ladies of whom I soon realised were of the Sapphic persuasion, and nothing wrong with that. I've often thought that I might be a bit of a lesbian myself. I once watched a movie where one of the female characters said to her girlfriend: "I want to lick every inch of your naked body". Bloody hell, I thought, so do I!

To my pleasant surprise one of the girls was English, and she gave me the grand tour of what was quite a chic and boutique style residence; recessed lights and scented candles decorating the way. With room for just a dozen or so bunks it was very cozy and homely, with wooden floors throughout and an open staircase leading to the upper floor.

It didn't feel like albergue at all, more like an alpine chalet. It was very nice and smart and all set in a beautifully renovated building, but my first suspicions were aroused by the absence of Wi-Fi and more importantly; there was no cold beer to be had!

This tiny *aldea* was arranged delightfully on the wide flood plain of the Río Valcarce, most of its few buildings sitting on the near side of the river I had tracked all day, and it was very picturesque. Hosed down, reshod and with what amounted to half a day still in front of me, I strolled along the one main street and was out of the village and into the next tiny hamlet in less than 5 minutes. Blink, and Las Herrerias was gone.

I took the opportunity whilst at the head of the village to get my bearings for my walk through here the following morning. On retracing my steps, I *just* managed to avoid being trampled to death under the hooves of a drove of horses, being corralled at top speed into a field by a shouting, arm waving *caballero*. Unbelievable! Where's that T-shirt Mario?

I stumbled shocked and trembling into one of the two bars in the village for a couple of emergency, restorative beers. As good an excuse as any, I suppose. I sat outside on the small terrace, admiring the sweep of this beautiful green valley and surrounding hills. It was close to a perfect moment. The air was fresh and clean, the heat of the afternoon sun beat kindly on my face, the silence was almost total. I had a chilled beer to hand, I felt relaxed, happy and very pleased with myself and my little world. It was a day I wished I could have bottled and preserved.

At that, with my heart rate normalised and thirst quenched, I decided it was time for a siesta. Spain's great gift to the world of lunchtime drinkers.

I had pre-paid for dinner on checking in, as I was unsure what else would be available in such a tiny, out of the way place. Sitting down at seven with a handful of other guests, I noticed we all had wine glasses but as yet, no wine. Mmmm, suspicions growing.

The food arrived soon enough and in the shape of a bowl of soup and three small pieces of rustic bread, topped with humus. Still no sign of the wine. I politely enquired as to its whereabouts; partly because wine was included in the *menú del día* deal, but mostly because my alcohol levels were dropping alarmingly. Pleading forgetfulness, our waitress returned with half a bottle of red - to be shared between six of us. Was she taking the piss? I can *spill* half a bottle of red down the front of my shirt on any given evening! My suspicions were off the scale!

Hungrily tucking in, I thought I wouldn't eat too much bread so as to avoid being overly full for the main course. I offered the young German lad opposite me (see what I mean) my unwanted pieces; but only on the strict understanding that as part of the transaction, he would agree not to join the Wehrmacht and invade Poland.

On finishing the soup, which was delicious by the way, our waitress then asked if we were ready for dessert. "Dessert? what about the main course?" we all cried, "you've just eaten it" she replied!

Stunned, I queried this and I felt on behalf of us all, whether she felt that a bowl of soup with bread and a small slice of lemon tart, was either value for money or sufficient fare for people who had been walking up mountains all day? Without blinking an eye, she considered it was both.

Getting just a *little* agitated by now I let it be known, with the solid agreement of the others, that we were far from happy and demanded more wine, lots more wine as compensation for this blatant rip off and disregard of hungry bellies. Reluctantly and red faced she scurried off, returning with a full bottle whilst mumbling platitudes and apologies. I should bloody well think so too. As it happened and to my ill-concealed delight, nobody else really wanted any more wine, soooo...........

Taking the opportunity a little later and by now quite calm, I sagaciously advised the young ladies that this albergue was kind of missing the point. They weren't providing accommodation and snacks for people shopping for shoes in Knightsbridge, but indeed, for tired and hungry walkers. And perhaps, should give a little more thought to putting something a bit more substantial on the table at 10 euros a plate. I don't think they got it, they looked at me as if I was I was from outer space!

I left them shaking my head in disappointment, and wondering if I could somehow sneak into their bedroom and steal the batteries out of their 'Rampant Rabbit', or whatever version of vigorously vibrating vari-speed they had secreted amongst their baby-doll nighties, the saucy little devils.

Always remember: revenge is sweet, but not fattening. Much like the dinners in this albergue, come to think of it.

Distance walked today – 23 Kilometres (583)

TWENTY FIVE

Las Herrerias de Valcarce

to

Triacastela

T he plan Captain Scott and I had carefully hatched yesterday, entailed me spending the night in Las Herrerias then tackling O Cebreiro in the early morning, and in doing so, I would avoid climbing in the heat that would surely be my close companion. So far so good, but I needn't have worried about the heat. I was awakened this morning by the sound of crashing thunder and flashes of lightening, brilliantly illuminating the darkened *dormitorio*. A wary peep out of the window confirmed it was pouring with rain too. Ouch.

Not remotely discouraged, I was all set and spattering out of the village by 7.15am. The rain wasn't too bad to be honest; steady rather than torrential, but the thunderstorm really was in full torment now; booming and flashing, with streaks of light lancing the cloud burdened skies.

The narrow tarmac road out of the village formed the early part of the trail this morning. Being lamp lit, it was easy and safe enough to follow in the dark so I was happy enough to crack on.

I passed in the merest moment through the tiny *aldea* of Hospital, at which point the ground began to rise quickly and steeply as I followed the road upwards. My eyes forlornly scanned the skies for signs of daylight or a let up from the storm, worryingly finding neither.

Climbing slowly but steadily, it was impossible to get any accurate sense of what was ahead through the stygian murk and my rain lashed specs. Yet, there was nothing for it but to press on, to get my head down, keep on walking and hope for the best.

A little further up the mountain I came across a hand painted sign on the road, indicating that cyclists should carry on and for walkers to spur off left, and onto a trail which led immediately into a dense and gloomy forest. Entering a little tentatively into the tightly enclosed woodland, I trudged carefully along the narrowest of tracks, as yet barely discernable in the near darkness.

The path at this point was very rough and uneven, and would get much tougher as the climb progressed. I wound my way steadily up a narrow track which was steepening with every metre. It didn't seem to be getting any lighter either, and it was now way past 8.00am. Concentrating only on the trail under my feet, I had to carefully pick out every step on the increasingly rough, slippery and demanding terrain, with a plunging fall to my right waiting to catch me in its hungry maw should I falter.

The rigourousness of the climb was unrelenting and it ticked all the boxes: long, steep, difficult and uncompromising. I had received fair warning about the challenges on this section of the Camino, yet despite the difficulty, I was thoroughly enjoying the moment. It was such an exhilarating and very different experience than anything I had encountered on the trail thus far.

Pausing for a brief rest to catch my breath, I reminded myself that I was engaged on a climb of over 8 kilometres and as yet, I had completed only a third of that distance and only half the height. I gave myself a good talking to, gathered myself together and climbed on. It felt as if I was little more than inching my way up the slippery incline, perhaps a little over-cautiously, yet always aware and fearful of the consequences of crashing down that precarious mountainside.

After the longest while the rain began to ease a little. The lightning storm too seemed to be moving away and at last, daylight, if you could call it that, was fingering its way through the trees making it much easier to see. Edging slowly but surely out from the thickly wooded glades, the trail eventually began to open up a little, and I was at last able to make out the shapes of the surrounding mountains, albeit shrouded in cloud and mist.

Looking back down the mountain through the mizzle, I could just about discern the ghost of the trail descending to the valley from where I had started, appearing lonely and lost in the enveloping gloom.

It occurred to me then, that the previous evening my albergue was full and the one close by must have been too, given the number of people I saw milling about. All these folk must surely have been making the climb that morning, and yet I had seen only one other person; a fit young lad cloaked in a red cagoule who had swept past me a little further down the track. Where was everybody?

I imagined with growing horror, everyone else sat snug and dry back in the albergue, drinking warming brews and saying: "That peculiar wine drinking fellow hasn't gone up to O Cebreiro in this weather has he, especially without a decent dinner inside him? I did notice he'd managed to get hold of some batteries for his torch from somewhere though". Dear me, get a grip of yourself man.

Along with the improving daylight, the rain had now completely stopped and I could thankfully take off my waterproof. It got bloody hot wearing it especially when climbing, and you could get just as wet with perspiration as you would walking in the rain without it, despite the manufacturers extravagant claims of the jackets 'Breathability'. I bet they never check these things outside of the factory.

Although still overcast with a swirling mist clinging to the mountain, I could now at least begin to make some sense of the surrounding landscape, as its stark beauty was gradually uncloaked. In these conditions the panorama appeared almost unearthly, like a distant and lonely planet in a sci-fi movie.

Resuming the climb, I soon encountered the tiny mountainside *pueblo* of La Faba. Astonishingly, there appeared to be at least a couple of bars and an albergue in this remote little outpost. Its narrow streets were deserted at this early hour though; the only signs of life being of fleeting shadows flickering across the dimly lit windows of the hostel as I passed by. 'What a lonely and gloomy looking place' I mumbled to myself as I left the village behind, pressing desperately onwards and upwards in search of the distant summit. What a melancholy old git! I'm sure it all appears very different and lovely in the sunshine.

With no remission at all from the ruggedness of the ascent, an aching tiredness began to creep into my legs. Consulting my book of mantras for inspiration I scornfully cast aside any discomfort, calculating that at this point there was only another four or five kilometres to climb before reaching the top of the mountain. I reminded myself immediately, however, that even after reaching the summit at O Cebreiro, there was a lot more climbing to conquer before this day would be done. How splendid.

Ascending through the *pueblo* of La Laguna Castilla, with a surprisingly large albergue amidst its farmhouses and outbuildings, I pushed assiduously on. Every step was now a little agony; my legs were aching terribly and my pack felt like a small building pressing on my shoulders. I rounded an obtuse bend and with the summit now in sight, fantastic though mist enshrouded views of the Cordillera Cantábrica mountains began to open up as I climbed ever higher. As I slogged up the final slope to the top another milestone hove into view.

I approached with quickening steps, the embossed and heavily graffitied stone plinth that marked the crossing from the province of Castilla Y León, into that of Galicia.

I paused here for a much-needed breather, realising with great satisfaction that I had now entered the last province on the Camino. This was the region that held Santiago itself. In every sense, I was now on the last lap.

Later on with my maps, I was able to check back over the enormous span of Castilla y León I had just traversed, reflecting with a mixture of disbelief and amusement on the many little adventures and grueling moments I had encountered over its length. I was not the least surprised to realise it had taken me sixteen, unforgettable days to cross this vast region. Make no mistake; the remorselessness of the Castilian Plateau had been indelibly stamped on my mind. It had however and without a doubt, been an incredible experience.

I had just a short push along a section of man-made track to complete now. At last, and with enormous relief I stumbled into O Cebreiro; the small but famous *pueblo* straddling the high mountain peak.

This village was not only recognised for its presence on the Camino, but also for its anthropological and architectural heritage. A large part of the village had been restored and preserved, and in particular, the ancient and circular straw roofed '*Pallozas*' of inhabitant's centuries past. The combination of Camino and historic site had created an irresistible tourist magnet, and I had been warned it can get very busy in O Cebreiro. I have to say though, there was little evidence of any visitor frenzy on this cool, murky and misty morning, with just a few dozen people pottering around the streets all wrapped up against the elements.

You may recall from earlier in this narrative, Don Elias and his yellow arrows of the Camino? The Don was the parish priest of O Cebreiro at that time, and not only did he dedicate himself to renovating the trail and introducing his famous signage, he was also the leading light in raising funds for the restoration of O Cebreiro as a sight of historical interest, *and* the rejuvenation of the village as a viable place to live. Don Elias was a remarkable and dedicated man with tremendous foresight, rightly remembered and celebrated for his achievements.

My plan was to linger just long enough for some recuperative hot tea and to get off my feet for a while. With this in mind, I headed for a short break to a café/hotel on the edge of the village. Inside the hotel and lined up against a wall were a number of expensive looking suitcases and bags. They were all labelled up and along with their owners, I presumed, ready to be whisked away by luxury coach to the next destination on some posh and pampered tour or other. I could have vomited on the lot.

Feeling much revived although on slightly shaky legs I cracked on, realising of course, that there was still a good bit more climbing ahead. So, firmly grasping the nettle in one hand and my ever-ready bag of clichés in the other, I began the long walk towards Triacastela. This, I truly hoped, would be the final stage-post on my long Camino journey today.

Skirting the mist enshrouded albergue at the head of O Cebreiro I turned sharply upwards, and once more into another densely wooded stretch of the trail. Although incredibly high up, with the tumbling mountainsides of the Sierra do Rañadoiro on either side, I could actually see very little. The mist was reducing visibility to just 20 metres or so in places, with the clouds beneath me completely obscuring what I knew would be stunning views of the valleys below.

It was very frustrating and *so* disappointing, I knew I was missing out on something very special here. Happily though I did get some reward, with occasional and breath-taking glimpses of the panorama appearing through briefly parting cloud. In these instances, I was fortunately able to fast-draw my camera gunslinger style out of my pocket, to take a few unsteady photos of these fleeting, yet wonderful views. It would have to do I guess.

Although not as fierce as the climb up to O Cebreiro, this was still tough enough on my groaning legs as the trail fell and climbed, twisted and turned, testing both stamina and willpower. On through Linares, looking bleak and empty on this misty morning, I strove ever onwards over the undulating terrain; focused, determined and unwavering. At least that's what I wrote in my journal.

At the heights of Alto de Roque boasting 1250 metres, the ascent levelled off briefly for some welcome respite. By this time, I was really beginning to feel my limbs rebelling against the terrain, but grittily casting aside my discomfort I pressed on. Not much bloody choice really.

In spite of the difficulties of the trail, I was actually delighting in its demands. This was part of the reason I was on the Camino; to be challenged and to overcome, to be tested and to prevail. I know it was hurting now, but I also knew it would be worth it in the long run. I was conscious that each hard driven step and every milestone passed, was adding to a wonderful treasure trove of experiences and memories, which I would always be able to look back on with enormous pride and pleasure.

With the trail now firmly adhering to the side of the road, I paused for a moment to admire the famous bronze of St James, cast here as a lonely, stooped and windswept figure on this high open peak. It was a wonderful and evocative piece of art and on this particular day, very appropriate. With just a little more climbing to negotiate I gritted my teeth, and in the manner of that immutable statue, I bent into the mist for the last push. Resolve and fortitude alone it seemed, driving me on.

The little *pueblo* of Hospital de la Condesa stood at the foot of the last short but seriously steep segment of climb, and I had a little rest here in preparation for the final slog. Dragging on my pack, staggering under the effort, I set off up the precipitous and winding road that, please God, would deliver me to the end of the climbing. Well it was hellish! So acute was the path towards the summit, I was practically bending over, like a ski-jumper in mid-flight!

My calves were on fire burning with lactic acid. Sweat poured stingingly into my eyes. My heart was thumping crazily, until at last, I rounded the final sharp bend, and collapsed exhausted into a chair outside the bar atop Alto do Poio, perched giddily 1337 metres up in the clouds.

I had finally made it! And as drained as I felt, I was also incredibly exhilarated and tremendously proud of the effort I had put in so far today. From the lower reaches at Las Herrerias de Valcarce to this high pinnacle was a long and challenging climb, and had taken me five grueling hours to complete. Now having surmounted and conquered, I allowed myself a brief moment to wallow in the fantastic feeling of accomplishment that now swept over me, and what a sensation that was. Nice one son. I think I deserve a sweetie from the tin after that, don't you?

I sat for a while enjoying a well-earned rest; refueling with a pot of green tea and a couple of bananas, relishing the thought that it was to be all downhill walking for the remainder of the day. I was also aware, however, that I still had around 14 kilometres of hiking to complete on very weary legs. It was I thought, going to be a long afternoon. Best get on wi' it then owd lad.

Feeling much better after a break and some food, I picked up the trail once more. It was a massive relief to have that great climb behind me, and I lumbered down the gently shelving slope and away from the peak with a little spring in my step. It was much easier going too, with the footpath now clinging tightly to the winding contours of the LU-633 highway.

In this way then, I began the long descent to Triacastela. The Camino now led me through many small and ancient farmsteads, each boasting herds of magnificent Galician cattle disporting their distinctive bronze-blond colouring and large horns.

It was amazing how the scenery seemed to have changed so quickly too, in crossing from one region to another. The day's preceding, had been mainly spent toiling in the vast openness of the Castilian plateau. Yet here I was now, as swiftly as stepping from one room to another it seemed, in the hills and valleys of rich, green and fertile Galicia. It was wonderfully soft and welcoming, and very pleasing to the eye too.

The trail regularly passed straight through the middle of farmyards and I always felt as if I was trespassing, yet nobody batted an eye as I sauntered through. Some of these farms looked as if unchanged for centuries; the stone lintel of one barn sporting the chiseled-on date of 1666. So long ago, it might have been etched during the very time London burned and Sir Christopher Wren sharpened his quills, imagining a new city out of the flames.

After all that elaborate prose, I bet somebody writes in to tell me it was all bollocks. The carving was just shorthand for 1st June 1966. I really should check these things you know.

The villages of Fonfría and O Biduedo quickly came and went, the trail falling a little more steeply now as the kilometres clicked by. I was almost in a trance by this time; unblinking eyes fixed on some blurred and distant point, awoken to my surroundings only as I passed through a farm or cluster of houses. My legs were working on autopilot too, crying out for relief, whilst at the other end my mouth was crying out for cold beer. Heeelp!

Still chasing the long climb down, the road continued to follow the undulations and twists and turns of the valley, with distant farms popping up here and there like little models spread over the sparsely wooded hillsides.

Passing under the peaks of the Serra do Oribio and towards Fillobal, a check of my map revealed just another 4 or 5 kilometres of hiking ahead, so I set myself resolutely for the last push.

The descent had become very steep now as it tumbled freely down the slope. Upon reaching the village of Ramil I stopped for a moment to look down the valley, catching a momentary glimpse of Triacastela, weakly lit in a twinkling of pale sunlight. It was *the* most wonderful and welcoming sight.

With the end now close, I felt infused with a final shot of vigour as I set off to complete the last couple of kilometres. I was completely hollowed out though, and fighting back tears of weariness, gratitude and relief as I finally reached the town marker of Triacastela. I wobbled down the last few metres along the main road into the town, spotting the municipal albergue sat just a few paces across the field to my left.

There was no holding me back as I let out a triumphant yell of 'yeeeeees!' to an audience of none. I couldn't have cared less, I'd bloody well cracked it.

Built from stone in two separate sections, the 'Albergue de la Xunta de Galicia' was a squat, modernish and fairly austere looking building (two buildings to be precise) but to me it had all the attributes of a palace as I checked in and collapsed on my bunk. I was completely and utterly shattered; but at the same time, absolutely buzzing with the achievements of this most memorable of days. The next trick of course, was not to lapse into unconsciousness before I had a celebratory pint - or several.

It was an effort of will to get freshened up and changed, thankful that it was just a short walk back across the field and to a bar by the side of the road opposite. It was now after 5.00pm, and today I had climbed and hiked and toiled for 10 hours, and all my desires were now firmly focused on beer, food and wine. Thankfully and with great gusto, I was able to find all three in this nice, friendly little bar, with the first exquisitely cold and sparkling lager disappearing without touching the sides.

I Sat outside to begin with. But the returning rain, quite heavy by this point, soon forced everyone indoors. The awnings over the tables performed better as shower heads than they did protection from the rain, so full of holes were they!

Generously sated with bacon, egg and chips Spanish style, sipping luxuriously on red wine, I looked back, brimming with satisfaction and contentment on the day just passed, and what a day it had been. Of the many great experiences I have had down the years walking and climbing, especially in my beloved Peak District, none had come close to giving me such elation and sense of fulfilment as this. As tough and demanding as it had been, weirdly, I was almost sorry it was now behind me. I had read other people's accounts of their expeditions up, over and beyond O Cebreiro and now having experienced it myself, I felt as if I could honourably join their club, happy and incredibly proud of my achievements.

It was a day that will live long in the memory. An unquestionable test of willpower and determination. An unforgiving examination of my mental and physical strength and endurance. I think it is safe to say, I discovered a little bit more about myself in those mountains that day.

A little drunk on wine and high on emotion, it was with a bit of a stagger that I headed back across the now darkened field to the albergue.

I found I had acquired three roommates in my absence but they were all out somewhere, still partying I had no doubt and good look with that. It was all I could do to take my clothes off! The burden of the day had finally won over, pressing me without resistance towards dark, delicious oblivion.

Distance walked today – 32 kilometres (615)

TWENTY SIX

Triacastela

to

Barbadelo

D espite the previous day's exertions I was, surprisingly enough, wide awake before 6.00am. The three young Spanish lads who had made up our small room of four were already up and about, quietly packing in torchlight and almost good to leave.

I heard nowt when they came in last night! If they had been a performing *mariachi* band, they still wouldn't have penetrated the depths of my unconsciousness. Feeling remarkably and unexpectedly fresh, no aches or pains beyond the usual, I assembled my kit and ambled across the field for some morning tea and to await a bit of daylight.

Today I was for Sarria, and at only 18 kilometres a stroll compared to yesterday. Dependent on how I felt as the day progressed, I would even consider pressing on a bit further.

With the first feathers of light tickling the dark belly of the night sky, I got under way on the serpentine road out of Triacastela. At the head of the village stood one of those occasional intersections on the Camino where you are offered a choice of trail for a while. I had already decided earlier that I would opt for the northern route. Although this involved some additional hillwalking it was about 8 kilometres shorter, and I was very certain that after the previous days toil, I would rather take on the climbing than the extra distance.

I crossed the main road rejoining the gravel path, and was immediately presented with a solid looking climb. The unshakeable rule of the Camino is: when you go up, you come down and vice versa; so I began the ascent up the opposite side of the valley I had staggered down yesterday.

A mixture of rough cobbles and gravel lay underfoot as the trail rose upwards into the growing daylight, tinged at its edge with ominously grey clouds drawing in from the Atlantic. This exacting climb over a distance of 3.5 kilometres and 230 metres in height was a real wake-me-up, and I was already sweating and puffing as I clambered through the seemingly deserted *pueblo* of A Balsa. The path steepened still further as I scrambled up to the peak at San Xil, before finally topping out at Alto de Riocabo at over 900 meters, and the grateful opportunity to take a moment to let my pumping heart settle.

From Riocabo, the trail meandered its way through broad high meadowland and open pathways. It had the uncanny look and feel of being in the Derbyshire Peaks and Dales, but without the sheep! It was absolutely beautiful. Compelling reminders of my oft' walked Wye Valley, Cheedale, Monsal Dale and Dovedale lay all around, and with the weather mild rather than hot, there was a real 'at home' feel to the walk. No chance of a decent pint of Best Bitter, alas.

Just a little note. In crossing into Galicia, not only the scenery changed but the language too. *Galego* is the tongue and dialect of this hilly region, and the *'El* and *La* and *Los'* etc. prevalent in the eastern provinces, would be exchanged by the prefixes of *'O* and *A* and *As '* etc. Galicia borders Portugal and *Galego* probably has more affinity to Portuguese than it does to popular Spanish, but I won't complicate matters further.

From Alto de Riocabo the Camino began to descend, gently at first, then becoming steeper and steeper until at times, I was almost jogging along. I wandered easily through a succession of farm villages, with the tangy whiff of cow shit persistently permeating the air. It was lovely to see the numerous herds of noble looking Galician cattle grazing lazily in the sun.

Mostly made up of small herds, although there were some larger ones too, these beasts were completely impervious to my presence as I marched on down the winding path through Montán and Fontearcuda. Here, the trail veered off onto a quiet tarmac road that continued on comfortably and uneventfully for the next 3k or so into Furela.

I paused here for a short rest and to check my map, realising cheerfully that once again I had made great time. Keen to cash in on my good progress, I quickly knocked off the 5 kilometres of twisting road through Pintín and Calvor, with just a short walk of little over an hour down the slope seeing me safely into Sarria.

From the heights overlooking the area where I now stood, Sarria appeared to be quite a large town, bigger than I expected in any case. This was my original destination on setting out this morning, the exertions of the previous day no doubt framing my thinking. It was however, not much past 11.30am, and I had completed the 18k to get here from Triacastela in quick order and with little difficulty.

Feeling certain that I should push on, I perused the map and thought Barbadelo would be a better-looking end to my walking day. I could be there in around two hours, still giving myself the opportunity for a good rest in the afternoon.

Whilst passing through Sarria, I thought I would take the opportunity to top up my wallet and purchase drinks and snacks. After leaving a small supermarket I must have taken a wrong turn and completely lost my bearings. I couldn't spot any Camino markers to put me back on track either. I followed a few likely looking streets, feeling certain I would stumble across some sign or other, when rather surprisingly, I heard someone call out my name.

Looking up the street I saw Berndt, the German chap I had shared a room with back at Castrojeriz, grinning and waving excitedly. We greeted each other warmly and he introduced me to the guy accompanying him. This was Rory; a gigantic Australian and fellow traveler with whom Berndt had recently teamed up with. Rory was well over six and a half feet tall and built like a house. He had the crooked nose and crushed ears that immediately marked him out as a Rugby or Aussie rules football player, and he had aggression written all over him.

Berndt told me, rather seriously, that they were both out shopping for new hiking boots. It transpired that at some point during the night, somebody had stolen their boots from the albergue they had stayed in the previous evening. Enquiries revealed no one else had been robbed of their footwear; just these two. This felt like a strange and unlikely occurrence to me. I asked if either of them had had a fall out with anybody? Berndt said absolutely not, Rory offered a rather less convincing "Well, not recently".

From my first meeting with Berndt in Castrojeriz, I got the impression he was a quiet and reserved kind of guy, and not likely to attract trouble. Within one minute of meeting the Aussie however, I could sniff danger and mischief leaking out of him; he just looked and felt to me to be a nasty piece of work and a magnet for grief. You know how sometimes, you can just sense these things?

As we were talking Rory slipped off into a nearby shop. I quickly took Berndt to one side and told him in the strongest terms (his English was superb) to drop his new friend as fast as he could and push on alone. I stressed to him that I felt certain that this Aussie monster was up to no good, and would bring him nothing but trouble.

With the colour visibly draining from his face, he nodded and said, "I think you may be right, but first I need to get back the 200 euros I have lent him to buy new boots" What??!! I was incredulous. Was this the story? Stunned at his announcement, I advised him to find the nearest police station and get some help immediately.

I didn't think I could be any further use to Berndt, and I definitely had no intention of mixing any poisons with the antipodean colossus on his behalf.

I left the two of them negotiating the next stage of their intrigue, feeling pretty bad about leaving a clearly naïve Berndt in the grasping clutches of the brute. I hope it all turned out ok for my German friend. I often think about that incident and wonder if I should have handled it differently? Still, there it is.

After all that palaver, I was still no nearer to finding my way back onto the trail. Distracted and a little upset by this unexpected drama, it took me several more minutes before, thankfully, I stumbled across a big fat yellow arrow daubed on the side of a building. With a twinge of guilt still nibbling away at me, and feeling the prescient words of Mario's T-shirt weighing heavily across my own chest, I gratefully returned to the comfort and familiarity of the Camino.

I was met immediately by a steep climb as I trudged my way out of Sarria, and I felt myself bending rather reluctantly into the ascent; still disturbed a little by thoughts of Berndt and his plight.

Predictably I guess, I soon began to feel the effects of yesterday's efforts re-visiting my legs, my pack too seemed to be weighing heavier than it had for a while and I looked back longingly at a fast disappearing Sarria, with its welcoming bars and soft beds. Ah well.

Striding on regardless, the trail continued its steep climb through thick pine forests, and along a stretch of track that was being improved and widened as I walked up it. To my delight, the ground workers on the job all paused from their labours to encourage me with a wave and a cheery 'Bon Camino' as I passed by. How nice was that? Eventually, the top of the climb gave out onto a broad valley, very high up, with small and distant looking farms scattered along both its sides. The dirt track eventually merged on to a paved road that threaded its way through the tiny hamlets of As Paredes and Vilei. This last village had a small general store and a modern, smart looking albergue and I was very tempted by it. With only a short distance to travel however, I bypassed this hostel and continued on down the narrow lane, arriving shortly after at the little *pueblo* of Barbadelo. I immediately spotted my albergue laying just off the trail to the left, sailing on a sea of green in the middle of a large, grassy meadow. Excellent.

I had arrived, with perfect timing I thought, just before the albergues appointed opening of 1.30pm. Meantime, I gratefully kicked off my boots, plonking myself under the cool shade of a veranda on the patio. There and to my delight, I spotted a glass-fronted fridge full of cold beers, superb. My joy was short lived however; the fridge was cruelly padlocked and guarded against my perspiring brow and trembling fingers.

1.30pm arrived along with a couple of young girl hikers, and I explained they would have to wait with me for the still absent manager to show himself. It transpired the three of us would be the only occupants here this evening.

2.00pm was approaching and still no sign of any one in charge. Feeling a need for action, I picked up a leaflet from a bundle by the doorway displaying the albergue phone number and gave it a call. In my best Spanish, I announced on pick-up that there were pilgrims awaiting; tired, hot and thirsty, heavily emphasising the thirsty bit. *'Tengo muy,muy sed!'*. The chap on the other end apologised loudly and profusely, he had fallen asleep! Easy enough to do in this quiet little spot I guess, and after all, it was siesta time.

The albergue 'O Pombal' as I have indicated, stood alone in the middle of a large green field, and was clearly a later addition to the much older farmhouse it adjoined. It was quite small; room for about sixteen in the dormitory and as always, smartly fitted out and comfortable. There was just the one downside; this hostel was equipped with just a single, communal shower/toilet. Luckily, with just the three of us occupying the bunk room tonight, that wouldn't be much of a problem. I bet there were a few crossed legs when the place was busy though.

Quickly refurbished, I treated myself to a couple of cans of the aforementioned and now liberated cold beers, finding a nice quiet spot in the spacious garden in which to enjoy them. I started with good intentions on updating my journal; I had nodded off before finishing the first sentence!

There was absolutely nothing to see in this tiny hamlet, apart from a very old and architecturally interesting looking church. Even as I entered the church yard, I had already convinced myself it would be closed. It was.

Remembering the albergue a couple of kilometres back down the way at Vilei, I strolled in the face of a strengthening breeze to check it out for dining potential later. Who knows, perhaps I might have a beer or two whilst there?

This venue turned out to be more of a motel/restaurant than a regular albergue, and it was a very nice set up indeed. I sat relaxing for a while on the patio refreshing beer to hand, happy and content and bugger all else to worry about. Lovely.

The earlier breeze had by now intensified into a very strong and chilly wind, the heat of the sun *just* about keeping it bearable. In no particular hurry I lingered for a while watching the place get busier and busier, and wishing I had checked in here instead of my quiet little albergue. It was no big deal really I guess, I would only be eating and sleeping wherever I lay my hat tonight.

It was amazing really, how in just a few short weeks on *The Way*, my needs and requirements had been stripped down to the basics. On arriving at my overnight halts, there was little fussing or faffing about which hostel to stay in, or where to eat etc. My routine was simply to find my albergue, clean up, see off a few cold beers, check out the local places of interest, eat, drink a bit more maybe, then climb into my bunk and collapse into unconsciousness.

It was warmly satisfying and very comforting to live this little life with its generally unchanging routine, cocooned in the safety of the Camino. I knew the real world was encamped on the outside of my current little world, watching and waiting to kick down the doors as soon as my journey ended. For now though, it would just have to wait. Reality? Never heard of it man!

I returned to my albergue feeling much better after a couple of restorative beers, deciding to extend my R&R with a late afternoon siesta in the quiet, empty dormitory. It was just the ticket.

Feeling quite refreshed and relaxed after my snooze and with nowhere else to go, I ambled my way back to the albergue at Vilei. There, and in the by now very busy restaurant, I enjoyed a substantial and tasty dinner of soup, pasta and dessert. It was grand. My lovely young *mesera* insisted, *insisted* I tell you! I should help the food along with a generous carafe of red wine. Like all good boys, I did as I was told.

By the time I left it was almost dark. Making my way back down the eerily quiet lanes to the hostel, a grey mist was already settling on the surrounding fields, soon obliterating any lingering daylight. My last thoughts before passing out were that all being well, it should be just six more days before I reached Santiago. Should I hug myself again? No, I'll keep it in reserve for a more auspicious, hug-worthy occasion!

Distance walked today – 26 Kilometres (642)

TWENTY SEVEN

Barbadelo

to

Portomarin

I was gently wakened at 6.00am by the shuffling, whispers and giggles of my two young roommates as they prepared to leave. Smiling to myself at their school girlish antics, I thought under what other circumstances would it be acceptable for a 60-year-old bloke to share a room, unchaperoned, with two 19-year-old girls *and* without causing raised eyebrows? Nothing else was raised either, I can assure you of *that*! It was all an unfortunate mix up in that little shower room, honestly. The Constable was very understanding too, after a small donation to the Police Station Christmas party fund.

The Camino is a great neutraliser in this respect. People of both (or more?) sexes and all ages, shapes, sizes and persuasions, living amongst each other night after night, all showing the greatest of respect and consideration for each other. Not once, had I witnessed any unpleasantness or uncomfortableness, or heard any reports of unacceptable behavior. This was indeed, true to the spirit of the Camino. Conduct outside of the hostels however was, shall I say, a little less honorable, with lots of desperate snogging and shagging occurring all over the place. And why not?

I lay for a while wrapped in my thoughts, nice and cozy under the blankets on what felt like a cool morning. There was no rush to be away too early.

The small town of Portomarín would be my destination today. Due to the extra kilometres I had completed the previous afternoon I had only around 18k left to walk, and I knew I could polish that off easily enough by early afternoon.

It felt strange getting my stuff together in a deserted albergue, with not a sound or person disturbing me as I stepped out into the early morning emptiness. I crossed over the dew-drenched grass of the meadow and was back on the trail at first light. My earlier suspicions were confirmed; it definitely was on the chilly side, a crop of goose bumps prickling my arms in confirmation. The surrounding fields and the valleys below were still shrouded in a thick mist, but I knew from the experience of recent days that it would soon burn off as the sun got to work on it.

Climbing out from the village, the trail continued to rise steadily but not too severely, and would follow the untroubling contours of the gently undulating hills ahead for the next 9 or 10 kilometres.

This really was the most exquisite of walks. The morning had turned into a beauty under azure and cloudless skies, but as yet thankfully, not too hot. The surrounding countryside was once again so reminiscent of my home county, as the trail weaved effortlessly through stone walled meadowlands and steep hills of the lushest greenness. It really was a perfect, pastoral picture.

The wonderfully docile Galician cattle were scattered throughout the fields. Some were dreamily chewing cud, ears twitching and tails whisking frenziedly at the ever-present swarms of flies. Others stood patiently at farm gates, awaiting their turn for morning milking. It was a complete joy to the eye; and after the initial climb it was easy enough hiking too.

Incidentally, what *do* flies see as attractive in a cow's arsehole? Particularly if whilst dining there they might get a good swatting. More so, when there are thousands of gallons of cow shit just lying around in fields to feast upon unmolested? Just mental. Still, good luck to them, they don't have much of a life do they? And as somebody once wisely said: 'It's ok to put zips on bananas, but it's cruel to sew buttons on flies'. So profound.

In regulation file I passed, replete with the joys of the morning, through sundry small villages and tiny hamlets. It was astonishing really given their size, that many of these tiny *aldeas* hosted a little bar and even a hostel. Villages such as Rente, Peruscallo and Belante, all came and went in quick order, some taking no more than a few strides to pass through.

At A Brea, I came across the esteemed Camino way marker indicating 100k to Santiago. With due deference to its importance, graffiti had been scrawled over every square inch and it was piled high with little stones. Not wishing to be disrespectful to this fine monument, I ceremoniously and solemnly added to the stone pile, but not of course, the graffiti. I didn't have a marker pen. And as a welcome bonus, I managed to stay on my feet!

Next along came Morgade and Ferreiros. Although both hamlets had bars and albergues, neither consisted of much more than narrow tracks through farm buildings and small cottages. Neither the cattle, dogs or farmers, nor the very few villagers I saw along the way, seemed remotely interested as I passed through. Quite right too.

I pressed on smartly through As Rozas and then on to Laxe, with the trail continuing its slow descent, twisting this way and that, quickening and become steeper as it went along. After a while and still very high up around Vilachá, I spotted the lustrous white buildings of Portomarín a few kilometers ahead, gleaming in the sunlight and overlooking a large stretch of water. From this viewpoint, it looked for all the world like a Mediterranean coastal scene.

Resuming its downward slope, the pathway opened up to give a broader view of the town; straddling the Río Miño and butting up against the huge Belezar reservoir. The bulk of Portomarín sat high on the west side of the valley, queening it over the surrounding tiny hamlets and the blue waters stretching out beneath it.

I made my way down the final metres of the hill, before crossing a long and very high bridge over the river. I have to say I felt a bit queasy on the traverse, and I had to stop myself from looking over the sides for fear of falling over! It was a most peculiar sensation, and I was very pleased to get to the opposite bank and into the main part of the town.

Following a walk up the steep hill into the centre, a helpful young lad pointed me in the right direction and I soon found the as yet to open municipal albergue. As I got closer, I could make out a neat chain of unattended rucksacks lined up on the patio. Clearly, I wasn't the first pilgrim in town today.

Needing to kill almost an hour before the albergue opened, I added my own pack to the collection and had a gentle stroll round the very pleasant looking town centre.

In a moment of rare and surprising abstinence I resisted temptation, deciding I would wait until I had cleaned up later before enjoying my customary, end-of-walk beer. This certainly was a surprise decision. I had neither discussed nor agreed this with myself at all! I really hoped I wasn't sickening for something again.

It wasn't long however before I became bored and restless so I decided to chance my luck, returning to the albergue a good half hour before its scheduled opening time. My luck was in! My arrival happily coincided with that of the albergue Hospitalier, and she was more than happy to sign me in ahead of the other still absent rucksack owners. Result.

This hostel was quite large and of a modern design and construction. Inside it was bright and spacious with very high ceilings. The ground floor comprised of a large kitchen and a capacious and comfortable communal area, the upper floor being made up of large, roomy dormitories and excellent shower rooms. It was a very nice place indeed, but I felt almost like an intruder as I settled myself in completely alone.

I was showered, changed and heading back out, just as a steady line was forming at the reception desk. The wide grin on my face hid nothing, as I smugly strode past the long queue and out into the hot afternoon sunshine.

I had hoped I would be able to connect up with the Alex, Alfredo and Fernando today, not least so we could stay in touch for the last few days of the Camino into Santiago. We had somehow gotten out of sync walking wise a few days ago and I was missing their easy-going company. I thought it would be nice if at the very least, we could walk the last day together. I was sure I could manage their more leisurely pace for a few hours!

Portomarín was a very nice-looking town. It snaked principally up one side of the steep valley and onto a pleasing little plaza, at the centre of which was an ancient church encompassed by municipal offices and a sprinkling of bars and shops. It was all extremely attractive and very bright too, as most of the buildings were either painted or clad in white or cream.

After perusing the notice boards detailing the towns history and its more prominent features, I discovered that the burg I was now standing in was relatively new. The old town further below, I read, had been swallowed whole by the new reservoir constructed in the early 1960s. Apparently, when the water level is low, the skeletons of the old town's buildings and the remains of the original Roman bridge, can still be seen.

Photographs of the old town, pre its own Noachian flood as it were, showed itself to be a very different kind of place, ramshackle and ancient. The new town seemed to be a significant upgrade; or at least, so it is said.

Several of the more important buildings were painstakingly dismantled and re-built higher up in the new development, the most impressive of these being the large church of San Nicolás which dominated the central plaza. Originally built in the 13th century and with some fine interior features, the entire church down to its minutest decoration was moved and reconstructed on its present site, looking now as if it had never existed anywhere else. An excellent piece of engineering.

Portomarín had a bit of a resort feel to it I suppose, sat on the edge of this large body of water; encouraged in this by the usual suspects of bars and souvenir shops that lined the streets. For me though it soon ran out of steam, and I was glad that I only had one night here, pleasant enough though it was.

With the evening stealing in I was beginning to tire and felt ready to call it a day, but first I needed to get a bite to eat before heading back to the hostel. From one of several small supermarkets in the vicinity, I bought some fixings for a little picnic to enjoy in a small park next to the albergue. Washed down with a couple of cold beers, it was spot on. I sat lazing for a while under the shade of a tree in the hot evening sunshine, with the humming of insects and rustle of trees providing a soft, lulling somnolence. Will somebody turn the lights out please?

Disappointingly, it seemed I had missed the Mexicans again. There was no sign of them anywhere; neither in the town or in any of the other albergues, and I had not seen anyone of a mutual acquaintance I could ask. A bit of a shame, but never mind, I was sure I would catch up with them soon enough.

After finishing up my little picnic, I felt no inclination to stretch my day out any longer. I felt so tired, and I really just wanted to lie down.

I had found I had become something of an accomplished expert at lying down. Good practice I suppose, for the eternal one waiting for me somewhere down the road. Not just yet though, please!

Distance walked today – 19 Kilometres (661)

TWENTY EIGHT

Portomarin

to

Palas de Rei

This morning I am happy to report, that despite an uninterupted nights practice at lying down, I am not dead. Thus encouraged, I was away from the hostel and trekking by 7.00am.

Although still fully dark, the first half hour or so of today's walk would be along lamp lit roads, so I was happy to wave my 'no walking in the dark' rule. On this particular morning, I set off in the company of quite a few other lone walkers and small groups all merging from different parts of the town, their numerous torches picking out the trail through the darkness. This was easily the most people I had seen on the Camino on any morning so far, clear evidence of the impact of those pilgrims beginning their journey in Sarria.

Sarria is a little over 100 kilometers from Santiago, and is very popular with pilgrims who wish to walk the Camino for just a few days. The Sarria/100k combination is easily explained. In order to receive a *'Compostela'*, the official certificate issued by the St. James cathedral authority confirming a successful completion of the Camino, you must achieve *and* prove, one of the following:-

That you have walked the length of any of the various Caminos, (as I have been doing, along the Camino Francés) and have collected the necessary number of official stamps in your Camino Passport or *Credencia*, certifying your progress along the route. You need a minimum of one stamp a day; easily available from the countless albergues, churches, points of interest and tourist offices etc. which can be found all along the Camino.

Or, that you have cycled the entire length of the official Camino cycling route, and have similarly collected your 'Passport' stamps as per walking pilgrims.

The cathedral authorities also allow the issuing of a special *'Compostela'*, if you have either completed at least 100 kilometers walking the Camino, or a minimum of 200 kilometers cycling. In either of these cases, you must collect at least 2 stamps per day, certifying your progress.

As Sarria is the first major town closest to the 100k minimum, it is the natural starting point for most pilgrims wishing to walk this section. This not only accounts for Sarrias popularity, but also meant for me of course, that the trail would undoubtably be a lot busier on this last leg of the journey.

Incidentally, to receive your '*Compostela*', it isn't necessary to complete your pilgrimage in one go. It is perfectly acceptable to take as long as you like, and return as many times as you like to the Camino. Thousands of pilgrims down the years have done just this; devoting say, a week or so each year to undertake a section of the Camino, then returning in future years to complete more sections, slowly piecing them together until they have accomplished the entire route. As long as you get your Camino 'Passport' stamped to prove your progress, you can proudly collect your '*Compostela*' no matter how long you have taken, or how many visits you have made. An excellent scheme if you ask me; but of course, nobody did.

After a short walk through the darkened, sleepy streets a dirt path emerged, immediately setting my fellows and I off on yet another early morning climb and up to the peak of Monte Torros. The path rose steadily into a rather thick fog, it's cloying fingers pressing damp on my face and beard, it was quite cool with it too. It was difficult at first to form an impression of where I actually was, as the track was also enclosed by thick stands of pine trees offering only occasional glimpses of the surrounding countryside.

The murkiness stayed close and heavy as the trail continued its ascent, eventually merging onto tarmac to become part of the main LU-663 road itself. By 8.30am, the fog was beginning to clear as the sun burned its way through, but it would linger long into the morning in the valleys below. Galicia I knew, is famous for its fogs, and I would certainly see why over the coming days.

Still climbing steadily I passed quickly through the quiet little *pueblo* of Gonzar, with the trail in due course easing onto a wide expanse of moorland above Castromaior, and it was here I took the opportunity for a short break. From this high point, I had spectacular views of mountains disappearing into the distance, the peaks of the nearer range appearing to hover over the fog filled valleys below. A young South Korean lad nearby was busy with his expensive looking camera, snapping off more shots of this terrain than I think I had on the entire journey. Easy enough to do now in this digital age I suppose, not having to fork out for expensive rolls of film.

Upon rejoining the road, and passing fleetingly through the many tiny hamlets populating this part of the Camino, I became aware of quite a number of dairy production units established along the highway. Some of these appeared to be quite large operations, with yards full of milk tankers festooned with corporate livery announcing their importance. Onwards and steadily upwards, the trail crested at Ventas de Narón, affording stunning views of the surrounding peaks of the Serra de Ligonde and beyond. The fog was still unmoving in the valleys below; perpetuating the strange, floating effect of mountain tops adrift on seas of mist.

Now began a fairly steep descent of around 4k, with occasional sharp little climbs to negotiate here and there to keep me on my toes. Feeling in good form I marched steadily on, passing swiftly through the village of Ligonde and several other little outposts along this busy part of the Camino. Airexe, Portos and Lestedo being the liveliest amongst them. A steady climb of a couple of kilometres up to Abenostre, and the sizeable looking town of Palas de Rei appeared on the slopes below. It was a very nice feeling indeed, to be closing in on the end of my days walking so soon.

As I had once again employed my early-morning-burst tactic, I had eaten up a sizeable chunk of the 25k scheduled for today by mid-morning. It was a leisurely walk therefore, that took me down the final slopes into the town, and on what had eventually turned into quite a hot day. On my way down, I paused briefly to have a look at the tiny *aldea* of O Rosario; a traditional halt prior to entering Palas.

Closing in on the town centre, I spotted a sizeable queue forming outside the large municipal albergue so I gave that a miss; as I did another nearby which appeared equally as busy. There were plenty of pilgrims in town already it seemed, and it was still relatively early in the day. More evidence of the Sarria effect, I thought. I really hoped I wasn't going to have problems finding a place to rest up. Memories of my struggles in Burgos were still fresh, and I didn't relish the prospect of having to move on to the next town in search of accommodation.

I crossed over the main street heading towards the edge of town, instinctively following a sign posted for an out of the way albergue. An inspired decision as it turned out. A few more minutes down the quiet back lanes, and in the middle of a spread of small allotments I found the hostel; a small barn conversion it appeared, and just a few minutes shy of its posted opening time.

In tried and trusted fashion, I kicked off my boots and sat relaxing on a bench for a while in the hot sunshine, lazily surveying the surrounding orchards and fields. Directly opposite, was one of the largest *hórreos* I had seen. I had occasionally spotted these odd looking structures on the cereal planes of Castilla Y León, but here in Galicia they were everywhere. These small buildings, usually supported on sturdy pillars or some other way raised off the ground, were long and narrow and usually built from stone or wood, or a combination of both. Most often, they were topped by a cross or other religious symbol and looked for all the world like a place one might place a coffin, or even several coffins. Surely not, at least not these days? No need to worry, my enquiries had revealed them to be food granaries; where harvested grain, fruit and vegetables could be stored away from pests and out of the sun. These simple but effective little barns, had been an important part of farm life in Galicia since the middle ages.

I had, yet again, nodded off! Dreams of fruit eating, skeletal corpses staggering from *hórreos* were flicking across my eyes, when I was suddenly awakened by the banging of the door next to me. A shiny bald head sporting a wide grin poked out of the doorway. This head was happily and firmly attached to the ample torso of my host for the evening; and now complete with legs, he emerged whole to offer me a warm welcome inside.

The albergue 'A Casina de Marcello' was a lovely little place. It consisted of accommodation for twenty or so in a neat dormitory upstairs, and a small farmhouse style kitchen and dining area below. It had a real homely feel to it, and I liked it very much. Marcello, the Italian owner of both the bald pate and the albergue, gave me a quick tour round.

Marcello was an interesting and amusing chap, with just the right amount of English and Spanish to enable us to have a good chat. Following the formalities, I completed my ablutions and headed back into the town. Prior to leaving, and having been convinced by Marcello's own description of his culinary skills, I reserved my dinner at the albergue and the promise of a home cooked Italian meal. It all sounded very appetising.

On first viewing, the centre of Palas de Rei didn't seem to be particularly impressive. It felt bereft of atmosphere to me, absent of any real substance and character. There was no grand plaza or central feature to admire, no tree lined walkways or leafy parks, nothing much at all really. It appeared to be just a warren of odd-looking streets, crammed with the usual small-town fare of bars, restaurants and souvenir shops; none of which held any great draw for me.

There *was* a square as such I suppose, straddling the main road with a loose arrangement of canopied shops and bars around it, but it was hardly impressive. Its principle feature was a 19th century period style Town Hall, unaccompanied by anything else noteworthy I'm afraid.

Before I am vilified for this less than gushing description of *my* brief impressions of the town, I will at say at once that I had read in brochures of the region, that there was much to admire in the vicinity of Palas, its origin dating back to Roman times. There appeared to be several historic churches, houses and castles in the surrounding area; the town having a military and strategic provenance, as well as one of some clearly long gone wealth. It all sounded very interesting and appealing, and in other circumstances I would have beaten a path to its various glittering doors. Just at that moment however, I had neither the time nor energy to drag myself around those interesting and noble buildings. My apologies, Palas de Rei.

One circuit of the town centre proved enough, and anyway, my feet were demanding a rest. I picked out one of the nicer looking bars opposite the town hall, sitting outside in the company of half a dozen of the local 'old boys'. These characters were all smoking away like chimneys, and shouting animatedly whilst waiting for their turn at the card school inside.

God knows what they were chattering about, their thick Galego accent made it impossible for me to follow; but it involved lots of arm waving, finger pointing and banging of tables. It was great fun to watch; and as one old party left to take his turn at cards to be replaced by a grumpy loser, the volume and excitement seemed to go up a notch as the vanquished poured out his sorry tale. It was absolutely brilliant, I could have happily sat and looked on for hours.

At some point during this engaging little rigmarole, an elderly looking couple arrived, joining me at my table. Ron and Joan were a husband and wife from Australia, though they were very keen to impress upon me that they had both been born in England. They were clearly very chuffed in relating to me that they were on their 6th week on the Camino, having walked all the way from France.

Sensibly, they too like my French friend from El Burgo Ranero, were having their packs road shipped between albergues, but they had walked every mile from St Jean-Pied-de-Port, and would continue to do so on to Santiago. Ron was 75, Joan was 73 and deaf as a post! It was like speaking through an interpreter, as the old girl was brilliant at reading her husband's lips, but useless at reading others. It all made for an eccentric, but very entertaining interlude.

What a lovely, interesting couple they were, and I enjoyed listening to them proudly boasting about their family and the life they had built in Australia; not without difficulty at times too, it seemed. After a while, a taxi arrived to take them to their accommodation just outside of the town. What tremendous characters there are to be found on the Camino, and those two were certainly amongst them. Bon Camino and good luck to them, I do hope they made it to Santiago safely.

Keeping my eye on the time and very much looking forward to my Italian dinner, I sat for a while longer in the pleasant evening sunshine, letting my mind wander and my thoughts drift. I was very conscious by this point, that I was fast closing in on Santiago and that this great journey would shortly end. There were many things I would have to consider in the coming days; not only concerning the immediate post-pilgrimage period, but also the days and weeks following.

I knew I had decisions to make regarding my situation at home, which could best described as 'fluid' and needn't burden the pages of this narrative. The problem was that I just couldn't escape the 'here and now'. I was so wrapped up in my Camino experience, that I seemed to have closed off all doors to the real world, if I can put it that way. I had found such solace and freedom during my time out here in this great wilderness, that I had developed a physical reluctance to face the realities of life at home. I found I was clinging, almost desperately, to the ridiculous notion that I could just carry on living in this bubble. Well, why the hell not?

I had recently read an account of a guy who had set out on a Camino pilgrimage a few years ago, and at its completion decided that wasn't enough, continuing his journey by walking from Santiago to Rome. On reaching Rome he felt he still had unfinished business, and off he went on an extended tour that took him far and wide, in search of whatever it was he was looking for. He may be still travelling; it would be nice to think so.

Yes, I thought, that would do for me! A never ending journey, safe and secure in my own world, and away with the rest. Maybe I should be spending a little less time out in the sun?

Returning to the albergue at 7.00pm as instructed, I found dinner had been delayed somewhat, but our host plied us with wine meantime which was very nice and very welcome. During my absence, a family of three had arrived. Mum and Dad in their early forties I guessed, and a young girl of around 12. Like Marcello they too were Italian, and had found this albergue via recommendations from fellow countrymen who had stayed in this hostel previously.

Dad, Andréa, was 80% wheelchair bound and didn't look at all well. Regardless of any impediments, they were still travelling along whatever route they could manage from Sarria to Santiago; with Mum Francesca and daughter Daniella, taking turns at pushing the wheelchair over a very tough 100 kilometres.

Witnessing all this made my own discomforts seem miniscule in comparison, and not for the first time on this journey, I was forced to reflect on how lucky I was in all that I had, particularly in being blessed with good health. I was filled with such admiration of their spirit and resolve, their clear devotion to each other, and the simple joy of life they exuded.

At dinner, Andréa produced a cocktail of pills to swallow with his food. He was clearly a very poorly guy, but nonetheless in great spirits and good humour. I sincerely hoped that this wasn't a journey with a darker burden for him and his family than was immediately obvious. I felt honoured to be able to share in their company that evening, listening to the story of their life at home and of their journey to Santiago. What a brave and determined man, and a loving, dedicated and inspirational family. Truly, truly humbling.

A plentiful and delicious dinner of salad, pasta and fruit was served by our host and thoroughly enjoyed by the entire company; all washed down of course, with rivers of red wine. Marcello certainly had an obligingly loose elbow in this respect.

The background entertainment to all of this, was a ferociously noisy thunder and lightning storm with accompanying torrential downpour, and Marcello opened the door on the fireworks so we could watch the show.

It was very late for me at 10.30pm when our little fiesta finally ajourned, and I had a little wobble on as I stumbled up the narrow staircase to my room. It had been a wonderfully warm and lively evening enjoyed in the very best of company, and one that I knew would live long in my memory.

It is moments like this and people such as these, that makes the Camino such a very, very special place.

Distance walked today – 25 Kilometres (686)

TWENTY NINE

Palas de rei

to

Arzua

With a long and tough day ahead of me, I made sure I was away from Palas just as daylight was breaking. I would be travelling 33 kilometres today and heading for Arzúa, where the Camino Francés conjoins with the Camino Norté. It seemed such a long time ago since I last crossed paths with the Camino Norté in San Sebastián. It was of course, less than a month.

There being no one else up or about at that hour I crept out of the silent albergue, closing the door quietly on what had been a wonderful and most memorable visit.

Having checked the route the previous evening, I noted that the Camino picked up again just yards from the albergue. So it did, and I was soon into my stride.

Through a close study of my maps, I knew that there would be a lot of climbing and descending today on a seriously undulating route. Well, that was just fine, I was prepared for anything by now. I had read in a pamphlet of the region, that due to the effect of the rivers that had forged and shaped the hills and valleys ahead, the landscape had sort of twisted around. Instead of being able to trace the contours of hills or follow valley floors, I would have to climb up and over every prominence. The Galegos had a name for this: *'Rompepiernas'*, translated as 'Broken Legs'. By the end of the day, I would know exactly what they meant.

Not long out from Palas de Rei the rolling nature of the terrain soon established itself, setting the pattern for the day ahead. The trail in this region was very beautiful; meandering through lightly forested hills and small agricultural plots, twisting and turning, rising and falling, dodging occasionally through shaded avenues of trees. It was blissfully peaceful and exquisite.

In a repeat of recent days, the Camino was hectic with many small villages and farmsteads, and I seem to be passing through one every couple of kilometres such was their frequency. San Xiao do Camino, Ponte Campaña set in the midst of the most spectacular woodland and O Coto, being amongst the most notable of them.

Huge dogs, sprawled in the middle of the road or tied up in farmyards, would very often be the only sign of life in these places, everywhere quiet and peaceful. Only the buzzing of nectar guzzling bees and the chirruping of hundreds of unseen birds playing amongst the trees, conspired to break the silence and my own reverie.

Regarding these dogs. They had been a constant feature since crossing into the cattle country of Galicia. I discovered later they were mainly but not exclusively, of the same type. They carried enormous heads on top of gigantic bodies, and were referred to as 'Can de Palleiro' translated I am assured, as 'Haystack Dogs'. They all seemed placid enough, and it would appear their job was to live amongst the cattle, for protection I assumed, but from what I couldn't guess. Usually, these great slavering hounds were happy enough just to give me a bored, sleepy eyed stare as I crept past them, or more often than not, show no interest at all and for which I was truly thankful. I was always mightily relieved to get past these drooling monsters unmolested; various muscles of the nether regions palpitating as I did so.

With the sun climbing slowly into clear blue sky but as yet without any great heat, I decided to stop for a short break at Leboreiro. I had renewed my early morning walking routine and had completed the 9k to this point in under 3 hours, so I was going along really nicely. Rested and refreshed I rejoined the trail, crossing a stout medieval bridge spanning the Río Seco, and to the repeating pattern of twisting and turning up and down the hills, all through the most delightful scenery. It was a pleasure to be afoot on this perfect morning and I was thoroughly immersed in it, uplifted by the beauty and tranquility of the surrounding countryside.

Passing quickly through San Xoan de Furelos, the trail led up a slope into the largish looking town of Melide. It was surprisingly very busy on this Sunday morning with a large market spilling into the streets, teeming with shoppers. It was really enjoyable to spend a moment or two having a little mooch round. I do like a good Spanish street market they are the real deal, lively and with plenty on offer, and of the kind so rarely seen in Britain these days.

What am I saying? You wouldn't see most of the foodstuffs displayed this way at a market in the UK. The Thought Police and Health & Safety stormtroopers, would have forbade any chance of food being presented without first being zapped, chemically treated and refrigerated, shrink-wrapped, ominously dated and guaranteed disease free. If my old mum, a doyen of her generation of market shoppers was alive today, she would be turning in her grave at such nonsense.

I browsed aimlessly amongst the stalls for a while but seeing nothing to tempt, I proceeded on through the town and back out into the country for the second half of the trek to Arzúa.

If anything, the varying undulations felt longer and perhaps a little more challenging than earlier in the day, and were becoming quite taxing too. Impervious to any tiredness on I went. Hammering out the trail, drenched in sweat, aching legs beating out a measured stride as the kilometres were steadily consumed.

On passing over an ancient bridge straddling a shallow river, I was soon through the village of Santa María. Re-crossing the river, this time via a set of large well-worn steppingstones, I came off the track and wandered on down a narrow lane. A sign at the side of the road announced I was now in the 'Consello de Arzúa', but knowing there was still quite a way to go to the town itself and with plenty of time in hand, I decided to have another short break. The mornings rigours were finally taking their toll on my legs, which not unreasonably, were nagging at me for a sit down.

I sat outside a pleasant little bar in the village of Boente, relaxing feet-up with a nice big pot of my favorite green tea. Sat at a nearby table was a pretty young lady of around 30 I would guess, and whom I vaguely recognised from the odd albergue on *The Way* thinking perhaps, she was English.

Catching her eye, I offered a cheery hello and a winning smile, at which she snatched up her phone and squeaked at me in a panic stricken voice: "I'm just trying to contact my boyfriend, I seem to have lost him but he *is* near here somewhere". I remembered her more clearly now and couldn't recall seeing her with a guy, but hey-ho.

She then leaped to her feet and pressing her phone to her ear, began a badly performed pretense of speaking to someone who clearly wasn't there. "Oh, hi er, er Bill? It's me. I'm just letting you know that I'm in Boente and I'll meet you in two minutes by the church, ok? Are you still with that group of karate black belts and Royal Marines? You are, brilliant......." Or some such nonsense. I quickly checked to see if I had a sign pinned to me that said, 'Beware! rapist and serial killer. Do not approach'. With blood draining from her face, she grabbed her pack and legged it across the road, checking behind her every ten seconds to make sure I hadn't followed.

Stupid bloody woman. Couldn't she see that I was incredibly lovely, harmless and far too buggered besides, to even *attempt* any ungentlemanly advances or chase her through the woods? Anyway, I didn't have my boots on.

Returning to my tea and cogitations I cast my mind towards the next stage of my journey, buoyed by the thought that I was now fast closing in on Santiago. The days since O Cebriero had simply flown by.

Feeling much better as always after a shot of tea, I cracked on for the last dozen or so kilometres to Arzúa.

Continuing the theme of the day, the surrounding countryside was simply glorious as I threaded my way through the corn fields and meadows. Scatterings of small houses and farms were strewn around like children's toys on a rucked green carpet of sumptuous hills, benevolently guarding the trail as it wandered through. It was nigh on being a perfect day.

I was in cruise control now as I zipped through the beautiful countryside along a moderate trail and I was soon into Ribadiso da Baixo, knowing I had but a short distance left to walk from there. Tackling the last and not too taxing 5 kilometre climb, I eventually eased my way into Arzúa at just past 3.00pm. What a glorious days walking it had been.

Ambling unhurriedly down the long main street, bypassing a couple of albergues that I didn't quite fancy, I eventually found an unlikely looking place on the ground floor of an apartment block near the town centre. As was often the case on winding down at the end of a day's walk, tiredness had quickly set in so I decided this would have to do.

It was actually very good. The 'Albergue Los Caminantes' was modern, spacious and sparklingly clean, and with just a few other hardy souls in the large bunk room, I was happy enough with my choice. The manageress who checked me in and showed me round the facilities was very nice, and quite beautiful too. This of course, had no influence at all on my decision to stay there. How could you even *think* of me being capable of such shallowness?

I quickly got myself cleaned up and changed and set off to see what delights Arzúa might hold, also, to scout out a decent place to eat later. It was obviously a large town, but once again and at risk of repeating my refrain, one without any real character or substance to it. There were no large communal areas, pleasant boulevards or impressive buildings; just a busy, knocked about main road, with dozens of straggly looking streets running at right angles to it.

Another modern town lacking a soul, or so at least it seemed to me. There was a small, attractive enough plaza, nicely dressed with shady trees and a couple of sculptures, but it was hard to get excited by it.

The one building of any interest to me was the 15th century church, alas, it was completely wrapped in scaffolding and sheets, the door firmly closed. How often these lovely and historic little churches had been closed to me on this pilgrimage. I'm a Roman Catholic for Christs sake! They should at least let us lot in, even if it's just to get out of the rain or have a snooze on the back pew. Both being long standing and traditional rites of practice for all devout Catholics and drunkards. Or devout drunkards and Catholics, if you wish. Same gig isn't it?

The whole place was so lacking in any visual attractiveness, I don't think I even took one photograph of Arzúa. I realise of course, that not every town can be dazzling, alluring and memorable, but come on Arzúa! At least make an effort!

On touring the streets I found the usual conglomeration of shops, restaurants and bars, none of the latter standing out really. Feeling pretty hungry by now though, I picked out a reasonable looking place on a corner where I could sit outside in the evening sun, and so settled myself there. This bar claimed to serve homemade pizza so I decided to give it a go. They did, it was, it was absolutely fantastic and I ate the lot. Oh, and I had some wine with it too. No really.

I decided to finish the evening off, with a further glass or two of the lovely local red wine in another bar close by. It was a bit on the rough side to be honest, but that was ok. After a month on the trail I was a bit knocked about myself, so I fitted in perfectly.

The young lady behind the bar had her kids in tow; clearly combining serving duties with child minding, and not being very good at either. I sat outside and watched the youngest kid, who would be about three, run out of the bar and dash up one of the nearby alleys. After a couple of minutes the mother came tearing out of the bar in a panic, asking if anyone had seen little Delores or whoever, and following a frenzied search, dragged the screaming child back inside. This little piece of theatre was to be repeated three or four times. Why didn't they just keep the kid inside, tethered to a beer bump? Or better yet, give her a job washing glasses? They looked as if they could do with the extra money.

By this point I was wilting a bit, deciding without much resistance that another early night was called for. After a pretty tough day clambering over the *rompepiernas*, my legs most assuredly felt pretty broken up. I returned to the albergue and on checking tomorrows journey, learned it would be a not *too* challenging 19 kilometre hike. No problem.

My pilgrimage was now fast reaching the end of its long road, the finishing line was in clear sight. If I could keep injury or death at bay for just a little longer (no certainty given my dalliances with danger over the last month) in less than two days, I would be in Santiago.

Distance walked today – 33 Kilometres (719)

THIRTY

Arzua

to

O Pedrouzo

Today honours the birthday of my beautiful and much-loved sister Pauline. God bless her and keep her safe always, what a star she is. A quick text, and my brotherly birthday compliments are completed for another year. It's hard to get my head round the fact that we are both now in our 60s. I still think of us as being in our twenties, and most certainly that is how we still behave!

I had decided on a slightly later start this morning as I only had 19 kilometres to polish off today, so I treated myself to a little lie in. The few people who had stayed in the albergue the previous night, had mostly left by the time I stepped out into the early morning sunshine.

Regaining the Camino on the far side of the town, I instantly regretted my tardiness, the way ahead was heaving. It was like match day at Manchester United, but with far fewer foreigners and tourists here on the Camino than at Old Trafford, obviously. This great swarm consisted mainly of Americans by the sound of it, the give-away being everyone under the age of 35 packing the word 'like', 6 times into every sentence. God knows where all these people had come from, they weren't remotely obvious in the town the previous evening, that's for sure.

Well, I just couldn't cope with all this noisy shouting and path clogging sauntering, so I put on a major spurt to get beyond the crowds. For the next hour or so, I dodged through and swept past dozens of people until at last, I was free of the mob and could see clear road ahead.

I became briefly held up behind one large group of Americans 'shooting the shit' as I believe is the vernacular in those parts. I overheard one of the young men say "……you just can't rely on history books, how do we know Julius Caesar was real? Maybe he is just a character in stories or plays …" I dearly wanted to stop and tell him that far from being a figment of immagination, he was actually walking along the ancient road first laid by the armies and slaves of Julius himself, over 2000 years ago! I bet those poor sods didn't doubt his existence.

I understand that dodging murderous gunfire in schoolyards might be a destraction to some students in the U.S, and occassional errors can be be forgiven. But believing Julius Caeser to be a fictional character?!! Oh dear.

It was very easy to become proprietorial about the Camino. I had been walking its length for nearly a month now, mostly on my own and thoroughly enjoying the peace, quiet and space. At the point when this idyll is suddenly broken, I'm thinking: "Who are these people, these Jonny-come-latelys? This is *my* Camino, fuck off!"

Really quite mental. Of course, they had every right to be there, also of course, you can join the Camino wherever you like. There are no rules of entry, it's there for anybody and everybody and for whatever motivation or purpose they may have. I have to admit however, I didn't feel quite so disposed to such grand principles on that particular morning, although I do promise you, I did give myself a good talking to later!

So, back to the trail. The usual 'good morning' hike out of Arzúa was quite tough in stretches, continuing on a pattern similar to the previous day, twisting and winding, rolling up and down. The setting too, was a prolongation of yesterday's abundant farmland, meadows and ubiquitous grazing cattle, with patches of woodland emerging here and there to offer a little variety.

Quite often, the trail would pass through thick, dark stands of pine, the eucalyptus like smell powerful and cloying but not unpleasant. The cooling shade that these avenues provided was most welcome though, as the sun rose into another cloudless blue sky, with the heat building predictably and steadily as the day progressed.

The folds and furrows on the Camino didn't seem as severe as the previous day, and I certainly felt a little more comfortable as I strode doggedly from one rise to another. Yet again, the trail was punctuated at regular intervals with lots of little *aldeas*, some consisting of just a few houses, yet amazingly, most seemed to have a bar or cafe of some description.

The first village after Arzúa was intriguingly named 'Pregontoño', loosely translated as 'Inquisitive'. You can imagine the conversation: "So, where do you live?", "Inquisitive". "Yes I am, but where do you live?".

I pushed steadfastly on, making my ground through what was still and would remain, predominantly farm country. Most were small concerns, but there were some quite substantial properties too, cattle and dairy production as expected, being the dominant activities.

Dairy farming in Galicia is a mainstay of the region's economy, and which I read later is undergoing major changes as it seeks to restructure and modernise. I sincerely hope, it's not at the expense of the wonderful little farmsteads that so beautifully adorn this province.

I had decided upon setting off this morning, whilst still feeling pretty good and full of energy I have to say, that I would attempt to knock off todays walk in one go, stopping only to buy drinks along the way. To that point at least, I was managing the attempt quite comfortably.

The little townships and villages seemed to pile up on one another today, with just a kilometre or so between each one. Calzada, Ferreiro and Salceda, making their way proudly into my notebook.

On the long hike down from the heights at Santa Irene, the one sour note and upset of my entire journey occurred. About halfway down the 3k slope, I heard a commotion behind me and what I initially thought was a car or some other vehicle, speeding down the hill. Seconds later, around a dozen cyclists came zooming past at breakneck speed, whooping and hollering and scattering terrified walkers to the sides of the trail. How they didn't hit or injure anyone was a miracle. I shouted some choice abuse after them, as they sped away. Selfish, reckless bastards!

At the bottom of the hill lay the small *pueblo* of A Rúa, and the crazy cyclists were gathered there; their bikes cluttering the path outside a bar as they jostled amongst themselves, smirking and laughing at their own antics.

These guys weren't kids, they were all in their mid/late forties and on reaching them I just lost it. I tore into them big time, hurling abuse and bollockings at their dangerous and thoughtless behaviour. As I raved on, attracting a small crowd as I did so, I became convinced I would get a punch in the mouth; but they all just stood quietly, accepting the vitriol I was spitting out as would naughty schoolboys in the headmasters study. I've no idea if they understood my words (I *think* they were Italian) but there was no mistaking my message. After a while, one of them held up both his hands and quietly said: "We sorry, we very sorry", which kind of took the wind out of my sails to be honest. I hadn't exhausted my lexicon of profanities yet!

I left it at that and stormed off, trembling like a leaf following my explosion of temper. The group cycled past me again a little further down the trail and my defences went *en garde*. I was alone and the path was empty of people at that point. If they were going to give me a good kicking, then was the time to do it. Mercifully they swept silently past, with neither a glimpse nor word in my direction. Phew!

From A Rua, I knew I was just a couple of kilometres shy of my destination for today, and the clock had only just ticked past 1.00pm. I was very pleased with myself which was just as well, as no one else seemed to care less.

On entering O Pedrouzo, it was but a short walk into the centre before I stumbled upon a very modern, quite chic albergue on the main road and which quite took my fancy.

I checked in, to the gentle and unexpected strains of classical music piping through the reception area, very bohemian. All In stark contrast I have to say, to the strains of violent wind piping through the posterior of the guy queuing behind me as I signed the register. Dear me! He made a game attempt to deflect attention from his malodorous trumpeting's with a tuneless whistle, which bizarrely, was just a semi-tone out from being in perfect harmony with his own anal arpeggio. I won't mention the nationality of this gentleman; but there was a thick whiff of smoked sausage and fermented cabbage polluting the air.

The albergue 'Porta de Santiago' was a step up from the usual offering. A tiled lobby gave on to smart wooden floors, with a plant filled glass terrarium nicely decorating the ground floor bunk room. A wide staircase led up to two further floors of accommodation and a sunlit terrace. It was all very nicely fitted out with comfy bunks and spacious lockers, and the shower block was top notch too. I thought it was going to be expensive, but no, just 10 euros for the night.

A quick shower and turnaround, a few minutes to update my journal in the lounge area and I was ready to explore. Espying a likely looking bar right across the street, I settled down with a cold beer and to watch the world go by for a spell, realising with growing excitement that this time tomorrow, I would be in Santiago.

I set my mind to trawling back over the events of the last few weeks: the grinding kilometres, the hard climbs and the countless villages, towns and big cities I had put behind me. But you know, I just couldn't seem to bring it all together. In a curious way, it all seemed too jumbled in my mind and quite inaccessible. I knew then, I would have to finish the pilgrimage before

I could assemble everything into some kind of order. In this respect, I was so pleased I had kept my journal up to date and in detail throughout. This, the many photographs I had taken and the countless scraps of notes I had scribbled along the way, would be invaluable when I eventually came to write a full account of my journey. This I definitely intended to do. But you know that, you're reading it!

I knew tomorrow would be a special and thrilling day, and I was happy to let my thoughts wander as I sipped my beer in the hot afternoon sunshine, conscious and uncaring that I had a ridiculously large grin plastered across my face.

O Pedrouzo was another uneventful little town really. Clean, neat and tidy as most places were in fairness, yet it was just another long strip of shops and bars etc. with streets striking off it hither and thither. There were some very nice and expensive looking houses around the outskirts, but a walk around the back lanes revealed little else. It was all very quiet and very sleepy and my cue for a siesta. A couple of hours looking at the back of my eyelids would be just the job.

Later, and whilst walking up the single main street in the early evening sun and browsing for a place to eat, it became obvious that this town too, as do so many, relied heavily on the Camino and its pilgrims for its business. Every other shop was a souvenir outlet of one kind or another, the spaces in between mostly filled by bars, restaurants, and a surprising number of hairdressers and beauty salons.

You could get manicured and massaged, your hair cut and coiffed. You could eat and drink your way along the entire length of the street, and buy enough tourist tat to satisfy even the most fastidious of Japanese. However, if you needed to buy a new shirt and pants for your cousin Enid's wedding? It appeared you wouldn't be getting them in this town.

I found a large, decent looking restaurant and chose a table outside, well shaded from the late evening sun which was still packing a mighty punch. Whilst perusing the menu, I realised I had been in Spain for over a month and had not yet had a paella, I *loved* paella! As this seemed to be the specialty of the house I indulged, selecting the sea food special. It was ok I guess, I've had better. I've cooked better myself to be honest. It was reasonable enough though; a plentiful pan of paella with chunks of beautiful rustic bread, accompanied of course, by a couple of very large glasses of red wine. The young *camarera* dropped a piece of paper on my table requesting 8 euros 60 cents. Not too much to complain about there really.

I decided on a final relaxing nightcap at a nice little bar next to the albergue. With my mind buzzing with the wine and thoughts of tomorrow, I was drawn into pondering on what I would do after I had reached Santiago? Well, I knew I would spend a couple of days in the city, resting and seeing the sights, but what then? There was an extension to the regular Camino; this entailed a three or four day walk to Fisterra on the Atlantic coast and then possibly, on up to Muxía.

I was very tempted by it, in a peculiarly masochistic sense I wasn't ready to stop walking yet! The best thing I determined, would be to see how I felt in a day or so and after I had completed the pilgrimage. No need to worry too much right then about what would happen next.

And so, already looking expectantly ahead to tomorrows journey, I retired to the albergue. Despite my head being filled with images of Santiago and a feeling of real excitement rippling through me, tiredness as always, doused the lingering flames of yet another tremendous day on *The Way*.

Distance walked today – 19 Kilometres (738)

THIRTY ONE

O Pedrouzo

to

Santiago de Compostela

I was wide awake super-early, instantly gripped by a feeling of excitement and anticipation reserved only for those special moments in life. This without doubt, was such an occasion. In the darkness of the bunkroom I could hear early risers readying themselves for the day ahead, and I too wanted to be away sharpish this morning as I had a strict timetable devised for today. Consumed by the most fantastic buzz for this last momentous day on the Camino, I set off eagerly in the pre-dawn darkness. My plan was to be in Santiago well before noon, so I really needed to get cracking.

A mixed porridge of reflection and speculation provided my food for thought as I got underway. Today would be my last on the Camino; the culmination of a long and challenging journey from the Pyrenees of eastern Spain, to within just a few kilometres of its Atlantic coast in the west. It was hard to put it all into perspective at that particular moment, difficult to give the journey a linear order in my mind. There were just too many thoughts fighting for prominence, in much too small a space.

At that point though, it was satisfaction enough that I perfectly appreciated that each step, every ounce of effort and drop of sweat, all the difficulties and challenges I had overcome, was *absolutely* worth the prize of profound experience and incredible joy with which this pilgrimage had rewarded me.

This journey had been simply amazing, way above anything I had previously experienced or indeed, expected. I have had more than my fair share of travel and adventure down the years, but this fantastic expedition had topped the lot.

I recalled the countless little villages, humble towns and great cities that I had passed through or stayed in. Each of them holding out the warmest of welcomes, and forging such treasured and indelible memories of even the briefest of visits. I reflected (with some disbelief!) on my month of daily walks; the physical and mental challenges, the agonies and ecstasies, and the wonderful satisfaction I felt at the end of each day. I remembered the stunning beauty and wonder of the scenery I was blessed with throughout; breathtaking, inspiring and unforgettable.

Amidst all the splendor and tranquility, this pilgrimage had afforded me the time and space I needed for serious contemplation and honest reflection. Over the course of this long journey, I had felt a gradual and widening disconnect from the stark realities of my personal world, creating and opening up this 'thought space' if you will. The mundanity, trivia and concerns of daily life, had certainly been pushed to the margins over the course of this last month. I willingly claimed this period of release and window of opportunity, for the kind of deliberation and self-examination that wouldn't be possible under normal circumstances. The wilderness, solitariness and peace of the Camino, combining to provide the perfect environment in which to do so.

Quite possibly, the watershed moment of reaching 60 had some bearing too, by adding weight to the certainty that there were substantially more years of my life behind me than in front. It wasn't a pessimistic or morbid viewpoint; simply an unmissable opportunity to pause and to take stock, to reflect honestly on my past, refocus on what is really important in life, and how I could best make use of the years and opportunities that, hopefully, lay ahead of me.

Throughout the pages of this book, I have alluded to the many occasions where I have felt a kind of mental shift in how I perceived certain situations in my life, or perhaps, experienced real clarity over troubling or long standing issues .

These were rarely sudden flashes or *eureka* moments, but rather more nuanced or complex; a product of an accumulation of thoughts and deliberations, and many hours talking to myself! As a result, I have found these processes and events much more difficult to write about. Not because I lacked the imagery or phraseology, but difficult because when I came to write of them, I wasn't entirely relying on clear memories or details of incidents as I had written them down. I was attempting to draw upon thoughts and emotions that even after a short period of time, was like trying to grasp hold of a distant memory, or accurately recall a fleeting dream.

I'm trying to be as honest and forthcoming as I can about this aspect of my writing. Easy enough when describing firmly fixed events, but less so when trying to recall strong and perhaps intangible emotions that quickly shape-shift over time, and removed from the environment in which those feelings were generated. I had to question myself very closely: "Did I really think that? did I really feel that? Did this happen in the way I am trying to reconcile and convey, *and* in the context I was so certain of during that time?" Complicated questions to ask, more so in trying to produce an authentic answer.

On a journey such as the one I had undertaken, when fatigue, emotional stress and a challenging and unfamiliar background all take their mental toll, how certain was I that the feelings and impressions I was trying to solidify, were not influenced by these very elements? There is plenty of evidence that exposure to hardship, isolation and a testing environment can conjure up extra-sensory thoughts or imagery.

I have mentioned my sense of 'disconnection' from my life at home; this was absolutely the case. This sense of disengagement didn't leave a vacuum though, but as I have mentioned, created an opportunity to explore and maybe face up to concerns or issues I had long been avoiding. For the first time in a very long time, I found I was able to confront these matters with perhaps a good deal more honesty than in the past, and I found the answers more readily forthcoming.

I won't bore you with chapter and verse or specifics. I'm not brave enough, in this book at least, to bare my soul and open up about very personal stuff. I most definitely lack the fame and appeal to make this even remotely interesting; I'm not Billy Connelly! I am prepared to say though, that throughout my journey, I was very aware that *something* transformative was working away, and completely outside the parameters of past experiences.

It wasn't troubling or disturbing, in fact, I found it to be profoundly satisfying as well as revealing. I also felt that this insight, if that's what it was, had gifted me with a feeling of great comfort and peace of mind. And I'll happily tell you; in my world I'll take that all day long!

More broadly, and whilst on the subject of the weird and wonderful. I do think it's so important, not to easily dismiss phenomena that are difficult to understand or rationalise. Nor do I think we should disregard the unfathomable, simply because it doesn't have a convenient pigeon hole in which to place and define it. I believe all of these singularities deserve our honest human curiosity, not the reflex of doubt or sneering cynicism. We shouldn't let apprehension or lack of imagination become limiting factors in our willingness to allow for the improbable, or explore the indefinable. Life would be very boring and predictable if we did, would it not?

Make of these meanderings what you will. Much of what I have expounded upon in these last few paragraphs is open to lively discussion, I accept that. But one thing I will say as a certainty: I would be in denial and less than truthful, if I didn't accept that something significant and meaningful had been brought to pass, on my long and very special Camino journey. For me, that was enough.

I would also add, less controversially perhaps, that I have felt genuinely enriched by this journey; be that in the nonphysical sense I have alluded to or by a more tangible heightening of the senses. A perception of seeing, hearing and thinking about things differently; more clearly.

My conversations with others had revealed similar and often more profound feelings. Many said their Camino experience had brought change to their lives or at the very least, their outlook on it. Of the many people I spoke to during and after our shared journey, I can't recall one person who didn't have a story to tell or experience to reveal, that exemplified these or similar emotions.

Historically, people would undertake a pilgrimage purely for religious and spiritual reasons. The hope was that through prayer and meditation, sacrifice and dedication, pilgrims could atone for their sins, find a blessing for a special cause, or simply become closer to their God. Most religions have a tradition of pilgrimage, particularly the Abrahamic (Muslim, Jewish, Christian) and whilst their theologies may differ, the purpose is generally the same.

Now I'm absolutely positive, that many modern day Camino 'pilgrims' do not set out with spiritual or religious motivations. Yet if questioned, most would say they hoped to *find something* on their journey, something about themselves maybe, or to find answers to specific questions or problems, or perhaps, to find enlightenment and a wider understanding of their world and how they connect with it. However secular these reasons may seem, they are not so far removed from those of religiously motivated pilgrims past and present, who also looked for change in their lives, for answers and inspiration; spiritual or otherwise.

The Camino de Santiago is not an esoteric entity. Whilst its origins may be embedded in medieval Christianity, the modern Camino is wide open to embrace any philosophy and belief, and therein lies its strength. It's overtones may still be broadly Christian, and that theme is stitched into the fabric of its offering, but it is not exclusive.

Surely, it has to be more important that the Camino provides the environment, space and opportunity for individuals to explore their own lives and the world that surrounds them, rather than to demand of them a fixed theology or ideology as a prerequisite?

Remove the labels and strip out the dogma. Be prepared to reach deeply into your mind, heart and spirit and the Camino will carry you along, helping you in your journey of contemplation, self-understanding and personal development. To my mind at least, it's as simple as that.

The Camino, if you allow it, can be a powerful force whichever way one chooses to analyse it; I have felt changed by it and I welcome and embrace that change. My sincere hope of course, is that I can become a better person for it.

It was a moment of some uncertainty too. For the last month, living and walking on the Camino was like being in a vacuum, remote and separated from the outside world, as it were. No TV, radio or newspapers, no home comforts or familiarities, and yet the routine became comfortable and reassuring.

All you had to do was walk the sections of the trail and keep yourself fed, watered and safe, knowing that at the end of each day there would be comfortable accommodation where you could clean up, relax and enjoy the very many and very different warm and welcoming places *en route*. By todays end though, all that would change.

All I had had was the Camino, all I *wanted* was the Camino. It grew on you day by day, gradually overtaking everything else, to the exclusion of everything else really. My total focus was on completing the journey, the determination to do so increasing almost with each step, and despite some really difficult and testing times, never giving up, never wanting to.

I knew I would miss it, I knew there would be a void in my life after it, and like many others before me I know, I was already thinking of returning in the future to do the whole thing again. Complete madness!

Leaving aside then, my homespun tu'pence ha'penny philosophy and musings! Here I was in the real world, shrugging on my backpack for the last day on the Camino. After all these weeks and hundreds of kilometres of walking and climbing, it felt as light as a wash-bag on my shoulders as I headed out from O Pedrouzo.   I felt at ease in mind, body and spirit and bursting with expectation.

I soon left the town behind, and for the last time on this journey headed into the by now much treasured fields, forests and hills of the Camino. I was anxious to get ahead of the crowds I was sure I would encounter today, as I imagined that this last stage into Santiago would be especially busy. On this early part of today's journey however, it wasn't bad at all in that respect. The trail was fairly quiet so far, but I expected it would liven up considerably as the day progressed.

The Camino began as it left off yesterday, in a cool, dark avenue of pine forest. The enfolding gloom had me reaching for my torch to light the way, with the sun as yet reluctant to escape the dark shadows of the hills behind me. To begin with, the trail wandered along easily enough through the many small farms and hamlets that marked its early course. It was just at the approach to Amenal that the path began to steepen, and I set myself for a stiff climb of four kilometres or so up to the heights of Alto de Barreira.

On passing through the little village of Cimadevila, the demands of the climb began to ease a little and it became a much more comfortable walk. That would be the last serious climb of the day, and indeed, of the Camino Francés. Just a few little borrows and hillocks lay in front of me now. I felt certain I could manage those!

It was on a pretty flat track then that I happily trudged on, passing through a continuation of little parishes and clusters of houses which would become increasingly more populous as I got nearer to the city. At San Paio, I decided to have a rest and a brew as I was nicely ahead of schedule. A quick check of my map revealed a little less than three hours would see me in Santiago. Perfect.

Refreshed and feeling light of foot, I pushed on through a large pine forest in the midst of which, I was suddenly and unexpectedly deafened by the roar of an overhead aircraft I could have reached up and touched! I was close to the edge of Santiago's Lavacolla Airport; and for the next few minutes all thoughts and sounds were drowned by the screaming of jets landing and taking off, as I skirted the airports northern perimeter.

At the edge of the forest and as yet still some distance off, I got my first tantalising glimpse of Santiago, it's buildings catching the early light of the sun on this perfect, blue-sky day.

This first sight of the city was for me, a peculiarly unsettling moment. Santiago had for so long seemed so distant and unreachable, yet here with the great prize now within reach, it almost felt unreal, like a mirage. How strange. I pressed on with growing urgency through the village of Lavacolla and up the short, steep incline to Vilamaior. I was continuing to make excellent time, and could see from my map that I was well over half-way to Santiago. Good lad.

Quickening the pace a little I marched on, eating up the kilometres now on the easy-going tarmac road. The trail, as I had suspected, was becoming increasingly busy after the relative quietness of the first hour or so, but happily not as crowded as I feared. Just about right I thought, to provide a nice atmosphere and to feel part of something special on the final road in.

Recognising with a rush of exhilaration that I was now on the last lap, I negotiated a final gentle climb leading up to the huge and prominent pilgrims park at Monte do Gozo. Within the park, I knew that there were a number of monuments and sculptures dedicated to the Camino which I really wanted to take a look at. Alas, my watch was telling me I would have to return to see them in the days ahead. I couldn't be late for my appointment in Santiago, the famed midday pilgrims sevice in the cathedral of St. James.

As I descended steadily down the track which ran alongside the park and towards the bottom of the slope, I could see a broad strip of motorway ahead, cutting across and underneath the trail. A glimpse of a sign by the side of the path showed there was just 4 more kilometres now to the city center.

By this time I was so pumped up, I felt I could have ran that last piddling distance! Sensibly though I reined myself in, continuing at a more sedatery pace as I climbed down a steep flight of stone steps, before crossing a wide bridge over the *Autopista*. From that point the city began to grow and thicken out, becoming busier and busier as I began the long, final trek through its outskirts.

Upon reaching a modern monument announcing the city limits, I pulled up as if stricken. Something wasn't right. Strangely and quite unexpectedly, I felt quite deflated. The excitement from earlier in the day that had fueled my progress so far had suddenly drained away, and I just couldn't work out why? It was a very peculiar feeling and I really hoped I would perk up a bit, and quickly. I thought I would be bouncing by now! I simply put it down to the strain and uniqueness of the occasion. How strange and contrary one's mind and mood can be sometimes.

The city continued to unpack itself around me as I ground my way through an estate of modern tenements, a handful of pilgrim albergues set down rather incongruously amongst them. Making a note of these hostels for possible use later, I nimbly negotiated a very busy intersection where the traffic crossed bewilderingly from four or five different directions. The pavements were hectic too in this busy part of the city; crammed with shoppers and tourists, and hell-for-leather pilgrims on their unstoppable race to the cathedral.

I made sure to keep a close eye on the Camino markers as I crisscrossed the busy and confusing roads, but I knew I was on the right track. One by one, I stepped over the inlayed shells of the Way of St. James, edging closer with every minute. I was almost there.

Slowly but surely, the modern city began to give way to the old, and I could feel a change in atmosphere with the transition. The groups of people around me too, were becoming noisier and more excited, tired limbs suddenly energised and filled with purpose. It seemed as if somehow we had all been turned into tiny, agitated specks of iron filings, each drawn irresistibly towards a giant magnet.

By now accompanied by a rapidly growing throng of fellow pilgrims, I crossed another busy road and was instantly swept up a paved incline, lined on both sides by buildings of a very different vintage. Confirmation at last, that I had entered the city's ancient and venerable heart.

Twisting my way through the narrow and busy streets, I burst suddenly onto a small, sunlit plaza, lively with people bustling about or sat outside the cafes around its edges. Picking my way impatiently through the crowds, I spotted the portico under the Palacio Gelmirez, which I knew led down a disappearing slope and on to the cathedral plaza. Moving slightly more cautiously now, I passed the massive side door at the north side of cathedral to my left, descended rather gingerly down a flight of well-worn steps and into the gloom of the large archway.

As if in greeting, there stood a traditionally dressed Galician piper; the skirl of his *gaita* droning out the lively tunes that heralded the last few metres of the Camino Francés, and of course, my own long journey.

I stepped rather hesitantly out of the shadow of the portico, and into the sunlit majesty of the Praza Obradoiro. As I inched further into the square, I physically felt my jaw drop, as the incredible and unforgettable sight of the cathedral of St James unfolded in all its glory to my left. Wow!

I had rehearsed this moment many times in my mind as I got closer to Santiago. I thought I should I have a few meaningful words ready, or perhaps, some significant gesture. It should at the very least, be something auspicious and fitting to the occasion. That was my plan anyway. In the end, just a single, simple phrase whispered from my lips.

'I'm here, I've made it!'.

I headed slowly towards the center of the enormous plaza, sidestepping my way through ever growing groups of pilgrims, all appearing equally as dumb-struck and transfixed. The stunning western façade of the cathedral completely dominated and overshadowed all else, gleaming massively against a background of cobalt blue sky. It was absolutely spellbinding. A few paces on and I was squarely front and center of the huge cathedral edifice, and shaken abruptly from my hypnosis, an unstoppable wave of emotion swept through me.

I dropped my pack to the floor, my knees quickly following, and buried my face in my hands. Great sobs shook through me, warm tears ran unstaunched through my fingers, I was completely overcome. Every step, every climb, the joys and agonies, all the great moments and adventures of my journey, surged forward in a tsunami of recollection. The entire emotional tapestry of my pilgrimage it seemed, sped across my mind like a fast forwarding film. It felt as if every single element of my long journey across Spain had been condensed into this one place, this single moment. It was just incredibly, unimaginably and quite indescribably moving.

After a couple of minutes I pulled myself together a little. Looking around the plaza, I could see plenty of others grappling with their own emotions too. Many were seemingly in shock, plenty of them too with tears cascading down their faces. Dozens were hugging, laughing and jumping up and down like excited children at Christmas. Others were holding their packs and even bikes aloft, like trophy winning captains on their finest day. Several lay unmoving flat on their backs, heads propped on packs, gazing in wonderment at the sight before them.

They too, were like the rest of us I'm certain; stunned at the realisation of their achievement, that they were at journeys end, and they really were here at the cathedral of Saint James, Santiago de Compostela.

These were the moments and emotions to treasure and remember. The sight of all those people, freed at last from the demands and hardships of the Camino, so filled with joy and celebration will stay with me always. The wonderful thing is of course, this wasn't an isolated event, nor an occasion with a beginning and an end. It was the continuation of countless thousands of days just like it before, and a rehearsal for the celebrations of all those pilgrims who will experience this fantastic moment in the days, months and years to come. Everybody here today, now had an inviolable link with all the Camino pilgrims past, and with all those unknown adventurers who's journey has yet to begin.

I felt immensely proud and privileged to be a part of this centuries old and continuing history, and felt a deep bond with all the people gathered here together, in this place and at this time.

I could hear the voice of a fellow traveler shouting exuberantly "we've done it, we've done it". I nodded and smiled in agreement, for I too had done it, I really had done it.

After a while I calmed down a bit, and I was able to properly take in the wonderful scene around me and make some sense of it. I could see that the enormous plaza was a mix of recently arrived battered and disheveled pilgrims, and groups of more smartly presented tourists of, shall I say, a less adventurous stripe.

There were more people arriving by the minute; rucksacks, boots and walking poles, bikes and helmets littering the cobbled square. Spotting a few familiar faces, teary handshakes and hugs of congratulations were exchanged, a few stories swapped. I got the feeling however, that most people were preoccupied by their own thoughts and just wanted to be alone for a while. I know I did.

◆ ◆ ◆

I referred to the ' battered and disheveled pilgrims' on the plaza, and this was absolutely true!

It reminded me of a story in one of Spike Milligan's wonderful war memoirs. In it, he describes the condition of his artillery battery after months of fighting in the deserts of North Africa in WW2. He portrays how upon leaving the UK, the regiment boasted brand new equipment and vehicles, all gleaming with fresh paint and military insignia. Its soldiers were outfitted in smart new battledress, clean and crisp, spanking new packs and boots, all polished and shining.

After several months chasing the Germans across North Africa and lots of hard and bloody fighting, Spike goes on to describe this once proud regiment, as now looking like a 'Caravan of Armenian refugees, fleeing the Turkish slaughter'. Equipment and vehicles were battered and dirty, parts missing, paint flaking, all held together with chicken wire and scrounged nuts and bolts. Soldiers were forlorn, dirty and disheveled. Once smart uniforms were hanging off skinny frames, ripped and badly repaired. Bits of packs were damaged or missing. It was a sorry, sorry sight.

This describes *exactly*, how a pilgrim looks after a month on the Camino!

The Praza Obradoiro featured large and impressive buildings on each of its four sides, the western façade of the cathedral completely outshining all else. Directly opposite, was the impressively porticoed and stately looking City Hall; the 'Pazo de Raxoi' and constructed in the mid-18th century. To one side, was the very swish, expensive and impressively named 'Palacio Dos Reis Católicos' (Palace of the Catholic Monarchs). Built originally in the 15th century as a hospital for pilgrims; added to in the 17th and 18th centuries, and now viewed as one of the world's finest hotels. Opposite the hotel on the southern edge, sat the 'Colexio de San Xerome', part of the University of Santiago and dating back to 1501.

All these buildings were very grand and imposing and, it is said, represent the four great powers of the city - church, government, university and commerce - and there is no doubt, that they each contribute separately and collectively, to the majesty and presence of the Prazo Obradoiro.

The exterior of the cathedral before me was essentially that rebuilt in the 17th century, although it was first consecrated on this spot in the 11th. Many of the buildings around it were generally of 15th to 17th century origin, although here and there was evidence of much older structures. The entire architectural cornucopia was fantastic; a dramatic scene exquisitely cast on a stage of perfection. It was everything and more than I expected, or indeed hoped for.

Conscious of the time I snapped off a few more photographs, capturing the moment I hoped. Time was pressing, so I quickly found a depository close to the cathedral where I could leave my pack for a few hours. I was running up the steps to the cathedral when it's great bells began chiming 12.00 noon, and I was fearful I wouldn't be allowed in. There was no such problem however, as I was nodded through by the security guard and into the main body of the cathedral which was absolutely packed, standing room only!

The mass was just under way as I fought my way through the crowds, trying without success, to get as close to the front as I could. It really was a riot! Tourists with no interest in the service, wandering noisily and obliviously amongst those immersed in it. Cameras and videos were held aloft, flashing and whirring away to the despair, waving arms and unheeded 'shushes' of the security people.

It was absolute bedlam, but really enjoyable for all of that; it brought real life into the church and to the service. All that was missing I thought, was a mess of livestock and a few chickens running wildly about, desperately chased by farmers in smocks. It then really would have been a scene, perfectly lifted from a medieval painting. Wonderful and unmissable.

It was difficult to follow the service with all the noise and distraction, but in truth, my mind was wandering all over the place, I was still preoccupied and buzzing with the morning's events.

Towards the end of the mass, the piece of theatre that many had come to see unfolded. The huge silver censer, the 'Botafumeiro', suspended on thick ropes and large wooden pulleys, was fired up with incense. Smoking away, it was hoisted up into the roof by a large team of attendants and swung dramatically along the transept, high into the eaves. It was then caused to swoop low along the aisles at terrific speed, time and time again, belching clouds of incense smoke as it swept its way through the spellbound crowds.

It was very, very impressive, and I could see why people talked about it so enthusiastically. This thing was the size and weight of a small child, and I couldn't help but to imagine the consequences if it came loose and went flying amongst the congregation, it would have been worse than a car crash! Still, there would at least be plenty of priests on hand, to administer last rights to the wounded and dying.

With the service now over, the altar began emptying its many concelebrants and acolytes into the aisles and most people began to leave. The cathedral remained very busy however, as more visitors began to arrive, quickly filling the spaces of those departing.

There were several things I particularly wanted to see and do in the church. It was a stunning building, both architecturally and artistically, absolutely packed with magnificence and beauty wherever one looked. At that point however, I decided I would return at a less congested time, when I could do more justice to a longer visit and better appreciate its many offerings.

I actually returned to the cathedral on several occasions over the next few days, it was a wonderful place and one I could never tire of.

Feeling very happy with life, and very pleased that I had managed to make it to Santiago exactly as planned, there were now two things foremost on my mind: cold beer and accommodation.

I decided I could do an internet search for the latter, whilst partaking of a few of the former. This I did at a large terraced bar to the rear of the cathedral which overlooked another grand square, the Praza da Quintana. The first large and ice-cold beer was beyond nectar, washing away the dust and heat of nearly 800 hard won kilometres. All together now ".…... I had never had a beer that tasted so good.…." Well, you know the script by now!

I expected that I might struggle to get a room in this pilgrim and tourist jammed city, but I was surprised at how quickly I was able to locate and book a place, and this just around the corner from where I was now sat. In truth, it transpired there was a large number and a wide variety of accommodations available in and around the city, and not too difficult to find a room to suit most people's taste and wallet.

The place I booked was a small, boutique style hotel, where I could have a private room and bathroom. I felt I deserved a little bit of luxury and privacy after my exertions over the last month, and again to my pleasant surprise, it wasn't that expensive.

The 'Hotel Badalada' was on the small side, 'Bijou', as I believe the vernacular of the tourist trade would have it, but nicely appointed and very comfortable. Squeezed into a terrace on a slope up from the cathedral, it seemed quite luxurious and a bit decadent following my month of nights in albergues, but I immersed myself into its comforts with grateful thanks *and* relief.

After taking my time over a hot, soapy shower, I changed into my one remaining clean shirt and took my tattered and dirty clothes to a nearby launderette. Machine loaded, I sat with a beer in a lovely little square around the corner whilst my clobber gargled, sloshed and spun; and where I cunningly prepared my body and brain, for a similar list of activities over the next few hours!

A little later, with the whole evening ahead of me and time now my own, I strolled leisurely around the city, joyously free of walking boots and backpack. It was so nice just to amble along taking in the atmosphere, embracing the moment of being amongst these ancient streets and squares, all busy and full of life on this beautifully warm, September evening.

Santiago is a fabulous city, instantly likeable and indeed I did take to it immediately. Of course it is very historic, its streets and buildings shout that and it *feels* ancient, but it is no stuffy museum piece either. The whole place was buzzing and vibrant, it's narrow streets and numerous, beautiful plazas throbbed with vitality. Bars and restaurants filled every street and square, tables and chairs spilled out onto the pavements; each one frantic with people eating, drinking and more obviously, celebrating!

It was dazzling; and I was absolutely enthralled by this lovely city that just a few weeks ago, seemed so distant and beyond reach. Definitely my El Dorado at the end of the Camino. Everywhere there was something to see and admire, something to remember and call you back, and I decided there and then that I had to spend a couple more days exploring Santiago. Apart from anything else, I was absolutely knackered, and desperate for a good, long rest.

I was by this time, feeling very hungry. Time to eat. I was lucky and a little surprised actually, to quickly find an empty table outside a very nice restaurant and I settled myself there, immediately attracting admiring glances from my fellow diners, and who could blame them? "Who is this lean, suntanned man of action?" They must be asking. "Who is this man, with the far-away look of a lone adventurer; windswept and mysterious?" I allowed a knowing smile to pass across my lips, running my fingers through my hair, catching the attention of one of the beautiful *meseras*, breathlessly hoping that *she* would be the one I chose. Coyly she approached and said, whispered really: "You can't sit here, this table is reserved. We have another table free 10 metres up the street next to the dustbins if you want it".

Actually, I couldn't fully understand what she said if I'm honest, her lovely Galego accent was impenetrable to me. I did pick up the 'reserved' bit though, so I reluctantly abandoned the table, cursing my luck once again. If it wasn't for bad luck, I wouldn't have any luck at all! Example: Shortly before embarking on this trip, I was cooking breakfast and cracked open a double-yoke egg. A certain sign of good luck I thought, *and* it was lottery day. I burnt my hand on the frying pan.

Gathering my dignity off the floor, I left with a haughty sneer trailing behind me, soon finding an equally nice place just around the corner. This time, by cleverly disguising myself as an ordinary person, I was invited by a mustachioed waiter, sporting a pink Alice band in his hair and waggling painted fingernails, to sit at a lovely table outside. With a flashing smile and a raised eyebrow, he draped my napkin tantalisingly across my knees and pursing his lips, asked what he could get for me. Mario, I really need that T-shirt now!

I ordered my favorite pasta and red wine, luxuriating in the knowledge that tomorrow I could sleep in and there would be no more walking. What a feeling that was. "Keep the wine coming", I adjured my lisping *mesero*, well, I was celebrating after all! It was wonderful to sit and unwind on this warm, still evening, soaking up the atmosphere and feeling pretty pleased with myself and my achievements, reflecting warmly on what had been an amazing and memorable day.

Often at this point in memoires such as this, the author takes the opportunity to take stock of the journey, to extol its virtues and measure its impact. Perhaps now is the time I should ask and try to answer the questions of 'Was it worth it?', 'What have I gained from it?', ' Has my journey effected any change in my life or my approach to its future?'. All of that and much more I suppose.

I considered however, that if I hadn't during the telling of my story and through the experiences I have related, given full expression as to the depth of influence and meaningfulness of my journey, then I haven't done a very good job as a narrator. If I need to explain and summarise my Camino adventure at this point for it to make sense, then I have fallen short really, haven't I? So, I think I'll leave it just there.

I do hope my story *has* been well told. I hope I have been able to properly convey what a wonderful and life enriching experience it has been, and what incredible fun and enjoyment I had along the way of this most fantastic of journeys. Most of all, I really hope you have enjoyed reading about my pilgrimage and its little adventures, as much as I have enjoyed writing about it.

I put all thoughts of what I would do next to the back of my mind for now. After all that had happened over the last month, I was happy just to savor the moment. I was going to enjoy my dinner, sip my wine and just relax in the ambiance of this lovely restaurant, in the ancient heart of this beautiful and historic city.

The food, the drink and my own contented musings, were the only companions I needed this night; this final night of an incredible journey, and one of the most wonderful experiences of my life.

Well, up to know at least!

Distance walked today – 22 Kilometres (Final total 761)

Please read on if you have the stamina. There are a few words to tie up loose ends!

AFTERWORD

Following my celebrations of the previous evening, I had fallen into my hotel bed in the early hours looking forward to an undisturbed and long lie-in. No chance! The ingrained habits and routine of my month on the Camino would not easily set me free and I was wide awake, although feeling a bit delicate, at exactly 6.00am.

There was no use fighting it so I got up, showered and dressed and set off in search of a hangover curing breakfast. A Spanish style English breakfast (eh?) soon put me right, and I sat with a large brew planning my day ahead.

As I was out and about early, I decided it would be a good time to visit the pilgrim office to collect my '*Compostela*'; the certificate of pilgrimage completion I have referred to earlier.

I knew the office opened at 8.00am and I also knew that long queues quickly built up, so it was better to get there early. I turned the corner on Rua Carretas just down from the cathedral plaza at 7.45, and there was already a line of around thirty people forming outside the office doors.

I realised this was as good as it would get, so I joined the queue and waited for the doors to open. At 8.00am prompt, a guard opened up and the line was sucked in through the opening. In the few minutes I had been waiting the queue behind me had lengthened considerably, I had time it just right.

With my much travelled and dog eared '*Credencia*', (Camino passport) to hand, I shuffled slowly along the line, waiting my turn to be invited into the accreditation hall. It was all very slick and modern, with electronic signs indicating the next available clerk. Within thirty minutes, I found myself inside the large hall and in front of one of about a dozen stations.

It was a bit like paying your gas bill, or signing on at the dole office in the seventies! I was called forward to be greeted by a very friendly but bored looking young lady, who without any preamble took my *Credencia*, asked a few confirmatory questions, established my name and how it was spelt and began typing. Satisfied all was well, she pressed a button on a machine and out popped my certificate.

Handing it over, she wished me a good morning and was already summoning the next in line before I had turned to leave. I was out of the building and walking back up the street in the blink of an eye.

Well that was rubbish! Where was the theatre, the drama? I had imagined being taken down into an ancient and darkened cellar by cowled monks, and led blindfolded through a secret passageway to a 1000 year old chapel or the like. Here, I expected to be greeted by the head of an ancient and esoteric brotherhood, who would reveal some great, life changing mystery, swear me to secrecy on pain of death and brand me on the arse with a sign known only to Camino veterans and the initiated. Alas no. I've had more moving experiences in doctors surgeries.

Still, it was nice to have my *Compostela*, even if only to prove I hadn't made it all up! Seriously though, and contrary to my expectations, I felt nothing in collecting my certificate. I realised I didn't need an ornate, Latin scripted scroll as proof or affirmation of what I had achieved. Everything I needed was firmly locked in my mind. It was enough. I was proud and happy, and my memories would always carry more significance than any piece of paper could.

Thoughts of my Mexican friends had never been too far from my mind. Although I had not managed to reconnect with them during the previous couple of days, I was as certain as I could be that they were only a day behind me in reaching Santiago. Whatever it took, I was going to set my stall out to greet them on their way in, even if I had to wait all day.

Knowing their routine, and also something of their plans for the run in to Santiago, I reckoned they would arrive in the city at around 11.00am. I knew they wanted to arrive in time for the noon mass in the cathedral too. There was a plaza I had passed through the previous day, that was a sort of intersection of the routes from the outskirts of the city to the cathedral. I knew if I stationed myself there, I would definitely see them as they passed through. To be on the safe side, I did a tour of the Praza Obradoiro, then took up station at a strategically placed café at my chosen point.

11.00am came and went as did midday. I was beginning to think I had guessed wrong. Abandoning my post, I popped back for another tour of the Obradoiro; they weren't there, so I returned disconsolately to my little plaza for another vigil. I decided to hang around until 2.00pm and if they were still a no-show, call it quits and try again later.

By 2.00pm, the disappointment was written across my face and felt in my stomach. I was sure I had anticipated correctly. Never mind, the sun had passed over the yard arm and I decided I had drank enough tea, it was time for a beer!

I sat outside a little bar on the plaza, and just as I was about to order another drink, a familiar trio rounded the corner. It was them! Alex, Alfredo and Fernando were amidst a small crowd, but unmistakable in their large Panama hats and cloaked in a variety of Mexican flags.

They hadn't spotted me yet, and I just stood in the middle of the pavement waiting for them to reach me. Suddenly, a Mexican yell split the air and Alex came rushing towards me, immediately followed by the other two. We fell into each other's embrace, hugging, jumping up and down, whooping and hollering like schoolboys. I was absolutely overjoyed to see them, as they were to see me, thankfully! It was a brilliant re-union.

After the briefest of catch-ups as to their to their last couple of days, they were of course, desperate to get to the cathedral plaza and draw a close to their own pilgrimages. I accompanied them over the remaining steps I had completed myself the previous day, and once in the Obradoiro left them alone for a few minutes, whilst they went through the emotions I was only too recently familiar with.

After a while, we got back together and snapped off a few photos. They wanted to go inside the cathedral for a few words of thanksgiving so I left them to it; showing them where they could leave their packs, and also, the bar in which I would be waiting after they had finished.

It was party time again! We sat for a couple of hours, swapping stories, drinking and laughing. It was a joyous moment and one to savour. I knew all too well, that tomorrow the boys had airplanes to catch and our time together would be over. But not before lots more celebrating!!

My *amigos* left after a while to find their accommodation and get cleaned up. I also needed to freshen up and perhaps have a little snooze. We all arranged to meet at 7.00pm to continue the party. I was very late, I didn't show up until 3 minutes past.

And so, we hit the city for a last few hours of merriment. We sampled several bars as we toured the centre, finding an excellent restaurant where the lads insisted on treating me to a slap up dinner. I knew they would want to maintain their Camino tradition of a great feast to end the day, and indeed, the pilgrimage.

I have no Idea what time we finished, but the streets were a lot emptier than when we started. We went our separate ways, appropriately I thought, in front of the cathedral we had all travelled so far to see. It was an emotional moment as we said our goodbyes, and we all had tears in our eyes in those final minutes. It had been a great honour and enormous privilege to walk the Way of St James with these fine, fine gentlemen. What pleasure and joy I had derived from their company. What memories I would carry with me of their friendship, kindness, wonderful humour and enormous appetites!

I spent two more days in Santiago exploring the sights, visiting and revisiting my favourite places until eventually, I knew it was time to move on.

During the last couple of days, I had definitely made up my mind to continue my journey to the coast at Fisterra, and possibly on from there to Muxía. I had spent time gathering maps and studying the route, and felt I could make the trip to Fisterra over three or four days, with maybe another day up the coast to Muxía.

The journey to both these places was considered an official Camino route, and had grown in popularity in recent years. Many pilgrims to Santiago continued their journeys to one or both of these destinations and as a result, a lot of new albergues had been established along the way, making it almost indistinguishable and seamless from the older and more established Caminos. Even the familiar yellow arrows and shells could be found along its way. Pilgrims could even acquire additional 'Compostela's' from both these places if they wished.

Personally, I didn't see this extra trip as an extension to the Camino or to my pilgrimage. That for me was completed, signed off, as it were. I definitely wanted to do the walking though, and was very much looking forward to it. For me though, this was a wind-down walking holiday and I intended to treat it as such.

From Santiago to Fisterra and from there up the coast to Muxía was about 120 kilometres of walking, and would take me into the province of A Coruña.

The terrain was across familiar ground and a microcosm of the Camino proper. There was plenty of climbing amongst forests and green hills, and long stretches through the most picturesque towns and villages. I took my time on the journey; walking at a nice steady pace, stopping off whenever I felt like it and for as long as I liked. It was very different indeed to the pressures of the Camino, and I took four luxurious days to reach Fisterra.

My route took me through Negreira, A Pena and Santa Mariña. Onwards to Olveiroa, Hospital and Cee, before reaching Fisterra on 18th September. Fisterra is on the extreme western edge of Spain, indeed Fisterra translates as 'Lands' End'. In medieval Spain however, this would have a more significant interpretation as 'Worlds End'. As Far as those ancients were concerned, after Fisterra, you fell off the edge of the known planet!

Fisterra was a really nice old fishing village, not too much changed as yet by the ravages of tourism and the new popularity of the extended Camino. I found a very cheap, and very comfortable albergue overlooking the port. They had an incredible offer of three nights for 20 euros. Far too good to turn down.

I did the traditional thing first, setting out to visit the lighthouse at the end of the peninsula which marked the true 'Lands' End'. The Faro de Cabo was a popular destination for Camino pilgrims and other tourists, and the long walk up the steep coastal road was pretty busy. One of the main attractions for a visit to the lighthouse was its spectacular views over the Atlantic, and in particular the sunsets, which are said to be stunning.

During the last two days my walking had been shrouded in

the thickest imaginable of Galician fogs, becoming denser as I neared the coast. Typical of my luck; on the day I marched up to the lighthouse it was a real 'pea-souper'. Once on the promontory that held the lighthouse, I could barely see six feet in front of me, never mind any spectacular views, or stunning sunsets for that matter.

The next day was much brighter and clearer, and I made a return trip. The views were indeed grand, and I enjoyed watching the mighty Atlantic assailing the rocks below with its relentless power. It's well worth the effort to visit Faro de Cabo and I'm glad I made the effort, twice!

I remember thinking that I had now walked entirely across northern Spain, and felt very chuffed I have to say. From the Pyrenees to the Atlantic, I had walked every blessed step. I never thought I would, I never thought I could.

I very much enjoyed my stay in Fisterra. There isn't a great deal to see to be honest, but it is a very nice, very quiet and picturesque fishing port, and I had a really relaxing time.

My prize for best bar on my entire journey actually goes to a pub in Fisterra, and I am happy to acknowledge the winner as bar 'A Galeria' on Rúa Real, high up and overlooking the harbour. It is a fabulous little place; cosy and full of interesting knick-knacks and oddments from around the world, all in a comely and eccentric setting. The beer is good, the food simple but tasty, and the owner is a top guy. What more can I say? If in Fisterra, bar 'A Galeria' is the go-to pub.

From Fisterra I set off northwards and up the Peninsula towards Muxía (pronounced Mooshia). It was a walk just shy of 30 kilometres, and I knocked this off easily enough during the course of the day. I never thought I would use the words '30 kilometres', 'walk' and 'easily' in the same sentence!

Muxía was another nice little fishing port, even smaller and quieter than Fisterra. I found another albergue offering a great two-night deal, and happily booked in. Two days I thought, would be ample to see all I wanted and more, in this remote little spot.

There was indeed very little to see in Muxia. It was a small place occupying a couple of curving bays on the Atlantic, with fishing and tourism at its heart. The port area was lively enough I suppose, with a few nice bars and restaurant's dotted around. The main attractions for me were to be found on the promontory; with a wave lashed lighthouse and a quite exquisite church, perched precariously on the edge of the ocean.

The 'Sanctuario de Virxe da Barca-Muxia' is dedicated to seafarers, fishermen and their vessels, and it is decorated with splendid models of sea-going craft, past and present. It had a simple but wonderful interior, with a special altar given over to St James himself, which is who this entire gig is all about really.

Legend has it, that after St James was beheaded by Herod Agrippa in Palestine in 44AD, his body was brought back to the Iberian Peninsula on a rudderless ship, making landfall close to Muxía. Following an adventure or two, St James body was transferred by ox and cart, eventually coming to rest at the spot where the cathedral at Santiago de Compostela stands today.

According to other accounts I have read, St James boat could have come to rest at any one of about 326 other points along this stretch of coast, each nearby village claiming their right of saintly provenance! It's historically certain that Herod did the dirty deed, and almost as certain that St James body was brought back to Spain, as for the rest?....Well, it all makes for good stories, and tremendous piss-ups on feast days!

Like Fisterra, I enjoyed a couple of days of gentle relaxation in Muxía, quietly reflecting on my weeks on the Camino and beyond. On September 24th, I left Muxía by bus and returned to Santiago. I spent two more days in the city,   re-visiting my favourite places and sealing my memories. I knew then, it was time to go home. Time to leave this fantastic pilgrimage and adventure behind me.

So, that was it. 6 weeks after I had left home, and 900 kilometres of the most incredibly rewarding walking and un-imagined experiences, I had achieved what I set out to accomplish. A long dreamed of journey across Spain, from the mountains to the ocean. Crowned of course, by the glittering prize of Santiago de Compostela and all that it meant to me.

Armed then, with the invigorating spirit of change and renewal the Camino had given me, I set off with real hope for the future in my own hands - and a pair of worn out boots on my feet!

pocket.pilgrim@outlook.com

Printed in Great Britain
by Amazon